HONEY FOR A
Woman's Heart

Also by Gladys Hunt

Honey for a Child's Heart
Honey for a Teen's Heart (with Barbara Hampton)

HONEY FOR A
Woman's Heart

Growing Your World through Reading Great Books

Gladys Hunt
Author of *Honey for a Child's Heart*

ZONDERVAN™

GRAND RAPIDS, MICHIGAN 49530

We want to hear from you. Please send your comments about this book to us in care of the address below. Thank you.

GRAND RAPIDS, MICHIGAN 49530 USA

WWW.ZONDERVAN.COM

ZONDERVAN™

Honey for a Woman's Heart
Copyright © 2002 by Gladys Hunt

Requests for information should be addressed to:

Zondervan, Grand Rapids, Michigan 49530

Library of Congress Cataloging-in-Publication Data
   Hunt, Gladys M.
   Honey for a woman's heart : growing your world through reading great books /
     Gladys Hunt.
     p. cm.
   ISBN-10: 0-310-23846-3 (softcover)
   ISBN-13: 978-0-310-23846-1 (softcover)
     1. Women—Books and reading. 2. Books and reading—Religious aspects—
   Christianity. I. Title.
   Z1039.W65 H86 2001
   028'.9–dc21

2001045576
CIP

Interior design by Beth Shagene

Printed in the United States of America

08 09 10 /❖ DC/ 10 9 8 7 6 5

To my friends—
traveling in the same company with me,
booklovers all,
generous in sharing,
enriching my life and yours
with their contributions in this book.
Come, best books, and lead us on . . .

Contents

Acknowledgments 11

Preface 13

1. For the Love of Books 19
   The Joy of Reading
   The Wonder of Words
   Why Read?
   Savor Your Memories

2. What Makes a Good Story? 31
   Scared of Books?
   Understanding Good Fiction
   What Fiction Can Do for the Reader
   Five Elements of Strong Fiction
   Questions for the Reader to Ask

3. The Brightest and the Best: Literature and the Classics 51
   Some of My Favorite Novels
   Let's Look at Some of the Classics
   First Books
   Memorable Reads from the Past
   The Great Nineteenth-Century Novels
   Twentieth-Century Classics
   Short Stories for Busy People

4. Something for Everyone: Genre Fiction 71
   Women Writers
   Mystery
   Historical Novels
   Western Stories
   Fantasy
   Science Fiction
   Religious Fiction
   Humor

5. The World and People Around Us: Nonfiction 101
   Reading Nonfiction
   Autobiography
   Biography
   Enjoying History
   Travel to New Places

Engaging the Natural World
Courage and Hardship
Parenting
A Potpourri of Interests

6. Piping Down the Valleys Wild: Poetry 127
   The Color of Metaphors
   Personification
   Let These Words Sing to You
   Nature Poems to Help Us See
   Reading Poetry Aloud
   Laughing Verse
   Feeling the Truth in Poetry

7. Honey from the Rock: Reading the Bible 143
   The Significance of This Book
   The Benefits of Reading the Bible
   Getting the Most Out of the Bible
   Bible Translations
   Where to Begin Reading
   Sharing the Bible with Others

8. Growing Up on the Inside: Spiritual Growth Books 155
   What Keeps Us from Growing Up?
   Handling Our Disappointments
   Learning to Forgive
   A Steady Life
   Hungry for God
   Talking with God
   Giving Meaning to the Word Christian
   Keeping Your Heart on Track
   Don't Miss This Author

9. The Company of Others: Sharing Books 175
   Furnishing a Home with Books
   On Being a Book Lender
   Reading Aloud
   Giving Books
   Sharing Books Leads to a Book Group
   Creative Book Sharing
   Finding Time for Reading

Afterword 191

Credits 192

Index of Authors 193

Index of Book Titles 199

Pleasant words are a honeycomb,
sweet to the soul and healing to the bones.

PROVERBS 16:24

Acknowledgments

I've been collecting short quips about reading and writing for some time now, and find some of them comforting, if not amusing. Peter DeVries, for example, said that he loved being a writer; what he couldn't stand is the paperwork! I can relate to that because books and paperwork cluttered my desk for months. I pulled books off our shelves to check out details and authors, made notes about books on slips of paper during the middle of the night—notes, papers everywhere, sometimes losing them only to find them later under something else. And books all needing to be shelved again, and me with no library assistant. Writing is easy, someone said, all you have to do is open a vein.

Now the project is finished and I owe a debt to so many. First of all to Keith, my everloving and helpful husband, who rescued me in computer problems again and again and encouraged me with food and wise words. And when he couldn't fix it, we called in our son, Mark. Thanks to my knights on white chargers!

Ann Spangler, always so full of good ideas, is the progenitor of the idea for this book. She got me started, had my proposal accepted, and set me on my way. Judith Markham and Evelyn Bence helped in refining the details in the book. My thanks to each of them.

My editors Sandra Vander Zicht and Lori VandenBosch encouraged my Dutch heart just looking at their names, to say nothing of the creative advice and wisdom that led to the manuscript reaching their desks for final editing. The book designers also get a vote of thanks for a well-produced product.

My wonderful friends, my companions in reading, came through with enthusiastic comments when they heard I was writing this book, and then helped by giving me their recommendations of favorite books, which you will find scattered throughout this book. I thank them for this gift of sharing with me and with you—each one so special.

Again and again I thank God for small kindnesses and large ones too. I believe in ministering angels. Where does it come from—this sudden remembering of just the right passage or just the right example or just the right book? Or just the right word? It's nice to be created in God's image for his good purposes.

Preface

The difference between the right word and the almost right word
is the difference between the lightning and the lightning bug.

MARK TWAIN

*R*eading is about words! I feel a sense of awe about words. I guess you could say that I am caught up in the wonder of words and all that words bring to our lives. In fact, I'm probably a bit in love with language, which is another way of saying that I like to read. I am not primarily an evangelist about reading, however; my hope is in something far more eternal than books. Yet words are connected to my real *evangel*, for words are a way to express truth; words are a gift from God. When words are put together in the right way they summon a wideness in our lives that pleases him.

My best hopes for this book involve you: First, I'd wish for you some new awareness of the way words go together and their potential in your life. Words are unique to human beings; using language is part of being made in the image of God. He speaks to us with words; we speak to him with words; we reveal ourselves with language. What color language brings to our lives! What a boon to be able to communicate and to read! Yet we often treat this incredible gift rather casually, showing how little we value it. We can read! Take responsibility for your giftedness. And we have books to read. Feel glad about that!

Second, I hope you begin to see what books can do for you as a reader. Books primarily tell stories. There is really only one Great Story in the universe. All other stories come from that one story. Our lives are stories; we tell stories, using our imagination to create narratives about people and events. Jesus was a master storyteller; he put his stamp of approval on fiction by doing this.

Stories tell us truths about the way the world is—about human longing, fears, and choices. We get inside the lives of others and contemplate the consequence of their actions and decisions. Stories are great teachers; we learn best from them because truth takes us unaware, sneaking up on us through our involvement in the story's characters and actions.

Third, I'd like to encourage you to read widely. Book ideas are spread throughout the pages of this book—all kinds of books. Indeed, I hope the chapters of this book sing out Robert Louis Stevenson's words,

The world is so full of a number of things,
I'm sure we should all be as happy as kings.

Book readers can go places without phoning a travel agent or starting the car. You can meet fascinating people in your own living room, people you would never know any other way. New ideas and concepts roll out of the pages of books into your own life, not because you have enrolled in school, but because you are reading. You can go on adventures you would never dare plan. Add to this the depth of feeling and beauty that comes from the right words in the right places—aah, who wouldn't want to be a reader! Reading enables us to see the world as richly colored rather than black and white.

Fourth, expect books to become "ministers" to your life, to say to you what you need to hear. It's amazing how the right book comes to rescue us when we are trapped by attitudes or habits. Books can give us the courage to root out some weeds so that we can get on with the real stuff of life. Relationships, often so tenuous, need insight and truth to make them flourish. The books recommended in the chapter on spiritual growth and the ideas for taking the Bible seriously could start a personal revolution.

It's risky, this business of recommending books. My "great books" may not end up being your "great books." When someone borrows one of my books or reads one that is high on my list of wonderful things, I make myself somewhat vulnerable as I wait for his or her response. Anatole Broyard in his essay "Lending Books" describes his experience in sharing books with others: "I look for agony or ecstasy, for tears, transfiguration, trembling hands, a broken voice—but what the reader usually says is, 'I enjoyed it.' *I enjoyed it*—as if that were what books were for!" When the book has left you all awash in strong feelings, another's placid response may be a letdown.

My All-Time Favorites

The Narnia Chronicles by C. S. Lewis

Great Expectations by Charles Dickens

A Tale of Two Cities by Charles Dickens

Quo Vadis by Henryk Sienkiewicz

Death Comes for the Archbishop
   by Willa Cather

A Child's Garden of Verses
   by Robert Louis Stevenson

Open Mind, Open Heart
   by Thomas Keating

RECOMMENDED BY MARILYN BAKER,
COMMUNITY LEADER AND READER

I'm not a literary expert. I am a learner, like you. I've written this book because I believe we are word-blessed people and our steward- ship of that gift is important. The world is so much with us, "getting and gaining," besides being very noisy and distracting. Everyone, including me, needs encouragement to take a look at what we read and how we read, to say nothing of whether we read!

I hope this book inspires you to become a reader of all things good—or at the very least to read more than you presently do. I'm a realist. Some book lovers will gobble up the latest authors and have read a dozen new books before others get around to finding the library. Because of this book, you may be one who will read three books this year instead of none. Either way, it's a start on *guarding your literacy*. Reading is not an escape from life; it is an exercise in living. *Enjoy!*

First Lines That Hooked Me

The first sentence is so well crafted, so precise, so intriguing it sticks in your memory long after you've read it. Recall the first line, and the whole book unfolds all over again.

Out of Africa by Isak Dinesen
I had a farm in Africa, at the foot of the Ngong Hills.

Chronicle of a Death Foretold by Gabriel Garcia-Marquez
On the day they were going to kill him, Santiago Nassar got up at five-thirty in the morning to wait for the boat the bishop was coming on.

Godric by Frederick Buechner
Five friends I had and two of them snakes.

Moby Dick by Herman Melville
Call me Ishmael.

A Green Journey by Jon Hassler
On the night before Christmas, a snowy night with wind in the forecast, Janet Raft arrived at Agatha McGee's house on River Street.

Pride and Prejudice by Jane Austen
It is a truth universally acknowledged that a single man in possession of a good fortune must be in want of a wife.

RECOMMENDED BY MARGIE HAACK, WRITER AND COLUMNIST

Francie thought that all the books in the world were in that library and she had a plan about reading all the books in the world. She was reading a book a day in alphabetical order and not skipping the dry ones. She remembered that the first author had been Abbott. She had been reading a book a day for a long time now and she was still in the B's . . .

For all of her enthusiasm, she had to admit that some of the B's had been hard going. But Francie was a reader. She had read everything she could find; trash, classics, timetables and grocer's list. Some of the reading had been wonderful; the Louisa Alcott books for example. She had planned to read all the books over again when she had finished the Z's.

A Tree Grows in Brooklyn by Betty Smith

Chapter 1

For the Love of Books

Book love. It will make your hours pleasant to you as long as you live.

ANTHONY TROLLOPE

I know what Trollope is talking about. I am a book lover. Crammed bookshelves spill over to stacks on the floor or on tabletops and counters. (Is it obsessive?) Sometimes I am reading three different books at the same time. I like the way books feel, the way the paper smells, and the anticipation of what the words will say to me. My idea of a delicious day is time to browse in a library or a bookstore, picking up a book and reading, putting back and choosing another until I find the one I want.

We recently moved to a smaller house. In our attempt to downsize we gave away a thousand books or more. It was a long process. We took one off the shelf, discussed whether we thought we would ever read it again, put it in a box, found another, and then retrieved the first one and put it back on the shelf. Moving was going to take forever, we said, because memories fell out of each book we handled. But we persisted, thinking of the gifts we were now giving to our younger book-loving friends, and also remembering how much it costs to move books.

Often when we put the box of books in the car for delivery, we took one or two volumes back out. It's hard to get rid of your friends.

I found it easier to give away the nonfiction books; I wanted to keep all the stories. My husband fought for the nonfiction and gave away some of the fiction. We kept almost all of the classics we had collected. But we still go to the shelves in our new house hoping to find some books that we gave away.

Our new condominium has fewer bookshelves, even though we increased the shelving before moving. We finally decided we did not need to keep the duplicates we had brought from our individual libraries when we married. (Why did it take us so long to come to that conclusion?) But whose copy of *The Complete Works of Shakespeare* would we give away? We each had sentimental attachments to certain books of poetry, so we were careful to keep some of the overlaps. My husband had emotional feelings about reading his copy of Tolstoy's *War and Peace*; I had never made it through to the end of mine, having lost my way with all those Russian names, so that choice was easier. We kept his. (I must try again! Maybe there is something magical about his copy.) But after the movers brought the furniture in, the first boxes we unpacked were books for the shelves in our living room, the library-den, and every other room where we had shelving. Then it looked like home.

It isn't as if we don't have access to a public library. We have a wonderful library within walking distance of our new location, and it already plays a significant role in our book discoveries. The problem is that when we are passionate about what we read, we either go to the bookstore or access the Internet to order our own copy so we can mark it up. The overload in our house is creeping back up to where it was before we gave all those books away!

We still read aloud to each other the passages that simply must be shared. Some passages we end up discussing; some we get wet-eyed over because the words are just too beautiful; some we laugh over together; others evoke a disappointed shrug of the shoulders when the book doesn't live up to the promises of the first pages. In many ways, but especially when it comes to books, we are glad we

My All-Time Favorites

Crossing to Safety by Wallace Stegner

Jane Eyre by Charlotte Brontë

The Wheel on the School by Meindert DeJong

The Ring of Endless Light by Madeleine L'Engle

The Loon Feather by Iola Fuller

Cold Sassy Tree by Olive Ann Burns

Across Five Aprils by Irene Hunt

RECOMMENDED BY PAT FELDHAKE, SCHOOL GUIDANCE COUNSELOR

married each other, because sharing books makes for a comfortable kind of companionship. Besides, if we didn't feel the same way about books, who would keep finding places to put more bookshelves?

But enough of such confessions. (I only shared this to make you feel less guilty about your own excesses.) Our house is probably slowly sinking into the soil beneath it because of the weight of our books. (Book collecting is not neat!)

It is not collecting, buying, or borrowing books, however, that make a reader; it is *reading* books. You don't have to own everything you enjoy reading. You may decide to avoid all that clutter. That's why we have libraries! Borrow; don't buy. Enjoy; don't complicate the dusting. If you choose a book you don't want to finish, it costs you nothing to take it back.

For many people in the world, a library is nothing short of a miracle. Imagine someone providing this incredible supply of books for you to explore! Don't take it for granted. Pioneer people were most often book-poor. Abraham Lincoln once wrote, "My best friend is a person who will give me a book I have not read." It was a fortunate family who owned a Bible. Even today in small towns and in the inner city, unless there is a persistent champion of reading, libraries may be dreary, poorly used facilities containing few books. Shout out a word of praise that we have so many treasures available to us in good libraries, free of charge.

But what good is a library if you never visit it?

The Joy of Reading

Mark Twain said that the person who doesn't read has no advantage over the person who can't read. It is awesome to be able to read, to learn that the letters of the alphabet have sounds, and that if you put the sounds together it makes a word! And words become sentences. And sentences become stories, and suddenly the magic happens. You can read! In *How Reading Changed My Life*, Anna Quindlen writes, "It is like the rubbing of two sticks together to make a fire, this act of reading, an improbably pedestrian task that leads to heat and light. Perhaps this only becomes clear when one watches a child do it."

One year I taught a class of first graders in the local public school when their teacher had complications from a broken leg. What fun I had! I watched a classroom of six-year-olds struggling at various levels to conquer the sounds of letters, putting letters together, forming words, and suddenly realizing they were *reading*. When we formed small groups to practice reading aloud, I watched stubby fingers stabbing each word, earnest faces mouthing silent sounds before committing the word to the airwaves. It was serious work—this business of reading—slow and tedious. After all, we were just beginning. Except for round-faced Abby who could hardly wait to read out loud. When it was her turn to read, something electric happened in the room. Abby seemed to size up a sentence before beginning to read; none of this word-by-word stuff for her. She read with drama, her

Great Read-Aloud Books

A Long Way from Chicago and *A Year Down Yonder* by Richard Peck

Peck's first book (1999 Newbery Honor Award) is about Grandma Dowdel through the eyes of her grandchildren, Joey and Mary Alice. The sequel (Newbery Medal 2001) continues the story with rich humor and strong characters. Mary Alice is sent to live with Grandmother for a year during the Depression. This is no ordinary grandmother! A real treat for all ages!

Vet in the Vestry and *Poultry in the Pulpit* by Alexander Cameron

True-to-life descriptions of veterinary practice in Great Britain (in the fashion of James Herriot's books), these books explore Cameron's life of faith as a minister of the Church of Scotland and his experience as a vet. The descriptions of both animals and parishioner are delightful.

Rilla of Ingleside by Lucy Maud Montgomery

Montgomery has written the wonderful eight-book *Anne of Green Gables* stories, but don't stop there. *Rilla* describes the agony of World War I and the heart-breaking involvement of the Canadians and British in this struggle, before the Americans enter the war. Then go on to read more. *Emily of New Moon, Emily Climbs, Emily's Quest, Pat of Silver Bush*, and *Mistress Pat* are tales of a different delightful Montgomery heroine with the same kind of unforgettable characters. Another small gem is *The Blue Castle*. Many of Montgomery's stories were discovered forty years after her death and are now being released in new collections.

RECOMMENDED BY KRISTY MOTZ,
LIBRARIAN AND STORYTELLER

voice rising and falling. When the dog ran, her voice warned of impending danger. When the character in the story said something as simple as, "Where did he go?" it became a melodrama, a moment of adventure for everyone in the room. This was *reading!* Every child in the room seemed filled with new hope about reading. I smile just thinking of the miracle I took part in that year. The wonder of reading; the magic of words.

The Wonder of Words

Reading and words obviously go together. Words rightly used have the potential of making us shiver with pleasure. Words are a God-idea. "In the beginning was the Word" (John 1:1)—that phrase itself says something important about words. It is no small thing that God has made us word-partners with himself. He communicates to us with words. He allows us to speak back to him with words. The wonder of this strikes me forcibly. What a gift from God to be able to communicate! All communication, the expression of ideas, the interface of human beings is dependent on words. I can transcend myself with words and attempt to let you into my personal world, telling you who I am—and you can do the same with me. All of which makes the world more habitable and less lonely.

The Bible says that the world was created by the Word of God. "God said, 'Let there be light,' and there was light" (Genesis 1:3). With the power of words, God spoke and created a world. In a lesser sense, we also speak and create a world—a world for someone else to live in. The harsh, destroying words of an angry father; the comforting, nourishing words of a loving mother; the name-calling bully in the school yard; the affirming words of a teacher about work well done—these are only examples of how people use words to create a world for someone else to live in. Words have enormous potential for good or for ill. It is likely that more lives have been destroyed by words than by bullets. More grace and joy have been brought to lives by words than by costly jewels.

Words not only create worlds; they give meaning to our lives. Some people use words; other people love words and see their potential. It really has little to do with talking or not talking; it is seeing what words were meant to do. Words name things. Words open up our imaginations. We clothe our experiences in words and save them. Writer Lynne Sharon Schwartz said that in school she was told that a picture is worth a thousand words. "But, to me," she writes in *Ruined by Books*, "the value seemed quite the other way around. Meanings might be embedded in the picture, but only words could release them, give them shape and specific gravity. Nothing was really possessed or really real until it was incarnate in words. Words contained the knowledge; words were the knowledge, the *logos*."

Words have a great attraction for readers. By *readers* I mean those whose eyes grab words wherever they appear, which is why people find themselves reading the same words on the cereal box morning after morning. But not all words have the same value because of the way they are used. Too many of them can overload and obscure an idea instead of clarifying it. Fuzzy thinking comes with fuzzy word choices. The challenge of using the right word is a healthy exercise of the mind and something readers learn to treasure.

In his commencement address at the University of Michigan, Soviet-born poet Joseph Brodsky told graduates, "Zero in on being precise with your language. Try to build and treat your vocabulary the way you treat your checking account—to enable you to articulate as fully and precisely as possible. Acquire a dictionary and use it on a daily basis." It may seem amazing that one would need to admonish university graduates about such an obvious thing, but the cheap and careless use of words has invaded our world like a virus and infected nearly everyone. Why not call people to honor and protect language the same way we call people to protect the earth?

Good literature is words at their best, taking words out of the mundane and demonstrating their wonder. It's all of a piece, this business of words and reading.

Why Read?

Reading is a sage way to bump up against life. Reading may be an escape, but it is not escape from my own life and problems. It is escape from the narrow boundaries of being only me. Reading in some wonderful way helps me find out who I am. When she was a young girl Patricia MacLachlan's mother urged her to "read a book and find out who you are." And it is true that in some way reading defines me as it refines me. Reading enlarges my vision of the world; it helps me understand someone who is different from me. It makes me bigger on the inside. We tend to see the world from our own perspective; it is good to see it from the eyes of others. Good literature

Novels That Broke My Heart

My Name Is Asher Lev by Chaim Potok
This book "told me" I *had* to be a writer, though it is a first-person account of a Jewish boy who becomes a painter. Moving story.

Jacob Have I Loved by Katherine Paterson
For adolescent girls of all ages who are not convinced of God's love. Full of biblical imagery, the story is told in the voice of a younger twin who perceives herself to be Esau, whom God "hates." It's set during World War II on an island in the Chesapeake.

Nectar in a Sieve
by Kamala Markandaya
A mother's hopeful survival through abject poverty in India. A book of "little graces."

Kristin Lavransdatter
by Sigrid Undset
See description of book on page 43.

The Poisonwood Bible
by Barbara Kingsolver
See description of book on page 177.

RECOMMENDED BY EVELYN BENCE, WRITER

helps me understand who I am in relation to what others experience. Far from being an escape from reality, good literature is a window *into* reality.

I read to feel life. Reading heightens my awareness on many levels. What the writer says and the way she says it give form and expression to my own feelings. When what I read is good prose or good poetry, it affects my own use of words. More than that, it makes my spirit soar. The right use of language is a gift for the heart.

A story should make you feel something. It's the opposite of how Thomas Gradgrind, in Charles Dickens's *Hard Times,* wanted schoolteachers to instruct the unfortunate pupils in his school. "Now, what I want is Facts. Teach these boys and girls nothing but Facts. Facts alone are wanted in life. Plant nothing else, and root out everything else." I remember reading that with a feeling of horror.

The cold facts contrasted against a skillful use of language to convey similar information demonstrates what I mean about feeling life. Leland Ryken gives a scientific description of a cold night:

Last night's low temperature was recorded as ten degrees below zero. Two inches of snow were measured. The sky was overcast with a cloud cover.

That's factual and precise. Then Ryken contrasts the scientific description with this poetic description in John Keats's poem *The Eve of St. Agnes.*

St. Agnes Eve—Ah, the bitter chill it was!
The owl, for all his feathers, was a-cold;
The hare limped trembling through the frozen grass,
And silent was the flock in woolly fold;
Numb were the beadsman's fingers, while he told
His rosary, and while his frosted breath,
Like pious incense from a censer old,
Seemed taking flight for heaven.

What a different experience the poem is from the weather report! One is factual and flat; the other surges with beauty and feeling. The right thing said in the right way, ah, that's the delight of good books.

I read for pleasure. The sheer luxury of reading and reveling in the world I live in is something I treasure. Life is more than meat and potatoes and duties. Learning to see, to laugh, and to enjoy encounter with others is reason enough to read. The world has comedy built into it; the ridiculous is but to be explored. Every reader knows the pleasure of being transported to another world in books.

Reading good books does not automatically make me a good person. Some people claim too much for reading. Does good literature necessarily give an adequate world/life view? That seems a lot to ask of a book; forming a world/life view is an exercise readers must do for themselves. I have read that those who tended the ovens in the Nazi concentration camps spent their free time reading Goethe's *Faust* and listening to the symphonies of Brahms and Beethoven. It takes an act far greater than reading or enjoying any art form to redeem a person. Books are not a savior, but they can lead to the source of salvation.

I read to learn. Good books instruct me about the world. I learn information; I gain perspective. I get a handle on history or people who have influenced the world. I have more breadth in my thinking—not a clinical detachment, but an involvement of myself so that it translates into my life.

I travel to places I might never visit in any other way except in a book. I solve problems in my life by sharing in the lives of others. I grow spiritually by encountering the wisdom of people who have thought through issues that still cause me to struggle. I share in the adventures of others and widen my own experiences.

Since every writer writes from a given view of life and the world, readers need to ask questions about the author's worldview and place all the ideas in any book on trial. "Is this true?" they must ask. The learning comes from confronting ideas and taking what is good and constructing a pattern for one's self. A worldview is simply a set of beliefs that tell a person what to think and how to act in any situation in life.

Books are wonderful ways to learn the possibilities of being human. We can define character traits with words, but they take shape only when you see what they look like in a person. How can we understand honor or valor or courage unless we have sometimes seen these traits in someone's life? Good literature may so move the reader that it seems impossible to verbalize about it. The experience is what counts.

Jane Stephens, an English teacher, puts it this way: "The fact that Stuart Little is a mouse rather than a boy is not a problem for children. They love him for his essence, his integrity and fortitude. I cannot talk to my students about these characteristics without trivializing them. . . . When we say that Stuart is 'just the best kind of mouse,' we are not talking about his clothes or his grades. We all know what we mean." (Ah, yes, I too have met Stuart Little and have seen what integrity and fortitude look like.)

The critical moment in a story may not be when we read what is happening to a character, but when that *character* begins to see what is happening and we ourselves enter into that character's life. It never hurts to stand in another's shoes. We learn to sympathize with

---

Children's Books I Read at Adult Dinner Parties

Chrysanthemum by Kevin Henkes
    A story about the conundrum of names.

Where the Wild Things Are by Maurice Sendak
    About the wildness in all of us.

Bedtime for Frances by Russell Hoban
    A hilarious portrayal of bed-time rituals.

I Can Hear the Sun by Patricia Polacco
    A brilliantly illustrated tale of wild geese and an unwanted boy.

Martha Speaks by Susan Meddaugh
    A dog learns to speak by eating alphabet soup and saves the day when a burglar enters the family home.

RECOMMENDED BY DARCY LENZGRINDEN, WEAVER AND WRITER

other people, but the real surprise is that we learn truths about ourselves that we had not seen before. In this sense literature does affect our world/life view. It does not always provide the standard; it provides the opportunity to see the responsibility of choice and the consequences that follow. It "extends our range of vision."

This is why an evil character in a story may reveal the real nature of evil more clearly than a sermon on sin. Reading stories is also a vicarious way to see how goodness and humility and honesty and beauty play out in life. Literature does instruct us, even though it may

Books That Inspire Courage in Me

Calico Bush by Rachel Field
Forced to become an indentured servant at age thirteen, orphan Maggie Ledoux travels to the New World with the Sargent family. Life in northern Maine is harder than Maggie ever imagined, but the harsh winter of 1743 proves her resilience and strength of mind and heart.

The Door in the Wall
by Marguerite De Angeli
A terrible illness leaves young Robin crippled and abandoned during the days of the knights. Though a nobleman's son, Robin's destiny is altered through his friendship with Brother Luke, a monk, who teaches him positive ways to endure what life may bring.

They Loved to Laugh by Kathryn Worth
At sixteen Martitia is left all alone when her parents die of typhoid fever in

Virginia during the 1800s. A kindly Quaker, Doctor David, takes her into his home where she meets his five big sons who tease and taunt her constantly. Martitia eventually learns to laugh along with them and also learns a lesson in love.

All-of-a-Kind Family by Sydney Taylor
Ella, Henny, Sara, Charlotte, Gertie are five lovable Jewish girls growing up in New York in the early 1900s—an "all-of-a-kind family." Then baby Charles is born and the fun begins.

Our Only May Amelia by Jennifer Holm
A headstrong young girl lives with her Finnish family in a remote settlement on the coast of Oregon. She copes with being the only girl in a family of seven brothers while proving herself capable of almost anything. Based on the author's grandmother's life.

RECOMMENDED BY SARAH JOY FELDHAKE, HIGH SCHOOL STUDENT

not be our main reason for reading. Malcolm Muggeridge wrote in *Jesus Rediscovered* that books like *Resurrection* or *The Brothers Karamazov* gave him an overpowering sense of how uniquely marvelous a Christian way of looking at life is, and a passionate desire to share it. Good books have a way of instructing the heart.

Life has a story-shape. Stories are built into the very structure of the universe. A good writer takes the materials of our experience and makes it into a story and helps us understand. "Out of the chaos of incident and accident," writes Eugene Peterson, "story-making words bring light, coherence and connection, meaning and value."

In Frances Hodgson Burnett's *A Little Princess*, the imaginative storytelling Sara so enthralls her less imaginative friend Ermengarde that she can hardly speak. She whispers, "O, Sara. It is like a story." To which Sara replies, "It is a story. . . . Everything is a story. You are a story—I am a story. Miss Minchin [the mean headmistress] is a story."

> ### Books I Loved as a Young Reader
>
> *A Girl of the Limberlost* by Gene Stratton-Porter
>
> *Black Beauty* by Anna Sewell
>
> *Peter Rabbit* by Beatrix Potter
>
> *Lorna Doone* by Richard Blackmore
>
> *Little Orphan Annie* by Harold Gray
>
> RECOMMENDED BY JAN KARON, AUTHOR

The Great Story of the universe can be told in many forms, and when it is told well it involves you and me, and makes us see that our lives are stories too. The stories always involve a view of truth and what we will make of the choices given us. A great novel can be a kind of conversion experience. We come away from it changed.

There are many other reasons to read. Read as a way to work through problems in real life; read as a way of celebrating your joys, read for enjoyment, read for entertainment, read because you love beauty. Read to savor your memories.

Savor Your Memories

Sometimes we need to turn the clock back and reminisce about what we read in our growing-up years in order to get our reading juices flowing, especially if the world has been overpressuring us. The flavors and memories of another way to live may inspire us to change our priorities to give more time to reading. Doris Grumbach, in an essay in *For the Love of Books*, brings back memories of her own childhood reading.

Before I was twelve I had read Johanna Spyri's *Heidi* again and again. I wept through the story, and cheered up magically only at the happy ending. Nothing that I can remember in my life before that year had moved me to tears, and then to a sense of delight, as did the trials and triumph in the life of Heidi. . . . This year before mailing off a copy of the book to my granddaughter, I read it again, and it was the same for me. Suddenly I realize that all these years I have gone on wanting a drink of warm goat's milk, to live in a hut on the top of a mountain, to sleep on a packed-hay bed, to have been orphaned at a young age and then to acquire, through the fortunes of a God-supplied plot, a gruff but beloved grandfather and the friendship of a lovely, wealthy, and generous family.

Maybe it's time to read *Heidi* again to remember the joy of reading. Children's books are some of the best out there! Have a grown-up romp through *The Wind in the Willows* by Kenneth Grahame; take an unabashed delight in associating with Rat and Mole and Toad. It gets better with age.

C. S. Lewis wrote that any book worth reading at ten years of age should be worth reading at fifty. If you've read the Narnia Chronicles you already know that he wrote that kind of book. Read Lewis's *The Lion, the Witch, and the Wardrobe* with the insights the years bring or, better still, read it aloud with someone you love. We read the series aloud as a family seven times, and then when our nest was empty, my husband and I began reading them aloud to each other. They are captivating!

Read *Little Women* by Louisa May Alcott again, or *Anne of Green Gables* by Lucy Maud Montgomery. You may find yourself shedding tears of nostalgia, and finding fresh pleasure in the love of books.

When little boys and girls grow bigger and older, they should grow from the outside, leaving a little boy or girl in the middle. . . . But some unlucky people grow older from inside and so grow old through and through.

C. S. LEWIS

Chapter 2

What Makes a Good Story?

The world of fiction is a world where there is no reality except that of the human imagination. . . . The imagination tells us things about human life that we don't get in any other way.

NORTHROP FRYE

*E*veryone loves a good story. The telling of stories is universally human. Stories are everywhere, giving us history, meaning, and purpose. Oral histories passed down through the generations give shape to our lives. "Your uncle always treated those who came to his general store with respect except for one man . . ." and thereby hangs a tale that pulls you into family history. Every family has stories.

In an essay in the book *Reading in Bed* (edited by Steven Gilbar), writer Sven Birkerts tells us how he came by his early interest in writing stories:

> My mother has a bottomless fund of anecdotes. "It was an interesting story," she says. "They were very happily married—at least everybody thought so—and they had a beautiful child, a son. But then, for some reason, nobody knows why, he began to drink. And after that things began to fall apart. . . ." The simplest of accounts would kindle me to ask Why?

Birkerts's curiosity over the *why* was what made him a good writer.

My grandfather, born on the Fourth of July, was an immigrant from the Netherlands. In the course of time he married and had nine children, who soon multiplied into a clan with many grandchildren. Always the family gathered on the Fourth of July to celebrate his birthday and, as the afternoon wore on, to listen to the same stories over and over, uniquely told in his Dutch accent. When wished a happy birthday, each year he proclaimed with amazement, "What a wonderful country this is! Here everyone celebrates my birthday!" Each year we laughed and listened and had a sense of belonging to this wonderful man, the patriarch of our family. The stories weren't new, but they were *our* stories.

We hone our own storytelling skills by listening to our family stories. Observing the large number of novels set in Depression years or the war years, I can picture families with a will and genius to survive retelling their adventures of hardship and triumph as they sit around the kitchen table, all the aunts and uncles pitching anecdotes into the mix of conversation. Many of these stories may already be larger than life. One of the listeners may someday take these tales and write stories that had their origins at the kitchen table. Good stories are laden with courage and endurance and the kind of decision-making that tells us what life is like.

Our love of stories is the beginning of fiction. Fiction is usually an embellishment of something that could have happened; some of it perhaps based on fact, but most of it made up. Such stories let the imagination explore the possibilities of what could happen. It is as human to make up stories as it is to tell them.

Scared of Books?

Words are powerful tools. Words in books herald new ideas, show readers new possibilities, or give readers the emotional energy to act—and this is sometimes considered dangerous. For one reason or another down through history some people have wanted to get rid of certain books. The Nazis lit up the night skies burning books that disagreed with their propaganda. Harassed Christians in China hid Bibles under floorboards or in the walls. Southern masters frequently forbade teaching slaves to read, and in some places severely punished those caught looking at a book. Hazel Rochman, now editor of the American Library Association's *Booklist*, tells of burying books in her backyard in Johannesburg during apartheid, fearing a police raid and a search for banned books. Books can be purveyors of truth, and the truth makes people free—and some people scared.

Others, besides tyrants, raise questions about literature. Plato himself (c. 400 B.C.) voiced three objections to literature: (1) literature is fictional and deficient in truth; (2) reading has a bad moral effect on readers; and (3) reading stories is not useful and therefore a waste of time. Later the early church fathers—Augustine, Tertullian, and others—transferred this thinking into the Christian tradition. These three ideas still spill into the reading arena and are worth a brief discussion.

Does Literature Tell the Truth?

Imagination and truth go together in good literature. Because a story is "made up" does not necessarily mean it is not true. It means it is imaginative. Fiction is basically literature about imaginary people and events (and includes mysteries, fantasy, drama, science fiction, and more). The definition of fiction is to shape, to fashion, to feign. Feigning is imagining—making visible images for invisible things. Why should I read fiction if it is just made up? I read it because it helps me pay attention to life. Reading good fiction is not simply a frivolous activity for those who aren't serious about life. I read because I *am* serious, and find that fiction says true things I might never hear any other way.

We struggle over a theology of imagination. We find it hard to believe that imagination is God's idea and that it is among the chief glories of human beings. Of all creation, human beings are the only creatures who have the ability to transcend the smallness of self and imagine something different than what they know. God is imaginative; we are made in his image.

Children are wonderfully imaginative; they are born that way. Bread crusts on highchair trays become trucks; dolls cry and need to be rocked. Imagination is to be encouraged, trained, developed, enjoyed. That is why we surround children with picture books that tell stories, and why we read to them about adventures in far places. Dr. Seuss lets them put their tongues and their imaginations around words that make up stories. Yet even before the advent of the book, people were drawing images in the sand and making up legends. Imagination is not only a human capacity; it is an awesome gift.

Imagination and truth-telling is an oxymoron to some people. Once, when I was giving a talk about children's books, a mother told me that she never read anything to her children that was not literally true. Since animals do not talk, she would not allow books that give speech or personality to animals. "I want my children to trust me," she said, "and if I give them untrue stories, they will suspect that I don't tell the truth about other more important issues." I felt sorry for her children because she had so little understanding of the role of imagination in enjoying the world around us. Her view of truth was too narrow, so narrow that she would have to conclude that the Bible gives us untruths when it speaks of the stars "singing together" or trees "clapping their hands."

Uneasiness about imagination leads to a narrow view of God and the gifts he has given men and women. In his book *Reversed Thunder*, Eugene Peterson writes, "Imagination opens things up so that we can grow into maturity—worship and adore, exclaim and honor, follow and trust. Explanation keeps our feet on the ground; imagination lifts

Books That Touched Every Sense of My Being

Isabel Allende makes you see, hear, taste, touch, and smell her words. Her exquisitely woven stories transport one into a different world. Many aspects of her novels are biographical.

The House of the Spirits, her first and arguably her richest novel, is set in Chile before, during, and after Pinochet's reign of terror. It tells the story of her family—in particular, her extraordinary grandparents.

Paula is the unsentimental but heart-rending story of Allende's journey in accepting her adult daughter's degenerative illness and death. As a mother, I found her story particularly poignant. Despite the bleak reality of her experience, Allende writes with characteristic humor, hope, and courage.

Daughter of Fortune is an enchanting epic novel set in the mid 1800s in a world possessed by gold fever. It follows the dangerous journey of Eliza Sommers, the spirited seventeen-year-old heroine, from Chile to San Francisco in search of her Chilean lover. Eliza has to reinvent herself in order to survive in this harsh new country. Her search for love turns into a journey of self-discovery and personal freedom.

RECOMMENDED BY ROSEMARY MOORE,
ATTORNEY AND MOTHER

our heads into the clouds. Explanation restricts and defines and holds down; imagination expands and lets loose." Christians have a large investment in the invisible and for them imagination is essential, for it is only by means of the imagination that we can see the reality of the whole.

The Bible is a book of literature; it is a work of art. It is imaginative. It is an anthology containing poetry, adventure stories, mysteries, stories about heroes, heroines, and villains, and romantic love. Ten verses in Job extol the glory of the hippopotamus and thirty-five verses speak of the strength of the crocodile. Morning stars sing for joy, trees clap their hands, and the sunrise is likened to a bridegroom coming out of his tent. Its words are marked by beauty; its imagery illumines the text. God seems to have an awesome regard for imagination and beauty in communicating truth.

"Does it make any difference," writes Clyde Kilby, formerly a Wheaton College English professor, "that the Book we look upon as holy comes to us in literary form rather than in the form of abstract doctrine or systematic theology?" Christianity is the most literary religion in the world—a religion in which *Word* has special sanctity.

Everyone has been gifted with an imagination that longs to be fed. Some are more imaginative than others and are a special gift to all of us. Without imagination there would be no new hypotheses, inventions, or experiments. Albert Einstein himself said, "The gift of fantasy has meant more to me than my talent for absorbing positive knowledge." Nobody lives in a totally objective world, only in a world filtered by imagination. Imagination allows us to soar and to wonder. Someone had to imagine everything that we take for granted, from a fork to an airplane.

How does imagination help us grasp truth? C. S. Lewis observed that a person can either have an experience or understand it, but never both at once. His theory was that only in a story do we have a possible solution to this dilemma. A story invites us to have, through our imaginations, a concrete experience of truth. Maybe that is why Jesus told stories. In a story I get to see my own experiences from a different angle and understand new truths about myself and the world.

Imagination can be tainted with evil or infused with good; whether it is good or evil depends on the heart of the person doing the "imagining." In that sense, imagining is like all our other gifts, to be used for good or ill. We don't worship imagination; we simply recognize the capacity to imagine as a uniquely human and God-given gift. The right use of imagination in writing can make truth come alive and jump off the page.

Does Literature Have a Bad Moral Effect on Its Reader?

Along the reading road we'll find books that strike us as being either too profane or superficial or even depressing to warrant reading. Even among the finest there is still a question of good, better, and best. At the same time, we don't give wholesale condemnation to all fiction either. Those who condemn fiction in general are usually not interested in reading anything that challenges their own comfort; they want to read books that tell them what they already know.

Some time ago I did a live radio interview about children's books. The person conducting the interview began the interview with an astonishingly negative statement posed as a question: "There are a lot of books out there we don't want children to read, aren't there?" Since my purpose in the interview was to promote the reading of books, I did a quick recovery and urged parents to investigate the world of good books and read to their children.

What struck me about the initial question, which was also evident in some of the call-ins to the show, was the fear of books and ideas that still exists in some people's minds. Fearful of the world, these people feel vulnerable. Truth seems "up against it" in the world of ideas; it needs protection. This leads people to a wholesale condemnation of good books—often without realizing that they are letting a spirit of fear overrule a sound mind (see 2 Timothy 1:7).

Certainly, if you read the Bible, you know that it has no quarrel with literary realism. It is boldly honest about human depravity. Sex and violence are in its pages; it presents reality the way it is; it records real experiences of real people. And it isn't always pretty. What it records, however, is in a context that exposes evil. It gives readers genuine insights into what the world is like. Its purpose is not to titillate or to tempt readers to base thoughts or actions. It neither condones nor revels in what it depicts.

So in reading stories that reflect real-life experiences, we need to take a close look at both the context and the behavior described. To get an accurate reading of what the book is saying, the reader may have to overlook some portrayals of sex or violence or profanity to get the point. Does it present a reality that illumines the point of the story? Would such a person speak like that? Does it add authenticity?

Read the whole book instead of stumbling over the specifics. The important question is, What is the story saying? What is its theme? British author Harry Blamires writes a true and profound statement: "There is nothing in our experience, however trivial, worldly, or even evil, which cannot be thought about Christianly."

Life is a pretty realistic affair, and fiction is supposed to be true to life. But if a story delights in evil acts or presents perversion as natural and right, well, then that author has a problem that becomes the reader's problem. We don't need to wallow in the slough of evil to get the point of a story. Personally I have a very low tolerance for four-letter words. I just don't want them echoing around in my head. And I can tell the difference between a book that includes sexual details as part of a larger picture or sex to titillate my senses, making no contribution to the theme of the book. Good books have a spiritual substance; they show the moral dimensions in life. That does not mean that the story will omit all questionable behavior or language, but what is described will fit the larger theme of the book.

Frank Gaebelein once said, "As a Christian I am responsible for the furniture of my mind." Everyone is. If a reader is attracted to unnecessary clinical descriptions of sex or any other unworthy thing that is out of proportion to the point of the story, that reader needs to check not only reading habits, but habits of the heart. Some writers deliberately attract readers who like salacious material.

If we reject a story, we should reject it because its excesses make it unconvincing, not because it makes us feel unsafe or uneasy. And we reject it for ourselves, not for someone else.

Is Reading a Waste of Time?

I like how Leland Ryken responds to this question: "Many of the most worthwhile things in life are of no practical use. What can a person do, in any utilitarian sense, with a sunset, or a snowy mountain peak, or mists on a summer morning or a beautifully shaped tree? The trees of Paradise, we must remember, were not only good for food, but pleasant to the sight."

Our work ethic says that a person has to do something worthwhile, and there is an underlying suspicion that reading is the opposite of doing something worthwhile. We need to "accomplish something," and reading does not seem like an accomplishment. I am "an accomplisher" myself, and it took some reflection on life before I could read a book in the daytime on a weekday. I am not alone in this uneasy feeling. One vacation Monday morning at 11 o'clock my husband looked up gleefully from the pages of a Dick Francis thriller and said, "This must be what it is like to be retired!" People don't read for pleasure on Monday mornings, do they?

Sven Birkerts, author of *The Gutenberg Elegies: The Fate of Reading in an Electronic Age*, fought this prejudice all his growing-up years. In the essay "Notes from a Confession" he writes,

> It is Saturday afternoon, summer, weather temperate. I am lying on the bed in my room reading a novel. I am ten, or twelve or fifteen—it doesn't matter. Once again, in my absorption, I have not heard my father come home from the office. Now he stands in the doorway. Not a word has been exchanged, but already I've put the book out of sight. . . . For we are both loath to go through the argument again. Because I'm not vertical, not engaged conspicuously with the so-called real world, I'm in the wrong. I know that. No use in my arguing the value of reading. "There's enough to think about with real problems," he would say, "why add on the problems of make-believe people?" . . . Behind everything, in spite of any high-flown pronouncements I might make, there is still the residual sense of something not altogether praiseworthy about my habit. (from *Reading in Bed*, edited by Steven Gilbar)

Oprah Winfrey, one of television's most popular entertainers, was shuttled back and forth between a father and mother who no longer lived together. The brokenness she found in home life was partly eased by the comfort of reading books. She told a *Life* reporter, "I remember being in the back hallway when I was nine—and I am going to try to say this without crying—and my mother threw the door open and grabbed a book out of my hand and said, 'You're nothing but a something-something bookworm. Get your butt outside. You think you're better than the other kids.' I was treated as though something was wrong with me because I wanted to read." Oprah's experience makes you respect and understand the passion with which she founded an on-air book club to encourage people to read.

We may pay lip service to the virtues of reading, but there is still a suspicion in our culture that those who read too much, whatever that means, are lazy, aimless dreamers, people who need to grow up and take part in real life.

Let's face it, reading can be a way to hide from the world. Life in a book can become more real than life outside on the playground.

I've seen a mother reading on the beach oblivious to the fact that her two children were about to drown each other. Reading, like television, can keep one from relationships!

But the other side of the argument urgently needs to be made. If we read well, good books do not let us cop-out of the real world. Instead they help us connect the material and the spiritual, the visible and the invisible, and thus make sense out of life.

I remember my mother often relenting at bedtime and allowing "one more chapter." I sometimes used a flashlight after the lights were turned out to find out what happened. And I remember being called away from a book to set the table or do some chore and answering reluctantly. Lynne Sharon Schwartz tells how her sister coped with this. "I envied my older sister her uninterruptability. While I looked up immediately from my book when my name was called, she had the uncanny ability not to hear. I would test her as she read. It was like addressing a stone. My sister appeared to be present, but she was in the book. This is a great and useful gift!" I agree.

Understanding Good Fiction

Good fiction seems to work by indirection, rather than by being overly explicit. This applies whether the subject is God or sex or even violence—which is not to say that the author necessarily avoids any of these. But as someone said, you can say a lot about God without ever mentioning his name. The same can be said about sexual matters.

All good stories are basically about brokenness or redemption, and the conflict between good and evil. Sometimes reading novels gives us a fresh realization of how broken life is for some people. We may need to let the story break our hearts as we ask ourselves, *Is the world like this? Is this truth?* It may lead to a new understanding of how complicated the world is. It could renew our passion for the message of redemption. Without changing our own values, maybe we need to be open to ask if there is more than one answer to a question. Franz Kafka spoke of a novel as "an ice-ax to break the seas frozen inside our souls."

Some people want to avoid the hassle of having to think about what they read; they want the escape of a pleasant story. To assure this, they read only books that come from religious publishing houses; they want what they call "Christian fiction." It's hard to define what Christian fiction is. Is Christian fiction simply a story I don't have to

A Significant Canadian Writer

Robertson Davies is a significant, serious Canadian writer, now deceased, and someone whose writing you may want to explore. He is funny, irreverent, and a master at creating intricate plots and odd but lovable characters. Although he doesn't write from a Christian perspective, he includes religious belief as an important aspect of his characters' lives and histories. He does not shy away from his characters' eccentricities or their sexual exploits (though never graphic), but the spirit of the novels is the desire to see his characters find their best selves. And "best" for Davies includes an awareness of one's weakness and baser instincts. My favorites from his writing are two trilogies:

The Deptford Trilogy: *Fifth Business; The Manticore; World of Wonders*

The Cornish Trilogy: *The Rebel Angels; What's Bred in the Bone; The Lyre of Orpheus*

RECOMMENDED BY MARIA BERGSTROM, LITERATURE PH.D. AND FULL-TIME MOM

worry about? Is it a book written by someone with Christian convictions?

Other hard questions hover over the discussion: Can an author without Christian commitment say true things with such skill that it impacts you deeply? What if the story is not addressing anything big enough to challenge the reader to think like a Christian? Is it subject matter that makes it Christian or is it excellence in literary style as well as substance? How would you classify Dostoyevsky's powerful writings? Struggling with these issues as a writer of novels, Frederick Buechner wrote, "If you are going to be a novelist you've got to be honest not just about the times that glimmer with God's presence but also about the times that are dark with His absence."

Baylor University English professor David Jeffrey writes that "the word 'Christian' suffers diminishment when it is not used as a noun. To be a Christian, strictly speaking, is to be a person under obedience to Christ." When I read this I wondered if the word *Christian* is on slippery ground when it is used as an adjective. It is interesting that the Bible uses that word only twice and never as an adjective.

"A religious novel at its best is a novel less *about* religious experience than a novel the reading of which *is* a religious experience," wrote Frederick Buechner. That statement provides a benchmark in evaluating fiction.

Chaim Potok, one of my favorite authors, commented that "religious" writers don't trust people of faith to make sense out of what they read; they want to fill all the empty places by telling them what to believe. They are not the only ones who do this, however. Issue-driven messages are all around us—in books, in the theaters, on television. Gay-rights writers, hawkers of victimization, feminists, hedonists, promoters of the irregular are among those who compromise excellence and slant their writing for the sake of the message.

Great stories are usually written in response to life's questions. They demand a response and make the reader stretch. Such stories give the reader time to discover, to mull over what the book is saying—and nourish the reader along the way, asking smaller questions a thoughtful reader cannot ignore. And smaller questions lead to bigger questions. Authors would do themselves a favor if they asked themselves, *Am I writing a simple narrative, or am I saying something significant about being human?*

The intent of this book is to promote books that meet the standard of both content and artistry, chosen by the merit of the book rather than by a checklist of moralisms (no sex, no language, no

Meet Van Reid, a Writer to Make You Smile

Maine writer **Van Reid** sets out to tell a good story and succeeds. He has a vision of people who are good, decent, and wise—and he knows how to portray them. Like the great comic writers Mark Twain and P. G. Wodehouse, Reid can make you laugh. And like his model, Charles Dickens, he features memorable and sympathetic characters. Tellingly, Reid shares his editor with another favorite current author, Jan Karon. If you love Karon you will probably like Reid.

Daniel Plainway: or the Holiday Haunting of the Moosepath League is set in Maine at the turn of the century and continues the adventures of the Moosepath League, a friendship club governed by no rules but kindness. Its founders are goodhearted men who have chosen the almost mythic Tobias Walton as their chairman—a man whose goodness so pervades all he does and is that even his lost homburg hat brings about good wherever it goes.

Reid's novels typically feature a page-turning plot, a missing treasure, a beleaguered orphan boy, a handsome and admirable man and woman destined for true love, and several digressive stories that embody the humor of a tall tale or the romance of a fairy tale.

Look for *Cordelia Underwood*, his first novel; and *Mollie Peer*, his second book—both of which received glowing reviews.

RECOMMENDED BY
LORI WALBURG VANDEN BOSCH,
AUTHOR AND EDITOR

violence). A good book has a genuine spiritual substance; it helps us see. Good fiction is made of that which is real and true, and reality and truth are difficult to come by.

What Fiction Can Do for the Reader

Fiction is about people and their relationships and their choices. (This is true even if the writer portrays the main characters as animals. Winnie the Pooh is more than just a bear. He is a character whose actions and thoughts mirror our own.) Getting inside a well-written story reveals our own self to us and surprises us with new insights.

Mark Twain wrote a profoundly moral and memorable story when he penned *The Adventures of Huckleberry Finn*. Not everyone thought so when it was first published, but it remains as instructive and full of pleasure today as when it was first written. A look at one part of this tale illustrates what fiction does for us.

In the story, Widow Douglas's kindness to the freedom-loving Huck becomes claustrophobic. Huck doesn't want to hurt her, but he wants out. So he stages his own death and escapes to an island in the Mississippi River. There he comes upon Jim, the runaway slave of Miss Watson. A close relationship develops between Huck and Jim, both runaways, as they raft down the river together. As this somewhat idyllic life goes on, it occurs to Huck that he faces not only the danger of being found, but also the danger of aiding a runaway slave. The bond of friendship with Jim is strong and conflicts with the way the culture around him views a black man. To shelter Jim is an unpardonable sin; yet Huck reckons that Jim seems better than most white people he has known. He argues with his conscience, but finally decides he had better turn Jim in. He writes a note to Miss Watson to tell her where she can find him. Listen to what happens inside Huck:

> I felt good and all washed clean of sin for the first time I had ever felt so in my life, and I knowed I could pray now. But I didn't do it straight off, but laid the paper down and set there thinking—thinking how good it was all this happened so, and how near I come to being lost and going to hell. And went on thinking. And got to thinking over our trip down the river, and I see Jim before me, all the time, in the day, and in the night-time, sometimes moonlight, sometimes storms, and we a-floating along, talking, and singing and laughing. . . . And then I happened to look

around, and see that paper. It was a close place. I took it up, and held it in my hand. I was a-trembling, because I'd got to decide, forever, betwixt two things, and I knowed it. I studied a minute, sort of holding my breath, and then says to myself: "All right, then, I'll go to hell"—and tore it up.

That's not the end of the story; both Jim and Huck face other problems. However, Huck's willingness to protect Jim challenges us. What choice would I make in Huck's situation? What choices am I making now? What is my view of other human beings? Would I risk my own plans for someone like Jim? Fiction asks questions about people and their relationships.

Favorite Books That Nourished Me

Kristin Lavransdatter by Sigrid Undset
    That Undset could win the 1929 Nobel Prize as a woman, while a mother of young children, is a feat that has my undying admiration. I have read this trilogy of novels three times and hope to read it at least that many times more; it has become my "companion on the way." Undset's extraordinary grasp of human experience, particularly that of women, is riveting. I don't just read this book; I live it. See also Undset's *Master of Hestviken.*

Taran Wanderer in the Chronicles of Prydain series by Lloyd Alexander
    These books are memories that warm my heart. We read them many times with our boys. Unforgettable characters, phrases that have become family code—just the joy of sharing good adventures.

Their Eyes Were Watching God by Zora Neale Hurston
    This book has my favorite opening line, and the enchantment never wanes. Hurston gives us the experiences of Southern, rural black communities in the early twentieth century. Grit, humor, and strong characters make me glad to know them.

Moses, Man of the Mountain by Zora Neale Hurston
    Black folklore takes on the story of Moses. Not for everyone, but I like it. See also her autobiography *I Love Myself Best When I'm Laughing.*

RECOMMENDED BY SANDRA FLANIGAN ZULL,
PASTOR'S WIFE AND TEACHER

Good fiction is about what is true. It takes the true stuff of life and helps us look at it. If the story compels a good reading, it probably raises questions. It brings life to life, as it were; it helps us see what is true and what is good and what is not so good. Everything we do has meaning; fiction helps us find meaning. Because fiction is about human beings and their lives, it cannot help having an ethical dimension.

In one sense, any discussion of good fiction is theological, even if God is not mentioned. The German philosopher Oswald Spengler once remarked, "Just as music is the only art that can convey the idea of God, so narrative or fiction may be the only art that can convey the idea of man or what it means to choose well as a human being." Good fiction cannot escape concern with morality.

One of the finest pieces of literature ever written is Tolkien's fantasy trilogy The Lord of the Rings. Reading it is a profound exposure to truth and beauty. Tolkien imagines and creates a whole new world and peoples it with creatures we come to love and know. A plunge into his world of fantasy can send a person back into the real world with fresh understanding of reality and truth. He says so many true things that it takes multiple readings to absorb the depth of his stories. A good story can teach us more about being human than we can learn in any other way. (If you find Tolkien a challenge to read, then look for the book on tape with Rob Inglis reading the trilogy and go on a long trip somewhere.)

Five Elements of Strong Fiction

Five things matter in good fiction: characters, action, plot, theme, and language.

Characters

Characters make the story. Long after we have forgotten the specifics of the story, we remember the characters—if they are solid characters like Huck Finn, Elizabeth Bennet, David Copperfield, Captain Ahab, Scarlett O'Hara, or even Winnie the Pooh. We remember them because in a novel we get to know the characters gradually as we read and observe them in action. The story often takes its time (like real life) and involves change and development of the persons in it, but when it is finished, these are people we know.

A basic requirement of a good story is vivid and memorable characters. This necessitates careful word choices—good prose. Some writers give us flat characters made of pasteboard and tell us what to believe about them. That's not good fiction.

Action

The characters in fiction are made real by their actions. We see what they do, the choices they make, their interactions with others—and we come to see what these characters are like. The Huckleberry Finn story is a good example. Twain does not tell us that Huck is impulsive but tenderhearted. He does not describe the moral code by which Huck lives. We come to know what is true about Huck through his actions—authentic actions that make him an interesting character. In fiction characters and action link together to give consistency to the story.

Plot

Where does plot fit in? It is closely linked to the action as well as to the theme of the story. Every story needs a plot; otherwise the story is simply a narrative, a sequence of events. Plot gives the story structure and works out the theme so that the story has meaning. Plot does not merely answer "What happens next?" It also asks "Why?" Plot is an intellectual formulation about how the incidents of a narrative relate to each other. Plot may well be the hardest part of writing a good novel (to which many poorly written books give witness). Yet it is critical to another element of fiction: theme.

Theme

The theme in a story helps us understand what is significant about the persons and events in the story. What do you make of this human experience? What's the point of the story? Theme always involves something about values and human conduct—whether good or bad, true or false—some concept of what and how human beings should be in the world. What does this story add up to? What does it mean? Unless the theme becomes evident through the characters and the plotline, you have no answer, only a tale told.

A story does not usually state its theme: "This is a story about . . ." or "This is what you should learn from this story." Everything about the theme is discovered as the story unfolds. Without it, there would be no coherence in the story. (Don't think of theme as the topic of the story. Topics usually mean pieces of information.) In a good book theme is not a kind of moralizing with illustrations. Theme is not a poorly disguised sermon. No, the theme or significance of the story comes from the characters and their actions. It's all one piece of work.

The theme of a story takes some thinking about. What answer would you give if asked about the theme of Shakespeare's murderous Richard III? Is this just a drama about an evil man? Or is the theme about power and its consequent diminishing of human lives? Is the theme about the arrogance of believing you can determine your own destiny, about the deceit of the human heart? Why is Richard who he is?

Authors of early children's books took no chances on a reader's ability to figure out a story's meaning and frequently had mini-sermons in the middle of the story addressed to "My dear little reader . . ." Children weren't fooled; they skipped those pages. Some authors are still doing a modified version of mini-sermons. Usually it means they have not worked out the story so that the theme is woven into the characters and their actions.

Language

The best stories employ creative or unique uses of language to convey their plots, characters, and themes.

"Never dare tell me again anything about 'green grass.' Tell me how the lawn was flecked with shadows," Robert Louis Stevenson once said. "I know perfectly well that grass is green. So does everybody else in England. . . . Make me see what it was that made your garden distinct from a thousand others."

That's the hard part of writing—to see and then to find words that let others see. Poets do this the best, but many others write prose that is almost poetry. The right word in the right place!

Good prose is like a windowpane. It is crystal clear; it is focused; it startles the reader with the view. Good writers hone down their sentences, using no extra words, few adjectives, and strong verbs. You can *feel* good writing.

In contrast, amateur writers often say too much. They tend to drown the reader with dialogue in an attempt to give reality to the story and its characters. I find myself wondering why I should care about these people to whom the novelist gives so much speech. Their story seems flat and thick, rather than lean and honed.

But when I read something like Alfred Kazin's description of the tenement kitchen of his childhood, I have a different experience. He writes in *Walker in the City:*

Ripeness filled our kitchen even at suppertime. The room was so wild with light, it made me tremble; I could not believe my eyes. In the sink a great sandy pile of radishes, lettuces, tomatoes, cucumbers, and scallions broke up on their stark greens and red the harshness of the world's daily monotony. The window shade by the sewing machine was drawn, its tab baking in the sun. Through the screen came the chant of the score being called up from the last handball game below. Our front door was open, to let in air; you could hear the boys on the roof scuffing their shoes against the gravel. Then, my father home to the smell of paint in the hall, we sat down to chopped cucumbers floating in the ice-cold borscht, radishes, and tomatoes and lettuce in sour cream, a mound of corn just out of the pot steaming on the table, the butter slowly melting in a cracked blue soup plate—breathing hard against the heat, we sat down together at last.

I have never spent a late afternoon summer day in a crowded tenement building, feeling the heat radiating from the walls in the room, except for this one time when I sat in Alfred Kazin's kitchen.

The Bible reads like this—such crisp word pictures saying so much more than it seems—so rich in texture that preachers have not exhausted its depths, sometimes saying poorly and meanly truths that should be read and listened to with a holy quietness. When language is used well, it reflects that we are made in the image of God.

Putting It All Together

While the biblical story of Joseph (Genesis 37 ff.) is history rather than fiction, it is story and a superb example of how character, action, plot, and theme can coalesce to create a compelling account. With an economy of words, we come to know the *characters* in the story from their *actions*. As the story develops, so do the characters; they change, they grow. The action of the story is climaxed in Joseph's revealing himself to his brothers, but the *plot* demonstrates how all of Joseph's actions and experiences (violent treatment, sexual assault, betrayal, imprisonment) have made him the man he has become. The *theme* is larger than we immediately grasp. God is using this family's trouble to save his people from extinction during the time of famine at the same time as he is making a man out of Joseph. The reader is affected by all the parts of this story, but particularly by Joseph's confidence in God, by his learned humility and forgiveness of his family. Because the central character in the story sees the big picture, we get a glimpse of it as well.

Heart-Warmers That Are Winners

At Home in Mitford; A Light in the Window; These High, Green Hills; Out to Canaan; A New Song; and A Common Life: A Wedding Story

Jan Karon has written an inviting series of novels on Mitford, a fictional small town in North Carolina, that have left millions of readers feeling deeply nourished and wishing they lived in Mitford. The books combine good humor, authentic characters, well-worked plots, and underlying truths that not only warm the heart but also leave characters living in the reader's memory like old friends. She takes on the complexities of her characters' lives with grace and good humor, stirring up something in our hearts that lingers long after the reading. Everyone who recommends these books seems to be smiling. This must tell you something. The fame of these books is largely the result of word-of-mouth recommendations.

Cold Sassy Tree by Olive Ann Burns

Will Tweedy is fourteen when things take a scandalous turn in this small Georgia town. His newly widowed grandfather elopes with Miss Love Simpson—a woman half his age and a Yankee. The story is exuberant, funny, and full of the sheer joy of living. As the book jacket proclaims, this is "a toothsome book with passages that will make you pucker with pleasure."

RECOMMENDED BY GLADYS HUNT

Questions for the Reader to Ask

How does a reader unravel this merging of characters, action, plot, theme, and language in a good book? Asking some basic questions may clarify what you are looking for; and if you are in a book group, discussing these questions can lead to some insights you might otherwise miss.

1. What are the characters like? Are they real and memorable?
2. What do they want and why do they do what they do?
3. What true things does this book say about the human heart? about the world?
4. How does this book stretch me and enlarge my world/life view?
5. What is memorable about the author's use of language?

Do you have to understand all these to read a good story? Not necessarily, but it helps. A good book is for reading. I don't favor analyzing the life out of it. I favor enjoying it. Yet if you want to be a thoughtful reader, these simple clues help you evaluate and understand why some stories are less than satisfying. Something happens inside you as you read a really good book, and its significance is what haunts you long after you have finished reading it.

If a book leaves you exactly where it found you, thinking and feeling nothing you hadn't felt or thought before, you are no different for having read it. The criterion for a memorable book is the hope of rereading it some day and a passion to share the book with someone else.

I once wrote a note to a friend suffering from depression and in a city far from her circle of friends: "Run, don't walk, to the nearest bookstore and buy Jan Karon's books." She trusted me and did exactly that. After reading them, this urbane woman wrote me a quick note of thanks. "Talk about authentic characters," she wrote, "the people in these stories are so real I found myself praying for them!"

That's evidence of what a good story can do.

Good prose is like a windowpane.

GEORGE ORWELL

Chapter 3

The Brightest and the Best:
Literature and the Classics

The classics are books that refuse to be eradicated from your mind and hide themselves in the folds of memory. A classic is a book that is never finished saying what it has to say.

ITALO CALVINO

*P*eople have always wanted advice about what to read, and such advice seems never in short supply. In 1771 Robert Skipwith, a future brother-in-law to Mrs. Jefferson, asked Thomas Jefferson, then twenty-eight, to draw up a list of books "suited to the capacity of a common reader who understands but little of the classic and who has not leisure for any intricate or tedious study. Let them be improving and amusing." Jefferson obliged with a list of 148 titles, mostly solid classical works, but including such practical volumes as *Horse-shoeing Husbandry* and *Compendium of Physic and Surgery*.

Among my many recommendations for your reading, none will be on horse-shoeing, physics, or surgery! However, I've been lying awake at night wondering if I am remembering to list all the favorites I want to share with you. I expect to hear someone say, "Why didn't you mention . . . ?" The books I miss are for you to share with your friends.

No one has read everything and few feel they have a handle on this thing called *literature*. I consider myself a reader, but I have only to be with other readers to be made aware of how much I haven't read—that there is more out there too good to miss. It's important to remind ourselves that the reason for reading it is not to gain a reputation of being well read. This book list is meant to entice you to follow your heart and enjoy what good books offer, not to become a member of a literary elite.

Some of My Favorite Novels

When it comes to books, my golden find may be your disappointment. In literature, as in love, we are astonished at what is chosen by others. Most people, however, respond to recommendations. It's chancy to wander into a bookstore and buy a novel without some kind of referral. The supply is mighty (fifty thousand new books are published each year!), but the worthy ones may be few. Throughout this

Memorable Novels

A Fine Balance by Rohinton Mistry

Set in India in the years following the partition of Pakistan, this is a riveting and wrenching novel of the horrors inflicted by religious and caste enmity. But it is also a story of the love and loyalty that manage to endure.

Mr. Ives' Christmas by Oscar Hijuelos

Mr. Ives' son is murdered by a New York street thug—a senseless event that shakes his life to the roots. He is forced to make sense of his world—and it is here that the carefully woven Christmas story emerges. Mr. Ives experiences an epiphany—reaffirming goodness in a dark world. A wonderfully moving story well told by a fine writer.

Mariette in Ecstasy by Ron Hansen

Into the ceaseless daily round of work, study, and prayer of the Sisters of the Crucifixion comes Mariette—seventeen years old, young, pretty, but "high strung," her father says, "given to unnatural piety." Her very presence disturbs the rhythm of convent life, and then Mariette begins bleeding from unexplained wounds. Is Mariette a saint? A lying, hysterical girl? Hansen never provides the answers, but the real miracle of the book is the exacting, achingly beautiful prose that Hansen writes. It is like poetry, with not a single extra word.

RECOMMENDED BY MARILYN BAKER,
COMMUNITY LEADER

book I have scattered recommendations from many different readers to supplement my own. The variety in readers' tastes should offer even more stimulus to reading.

High on my list of favorites is *To Kill a Mockingbird* by Harper Lee. This novel is a work of art—perfectly conceived and presented—the only book Harper Lee ever wrote. Set in a 1930s small town in Alabama, the story covers three years in the lives of lawyer Atticus Finch, his two children, Scout and Jem, and their black housekeeper, Calpurnia. Told in the Southern voice of Scout, six years old when the story begins, the novel hinges on Atticus's defense of a black man accused of assaulting a white woman. It's a growing-up-in-a-small-town story as we watch Scout, Jem, and Dill Harris, a neighbor boy, enjoy kid stuff—enacting *Dracula* and telling scary tales about the town's bogeyman, Mr. Arthur Radley, whom they call Boo. Scout and Jem are caught up in events beyond their understanding as their father defends Tom Robinson in court, and later from being lynched by the town's racists. When Atticus warns Jem not to shoot at any mockingbird because, "It's a sin to kill a mockingbird because all it does is sing its heart out for us"—he uses the metaphor that ties together the deeper meaning of this unforgettable book. I first read this book in the 1960s and have read it twice since then. It's not a new book, but if you haven't read it, it's as good as ever today. On a recent car journey we listened to an audio-reading of the book from the library, read perfectly in Southern voice. When we got home we rented the video to see it once more on the screen with Gregory Peck in the role of Atticus.

Cry, the Beloved Country by Alan Paton was the first book to broadcast the pain of racial conflict in South Africa; it was like a shot heard around the world. It is a tender story of two fathers, Reverend Stephen Kumalo, a black pastor, and Jarvis, a white plantation owner, both victims of apartheid, who each loses a son. Absalom Kumalo, caught in a vice ring in the black townships of Johannesburg, accidentally shoots Mr. Jarvis's son. In this heart-breaking story of grace and forgiveness I saw the terrible price exacted by racial prejudice. We have also listened to this on audio-tape while on a long car journey. It's one of the books that can be read again and again.

When I read Chaim Potok's *The Promise* and *The Chosen*, I was drawn into the lives of Reuven Malther and Danny Saunders in the Brooklyn of 1940. Despite their different backgrounds, these two boys form a deep friendship and try to understand each other's families.

Reuven is a secular Jew with an intellectual Zionist father, while Danny is the brilliant son and rightful heir to a Hasidic rebbe. The intellectual clashes between the fathers, between each son and his father, and between the two young friends allow us to explore the issues in these relationships. Ultimately and movingly, in the end they trade places in their convictions. Chaim Potok is one of the great writers in the United States. His books span a long career; he is still writing, and I am still entering into the hearts of his characters and understanding Jewish life the better for it. Look also for *My Name Is Asher Lev* and *The Gift of Asher Lev.*

Staying in the home of a friend in England, I picked up *The Heaven Tree* by Edith Pargeter from the bookshelves in their library and began to read it one night before going to sleep. I quickly got involved in the story and the hours flew past. At breakfast I learned *The Heaven Tree* was the first of an epic trilogy—one of the most compelling reads ever—and one I had to leave unfinished until back home in the United States. I found it published here in one volume under the title *The Heaven Tree Trilogy.* In the twelfth century in the west of England near the Welsh border, Harry Talvace, a gifted stonecutter, is taken a virtual prisoner by the powerful and brooding Lord of Parfois, Rolf Isambard, who sponsors Harry's monumental creation of a cathedral. The story interplays the integrity and grace of Harry, the young stonecutter, with the uncontrolled passions of Isambard. The three books take one through many page-turning adventures, and the ending leaves the reader breathless! Pargeter considered this her finest writing, and so do I.

Edith Pargeter is also the real name of the person who writes as Ellis Peters. Her appealing Cadfael mysteries are noted in the mystery section of this chapter. A prolific writer before her death in the late 1990s, she seemed to like trilogies and even quartets, setting much of what she wrote in the twelfth century and along the Welsh border. Her war novels are among the best ever written to chronicle the failures and successes of World War II. Pargeter wrote almost contemporaneously with the action of the war—both a painful and glorious account. Look for *The Eighth Champion of Christendom* as the first of the war trilogy. Look also for *A Means of Grace*, the story of a woman's return to a country divided by communism.

Wallace Stegner's *Angle of Repose* (1972 Pulitzer Prize) tells the story of a lonely historian, just past middle age and beset with a debilitating bone disease, who struggles to give his waning life significance

check?
out

by writing the story of his pioneering grandparents—Susan and Oliver Ward. "Angle of repose," a geological term describing the angle at which matter settles after an avalanche, is the metaphor in Stegner's exploration of the emotional terrain in the lives of his grandparents. Although his writing has a grim reality to it, Stegner's depth of insight and beautiful prose captivate me. He is one of those "I bought everything he has written" kind of authors. I liked his *Big Rock Candy Mountain*, a novel about a transient, rootless family in the American West in the early 1900s. Bo Mason is the book's most dominant character, who is obsessed with finding the Big Rock Candy Mountain where "the bluebird sings to the lemonade springs," a land of futile dreams. Another of Stegner's novels is *Crossing to Safety*, the story of a lifelong friendship of two academics and their wives who meet at the University of Wisconsin. It's deceptively simple and terribly moving.

Kazuo Ishiguro captures the tragic story of the perfect English butler in his repressed and fading world in post-war England in *The Remains of the Day*. Stevens the butler "inhabits his profession," so caught up in the past that he cannot embrace any life-affirming love that would help him know what to do "with the remains of the day." A must-read for Anglophiles.

Willa Cather's *My Antonia* makes the reader feel the burning sun, hear the waving grasses of Nebraska, and experience the hardships of pioneer life for the immigrant settlers. Jim Burden goes to live with his grandparents in Nebraska and becomes fascinated with the life of a simple and courageous young woman from Bohemia, Antonie Shimerda, and tells her compelling story in his voice. Cather's fine prose stirs the heart and the senses. Read her *O Pioneers, Death Comes for the Archbishop, Song of the Lark,* and *The Professor's House.*

Johanna Greenberg (who also writes as Hannah Green) says she wrote *I Never Promised You a Rose Garden* during the 1960s and 70s when people were taking LSD to simulate what they thought was a liberating experience. There is no creativity in madness, says Greenberg, writing partly to dispel the romanticism of being out of your mind, while at the same time dealing with the stigma of mental illness. The book confines the reader to an insane asylum. No one does a better job of standing you in another's shoes than Greenberg does. *In This Sign* is her moving story of a hearing child of deaf mutes. Both of these books expanded my compassion and understanding.

So Big, a 1924 Pulitzer Prize winner, is Edna Ferber's best book. Set in early twentieth century in rural and urban Chicago, this is the story of spirited Selina DeJong and her struggle to raise her only son Dirk (called So Big) and teach him what is valuable in life. Although she is undaunted in the struggle to give advantages to Dirk, he misses the point of his mother's life and becomes shallow and selfish. It's an engrossing, highly readable tale by a fine storyteller. Her *Cimarron* and *Giant* are noted in the Western book section.

At this point you may be thinking, *Her favorites were mostly written in the first half of the twentieth century!* Yes, they are timeless in impact and writing skill. The daily papers will push all that is new. I owe it to you to recommend at least some old books that you might otherwise miss. But that is not all there is!

I liked David Guterson's *Snow Falling on Cedars* because of his skillful prose and the way he led me to feel and see the lush rainforest of an island north of Puget Sound, as well as his sensitive review of the Japanese history of that island. Beautifully written (but with some unnecessary sexual scenes), it is the story of a drowning and the Japanese American charged with the murder. *Obasan* by Joy Kogawa is another telling of the incarceration of Japanese families in the West—events that destroyed families and culture and a way of life. It is a bitter, haunting story.

Jayber Crow by Wendell Berry catches the flavor of a slower-paced, more thoughtful world in a novel with characters so real that you already know some of them. An orphaned boy who feels called to the ministry cuts his seminary days short because of questions of faith he cannot answer. Instead he becomes a barber in Port Williams and finds himself listening to the stories of his customers and discovering answers that eluded him before. Downright wonderful writing.

Mark Helprin's writing almost takes your breath away with his descriptions and multilayered plots. *A Soldier of the Great War* is an epic tale that includes everything that makes a

A Gem of a Writer

Louis De Bernières—what a gem of a writer to discover! His style is charming, combining comedy and tragedy in novels that touch the heart.

Corelli's Mandolin—probably De Bernières' most enthralling novel, set in 1941. Captain Corelli is a young Italian officer posted on the Greek Island of Cephallonia, part of the occupation forces. Corelli, with his gentle disposition and sense of humor, is a lover of peace, beauty, music, as well as the local doctor's daughter! This is essentially a wartime love story—moving, funny, and angry—told in lyrical language.

Señor Vivo and the Coca Lord—similarly humorous and satirical, with De Bernières' anger directed at the drug trade in Colombia. Passion, love, and humor are juxtaposed with appalling violence and wanton cruelty.

RECOMMENDED BY ROSEMARY MOORE, ATTORNEY AND MOTHER

story good reading: humor, memorable characters, and fine use of language. Woven into the storyline we find concern for moral issues, spiritual issues, beauty, and love, as Helprin gives us a fine example of what significant fiction can do: leave the reader profoundly moved.

Every reader has favorites to share. Maybe over lunch you have scrawled out some recommended titles on an old napkin or envelope that now lies crumpled in the bottom of your handbag—authors and books you need to explore.

Let's Look at Some of the Classics

This is probably the last place you would choose to look for a good, readable book. The classics have been given bad press. Most people aren't sure they know what they are and why they are classics. Samuel Clemens (Mark Twain) said in jest, "A classic is something everyone wants to have and nobody wants to read." Ask average readers what they think about reading the classics, and they immediately conjure up a high school English class where they languished in ennui during their teenage years. If even thinking about them turns you off, skip this section and go on to the next.

Why am I touting the classics? Because they give you a standard to distinguish between what is inferior and superior in a day when we tolerate so much of what is mediocre. It is contact with greatness. You may not like the ones I like, but these stories will stick with you and instruct you for life.

Classics, in book language, simply mean that the stories are so good that they can bear reading and rereading. The dictionary defines *classic:* "of the highest class; being a model of its kind." It's a product of enduring excellence. It has become commonplace for reviewers to call new books classics, but that only describes their hoped-for potential. Most classics are over a hundred years old, and you have to be good to last that long! Reading the classics is an acquired taste; you can't be captivated by what you haven't tried. Once you begin, the classics can be trusted to win us.

A word of advice about classics: the first fifty pages are usually the hardest. In a visual age we find movies and television assaulting our minds with so much action in the first few minutes that we sometimes don't know who is who. Readers of character-driven books need to step back and let the author set the scene, allowing your imagination to work. Don't give up until you have read at least fifty pages! What's the hurry? Relax. Walk through the scene and mood the author is building: look and feel and listen. This warning applies to many books—wherever the author is building something of depth.

I remember when I chose to read Victor Hugo's *Les Miserables*, admittedly with a sense of doing something noble and sacrificial as I held this 1,400-plus page book in my hands. Before I knew what was happening I was swept away with each new character I met in the story—from the valiant Jean Valjean to Fantine to Inspector Javert and the inspiring Enjolras who leads the student revolution. I could scarcely put the book down. I began to hound my friends about reading it. I even gleaned bits of humor and wisdom in memorable lines: "A girl who knows herself to be pretty is less likely to become a nun, the sense of vocation varying inversely with the degree of beauty." Reading the book heightened my enjoyment for the musical, which I admit to seeing three times and would gladly go again. What a story!

Having finished that weighty tome and finding such delight in reading it, I could relate to Alice falling down the rabbit hole, down, down, down, and thinking to herself, *Well, after such a fall as this, I shall think nothing of tumbling down stairs! Why I wouldn't say anything about it, even if I fell off the top of the house!* It made reading some other classics a piece of cake.

First Books

The classic that began it all is Homer's *The Odyssey*. Katherine Paterson, the noted children's author, said, "I was always told that I should read *The Odyssey*. But somehow I never got around to the whole thing until I was forty-six years old. I gave myself the assignment to read *The Odyssey* (Rouse's translation) all the way through from the beginning to end. Do you know why *The Odyssey* has lasted for nearly three thousand years? Because it is a simply marvelous story. Why did people keep telling me that I ought to read it so that I could be an educated person? I can't imagine anyone who had ever really read it, telling someone else to read it because it was good for him. Read it because it's one of the best stories you'll ever read. Read it because it's one of the best stories I ever read." Both *The Odyssey* and *The Iliad* by Homer have new translations. I like Robert Fagle's new translation.

The Best Novels from Around the World

In each of the following novels, the particular social or political situation is critical to the characters' dilemmas. Their voices bear witness to how people can remain human under extreme conditions. Do not be surprised that the characters' sexuality is graphically displayed in a couple of them because, for people without an ultimate hope in God, human love is often their only solace, or as Allende puts it, the way to "save themselves from a banal existence."

One Day in the Life of Ivan Denisovich by Alexander Solzhenitsyn

The book that shook the Soviet Union four decades ago traces an ordinary winter day in the life of an ordinary peasant-prisoner in a Siberian work camp. On this one day of his 365 days of imprisonment, Ivan maintains his inherent dignity and hope for survival by doing the best work he can and sharing his meager resources with his fellow zuks.

Things Fall Apart by Chinua Achebe

When the missionaries first penetrate into Igbo country, they upset the delicate balance of social mores and religious rituals that determine both individual and community roles. Okonkwo's desire to achieve success precipitates his calamity just as the clan life is being altered by outsiders. This Nigerian classic is still the best entrée into African literature.

The Unbearable Lightness of Being by Milan Kundera

Kundera explores the philosophical question of whether what we do in life has any meaning if physical existence is all there is (the "lightness" of the title). He works this out on a personal, existential level in the lives of two sets of lovers. The question ironically assumes great weight on the political level because all four are Czechs enduring the Soviet occupation in which the government makes decisions for its citizens. A difficult book to read, but worth the effort to understand the forces of modernity that shape all our lives.

Silence by Shusako Endo

Endo, a Christian and Japan's best known novelist, plunges his readers into the dark despair of a sixteenth-century Portuguese priest who returns to Japan to help the believers being tortured by the shogun. His dilemma: to renounce his faith by stepping on the fumie (a medallion bearing the face of Christ) so that the faithful can be set free or to refuse to recant so that they die. He longs to hear Jesus break the silence that engulfs him. No one can read this book and be unchanged.

Of Love and Shadows by Isabel Allende

Based on an actual incident of military brutality in Chile during the dictatorship of Augusto Pinochet, Allende tells the story of three families sucked into a shared tragedy who learn the meaning of love through suffering. Allende, considered one of Latin America's best contemporary authors, now lives in the United States.

RECOMMENDED BY BARBARA HAMPTON,
TEACHER AND WRITER

Can you imagine *Beowulf* on the best-seller list? The Irish poet Seamus Heaney recently won a coveted prize for his updated translation of the timeless Anglo-Saxon epic *Beowulf.* It's a wonderful translation and begs to be read aloud. Or listen to the audio version, where Seamus Heaney himself reads these wonderful tales of heroism that were written over a thousand years ago.

Memorable Reads from the Past

If reading Shakespeare has not been your thing, but you'd still like to get the gist of Shakespeare's plays, then by all means get a copy of the wonderful old book *Tales from Shakespeare* by Charles and Mary Lamb, a brother-sister team who faithfully and simply tell the stories of Shakespeare's plays. This book was written in 1807 and still is in bookstores today!

Pilgrim's Progress by John Bunyan deserves an adult reading. We read this book aloud when our son was fourteen. We waded through the original King James English on purpose (we had already read Helen Taylor's *Little Pilgrim's Progress*) because we were fascinated by the imagery and allegory. Christian's dangerous journey to the Heavenly City, often waylaid or detoured in places like the Slough of Despond facing almost certain defeat, gave us much to talk about for our own journey. John Bunyan's antiquated sentences have been updated in several different versions. No excuses are valid anymore for omitting this relevant journey from your reading list.

Don Quixote by Cervantes takes the reader on a journey on horseback chasing windmills. The friendship between Quixote and Sancho Panza and their affectionate debates make up the heart of the story. Quixote's visionary madness and Panza's shrewdness play off each other in humorous ways. Don Quixote, referring to knights that go mad because of a lady's rejection, says that he has it worked out beautifully. "If a knight errant goes crazy for good reason, how much is that worth? My idea is to become a lunatic for no reason at all." I recommend an abridged version done by Walter Starkie because of wandering passages that only divert the reader. It's a great adventure story, comparable to *The Odyssey*, very funny and satirical. King Phillip III of Spain, noticing a man reading beside the road and laughing so much tears were rolling down his cheeks, said, "That man is either crazy or he is reading *Don Quixote.*"

The Great Nineteenth-Century Novels

Jane Austen wrote her five great novels—*Pride and Prejudice, Persuasion, Mansfield Park, Emma,* and *Sense and Sensibility*—in about five years' time. Many call her the finest woman novelist in the English language. *Sense and Sensibility* and *Pride and Prejudice* both have protagonists with wise insights into men and sufficient courtship intrigues to delight and lead to second and third readings. Something about the

Why I Never Tire of Reading Jane Austen

Jane Austen (1775–1817) started writing when she was twenty-one years old and died when she was forty-one! She lived her whole life in the circle of her family in the parish where her father ministered and had no contact with the London literary world. Yet she is considered by many to be the greatest woman novelist of the English-speaking world. Her novels are largely novels of manners; no earth-shaking events take place, but this allows her characters' lives to stand out in bold relief so that they translate well into today's world and seem as vital as ever.

Her detailed conversations between friends and sisters are particularly memorable. In *Pride and Prejudice* Elizabeth and Jane delightfully share the details of each other's lives—their secrets, household problems, family situations, relationships with acquaintances and friends.

Her insights into the human heart regarding love—romantic and familial—and God's role in our daily lives still span the centuries.

Her satirical wit creates some very funny characters. She finds comedy in everyday occurrences of life and relationship. Some are tragically funny like Mrs. Bennet with her hysterics and constant whining.

Her keen insights into the moral climate of society and her characters are still valid today. In *Pride and Prejudice* Jane remarks to Elizabeth, "One (young man) has got all the goodness, and the other all the appearance of it."

Her convincing characters are interesting enough to make reading the books several times a pleasure. I greet her characters as friends and never tire of them.

While she sometimes uses biting irony, Austen's descriptions of eighteenth-century culture remind us that we also have rules, pitfalls, and comedy in our own ways of relating.

RECOMMENDED BY MARIAN HUNT,
ONCOLOGY NURSE

wisdom and beauty of manners and courtship, plus Austen's sly and unfailing wit, attract women readers in our age of casual living. Fadiman says of her, "She was born to delight readers, not to shake their souls."

Leo Tolstoy's *War and Peace* is still on my list to conquer; it's long and complicated, but may well be one of the greatest novels ever written. It is a gigantic story of the impact of Napoleon's invasion on a whole country; it is honest and perceptive. I started it once many years ago and got lost in the complex cast of characters. Now that I am a more experienced reader, I need to try it again. I found Tolstoy's *The Death of Ivan Ilych* (using Aylmer Maude's translation) a powerful and beautifully written story about the meaning of life and death. It cuts aside all sham and, with Ivan, the reader must face the truth.

Tolstoy's less demanding *Anna Karenina* is probably his most widely read work—the story of a woman who discovers too late that she has thrown away all that makes her life meaningful to follow her lover. In the end it becomes nothing; her sorrow overtakes her and she ends her life. It is Russian all the way, reflecting life under the czars, and is a very powerful comment on choices.

And then there is Fydor Dostoyevsky's *The Brothers Karamzov*. It is hard to think of a book that more clearly gives a picture of fallen humanity and the great grace of God than this book. It is a story that remains in your heart long after the reading is finished. His *Crime and Punishment* remains the best of all murder stories almost a century and half after it was published. If you feel reluctant to try a complete novel, let me put you on to a book that will give you a taste of what makes Dostoyevsky so timeless. I recommend *The Gospel in Dostoyevsky*, available from Plough Publishing House. It contains some of the most unforgettable passages in Dostoyevsky's writings. It could whet your appetite to read a whole novel.

Charles Dickens is a household fixture, with great popularity around the world. His memorable characters and descriptions of weather and landscape make all his descriptive passages worthwhile for me. Passages like "A cold silvery mist had veiled the afternoon, and the moon was not yet up to scatter it. But, the stars were shining beyond the mist and the moon was coming." I especially urge you to read *The Tale of Two Cities, David Copperfield, A Christmas Carol*, and *Oliver Twist*. No other writer has written so convincingly of the injustices of the Victorian period, especially the hardships inflicted on children. *David Copperfield* is a sentimental gem. His characters are so vividly developed that the best way to recommend Dickens is to mention the Artful Dodger, Fagin, Mr. Micawber, Uriah Heep, Miss Havisham, Mme. DeFarge, the lovely Agnes, innocent Lil' Emily, or Pegotty whose buttons keep popping off, or Barkis, who is willing. The reader knows these as unforgettable human beings, and a mental curtain goes up at the very mention of their names.

Jane Eyre by Charlotte Brontë captures a romantic's heart, making it many women's all-time favorite book. It has all the drama, suspense, and happy ending a reader longs for in a story—a spirited orphan heroine to admire, employment as a governess at Thornfield Hall, the handsome father's troubling secret, and Jane's unrequited love for him. The other Brontë sister, Emily Brontë, writes with a wild passion, maybe reflecting the Yorkshire moors of their childhoods. *Wuthering Heights* is a nightmarish book with many twists in the plot, a story set in the cold sweep of the Scottish moors and threaded with violence. It is sheer melodrama and yet has captured the imagination of readers for two centuries.

Thomas Hardy's novels give us characters painted in bold colors on the dreary heaths of nineteenth-century England. In *The Return of the Native* Clym Yeobright returns to Egdon Heath and marries the wrong woman. It is the story of a love triangle with the least likely fellow having the truest, kindest heart. *Far from the Madding Crowd* left me wanting to warn the pure-hearted Gabriel about the coquetry of immature Bathsheba. *Tess of the D'Ubervilles* is one of the most tragic heroines of classical literature. Discovering that she is from a noble birth only brings her grief and places her in bondage to the D'Ubervilles. It is a tale of love gone astray. Many believe this is Hardy's best novel. Hardy captures readers almost unexpectedly. Fans such as English professor Henry Zylstra declare, "There is more of you, after reading Hardy, to be a Christian with than there was before you read him, and there is also more conviction that you want to be it."

"Above all, give me Anthony Trollope, from whom I have received so much pleasure. Of those who minister to the tired, nightwelcoming mind, Trollope is king. He is the perfect novelist for the bedside." So writes reading guru Clifton Fadiman. Look for Trollope's character-driven stories, such as *The Warden*, the first of many novels set in Barset, *Barchester Towers*, or *Phineas Finn*. Trollope, a British postal official (he is the father of the mailbox; before his time everyone had to go to the post office), arose before dawn each day to write by candlelight for three hours (writing a thousand words an hour!) before going to the labors that kept his family fed. He gave us characters to love and characters to hate, with themes of power struggles, greed, love, desperation, and generosity. His stories are funny, moving, and about real people.

George Eliot was really Mary Ann Evans, writing as a man so that she would be published and read. *Middlemarch*, a story of an unhappy marriage, develops the author's frustration over the confines of women in the middle 1800s. Dorothea Brooke, searching for some worthwhile fulfillment for her life, calls herself "St. Theresa of Nothing." It's a challenging book of nine hundred pages, but full of lines you will want to stop and reread to ponder her insights into human nature. You will find yourself referring to Eliot's characters in your conversations.

The Scarlet Letter by Nathaniel Hawthorne, set in seventeenth-century New England, deserves an adult reading. In the story Hawthorne gives the Puritan world a more uptight climate than has since proven to be true. (Research has shown the Puritans were joyful,

Big Books I Liked

Les Miserables by Victor Hugo
    The story of Jean Valjean, the most famous peasant in classical literature, who was imprisoned for stealing a loaf of bread. No one should miss this.

A Suitable Boy by Vikram Seth
    At the center of this vivid look into Indian culture are Mrs. Rupa Mehra and her search for the right husband for her daughter, Lata. The portrait of four families caught in a web of love and ambition requiring the most delicate social etiquette and the most appalling violence.

Lonesome Dove by Larry McMurtry
    An epic of the frontier West. Full of unforgettable characters: heroes, outlaws, ladies, Indians, and prostitutes—real and unromanticized. Contains powerful metaphors of Christian life and truth. (Language, violence, and sexual situations)

The Brothers K by David James Duncan
    A thread of redemption runs through this novel about four brothers coming of age in the 1960s. But, oh, what a price they pay for the wisdom gained. No contemporary author moves me like Duncan. The range of emotion he evokes—from hilarity to sorrow matches real life as it exists. (Language and some sexual situations)

Kristin Lavransdatter by Sigrid Undset
    See description of book on page 43.

RECOMMENDED BY MARGIE HAACK,
WRITER AND COLUMNIST

relaxed people; howbeit with a morality befitting their faith.) Rather than a discussion of Puritan hypocrisy, this is a parable of the human heart and its hidden guilt and fears. It is only incidentally a story of the bitter fruits of adultery. Hawthorne's characters—Hester Prynne, Roger Chillingworth, and Arthur Dimmesdale—are seen with new eyes and raise even bigger questions. Which is the greater sin? Adultery or deception? Which is the greater punishment? Public humiliation or guilt? Try to find this on audio-cassette and listen with new ears.

Someone has said that *Moby Dick* by Herman Melville reads like "an organ with all the stops pulled out," an apt description of the magnificent prose of this book. It is a superb story in which obsessive Ahab rallies his whole crew in his revenge quest to kill the menacing Moby Dick, the snow-white sperm whale. All but Ishmael, the narrator, are destroyed by Ahab's insane venture. Reading it is not a small venture, but I know of people who have read it many times—not just for the adventure of the story, but to grasp the multilayered themes in the book. Is this something a woman would want to read? Why not? You will never forget it.

Twentieth-Century Classics

Rudyard Kipling wrote marvelous tales for children, a quantity of good poetry and *Kim*, the story of a half-caste Indian-Irish orphan boy who grows up in Lahore. He attaches himself to a wandering holy man in search of a river that will wash away his sins. Along the way he becomes a secret agent for the British Colonial government. Enough said. His adventures are captivating.

Certainly on its way to being a classic is Thornton Wilder's *The Bridge of San Luis Rey*—the story of the collapse of an eighteenth-century bridge in Peru, killing five people. Who were these five? Was it an accident or a punishment from God? Brother Juniper searches out their intertwined lives, believing that "either we live by accident and die by accident or we live by plan and die by plan." Look also for *Theophilus North* and *Our Town* by Wilder.

Jessamyn West did us all a favor when she wrote *Friendly Persuasion,* the story of the Birdwells, a devout Quaker family in southern Indiana before the Civil War, who live by rules with a pervading sense of joy and playfulness. The father's free spirit and love of singing and horse-racing sometimes clashes with the more serious, practical mother, and thereby hangs part of the tensions in the story.

From English Class to the Bookstore: Toni Morrison

I first read **Toni Morrison**'s novels in a college English class and found her writing compelling. Her novels can be challenging because she switches perspective and narrators without warning. She lets each major character have a "say," which makes quick, easy judgments difficult. (Coarse language)

The Bluest Eye is probably the most accessible of her novels—the story of a young black girl who wishes for blue eyes, which she thinks would make her happier. Difficult situations occur—a rape lies at the center of the book—but Morrison leads the reader through, tracing the ways love can be damaged and twisted, but still remain resilient.

Sula. Two girlhood friends made choices that lead to very different lives. One stays rooted in family and community, the other becomes rebel and critic. In the end they confront each other and their choices—and face up to ways they have hurt each other and the ways they still love each other.

Beloved is the best of Morrison's novels, in my opinion. The story can be hard to follow because of its shifting narrators, but the book is worth the struggle. It focuses on a young woman who escapes from slavery but lives constantly with its terrible consequences and impossible choices. A very powerful book.

RECOMMENDED BY MARIA BERGSTROM, LITERATURE PH.D. AND FULL-TIME MOTHER

I first read *Giants in the Earth* by Ole E. Rolvaag when I was in high school. I copied all the beautifully written passages into a notebook to read again and again. It's the story of Per Hansa and his family, Norwegian immigrants who settled in southeast South Dakota during the latter part of the nineteenth century. There has never been a better book about the joys and sorrows of the early pioneers settling on the northern Great Plains.

A Farewell to Arms by Ernest Hemingway is a novel about the Italian front of World War I where Henry, an American ambulance driver, falls in love with Catherine, a British nurse. Henry, cynical about war and uncertain about Catherine as a permanent attachment, later deserts to join Catherine and escape from behind the lines. You may also enjoy his novella *The Old Man and the Sea*, plus his many short stories found in many collections.

The Pearl by John Steinbeck, a short novel, tells the story of a simple peasant named Kino who dives for clams in the waters off Mexico and finds the pearl of great price. His joy over this provision for his family is short-lived because the pearl begins to change him, bringing greed and treachery with it.

A Tree Grows in Brooklyn by Betty Smith is Francie's story and told through her unbiased eyes. Francie is a book-loving girl determined to read every book in the library and be educated. The story has plenty of poverty and physical squalor, and some moral squalor as well. But like a Tree of Heaven, Francie manages to grow out of the cement in her slowly changing twentieth-century Brooklyn neighborhood.

Lamp-Lit Souls: Southern Writers

The American South produces an abundance of good writing. It is a region of the country where the Bible is still seen, felt, heard, and for better and for worse, used and abused. Nearly ninety percent of people living in the South, natives or not, claim some religious affiliation. Vacation Bible school banners billow up and down neon shopping strips and farming back roads the whole month of June. Street preachers still get arrested for disturbing the peace, and revivals are advertised on roller-signs at the highway's edge. To be fluent in contemporary Southern culture is, to some extent, to be conversant with the church and the Bible.

One of the reasons this region produces so much good fiction is that these writers, raised in the Bible belt, grew up hearing the Judeo-Christian stories over and over again in Scripture, songs, hymns, and dramatic pageants. If, as has been said, there are no new stories, then it follows that some of our most accomplished and promising contemporary writers are well versed in the Story. In recommending these books I make no claim to understanding the personal faith of any of these writers, but there is an unmistakable connection between the Bible as a source and wellspring for these storytellers.

The reason these stories are worth reading by busy, overworked modern women interested in lighting the lamp of their souls is simple: they are good stories that tell something truthful, grant us strength, and sometimes even give us the ability to love. It's food for the soul.

CONTRIBUTED BY SHERYL CORNETT,
UNIVERSITY LECTURER AND WRITER

Meet Three Contemporary Southern Writers

grand humor and insight into human nature have won him awards and a following of loyal readers. His entertaining stories and the way they are written show us ourselves and keep us laughing. Women readers love Edgerton.

Raney chronicles the "first two years, two months, two days" of a modern Southern marriage between Southern cultural opposites.

The Floatplane Notebooks gives a glimpse through multiple points-of-view of life's unpredictables (from unwanted pregnancy to Vietnam War casualties) in the lives of an extended family in a small Southern town.

Walking Across Egypt is an up-close experience of a lovable grandma who takes seriously the gospel teaching "whatever you do unto the least of these" and adopts a juvenile delinquent to "train him up in the way he should go."

Killer Diller carries on the cast of *Walking*, and looks hard at what is often unchristian about Christian institutions—in this case a fictional Baptist university.

Memory of Junior blesses us with those multiple storyteller points-of-view. There's always more than one side to every story.

Trouble Sleeps—my personal favorite—comes again with a community viewpoint, arrived at via individual tellers of the tale of the town of Listre, North Carolina, summer 1950s.

Doris Betts received the Lifetime Achievement Award from the Conference on Christianity & Literature for her contributions and support of "connections between Christianity and literature." She has a reputation for creating haunting stories of quirky, endearing people.

Souls Raised from the Dead takes us into the heart of a blended, imperfect modern family as they deal with the illness and death of an only child.

The Sharp Teeth of Death is a healing journey that doesn't shy away from violence and its purging, which is often a part of significant cleansing and transformation.

Other titles—*The Gentle Insurrection, Beasts of the Southern Wild, The River to Pickle Beach, Heading West*—are worth investigating. Betts's understanding of the human heart is powerful.

Lee Smith, a prolific storytelling woman, writes straight to the heart of her readers. Her main characters' (chiefly women) struggles, triumphs, and courage mirror and inform our own. *Oral History, Family Linen, The Devil's Dream, Fair and Tender Ladies,* and *Saving Grace* are all titles I unequivocally recommend. She writes break-to-heal-your-heart novels and short stories. *Me and My Baby View the Eclipse* and *News of the Spirit* are short story collections. *Fair and Tender Ladies* spans almost a century of living in Appalachian Virginia; the moving and tender story is told through letters. Wonderful reading.

RECOMMENDED BY SHERYL CORNETT, UNIVERSITY LECTURER AND WRITER

Lost Horizons by James Hilton is an exciting tale of three men and a woman trying to escape from political upheaval in the Orient who crash on a Tibetan plain and are taken to Shangri-la, where life is stress-free. Or is it? This old book proves very relevant for our stressed-out lives.

Short Stories for Busy People

Short stories might be what you are looking for. Don't neglect this genre, especially if you are short on time to read. Short stories are not just abbreviated novels; they have their own characteristics, such as concise language that compels the reader to make moral judgments with a minimum of detail. The writer avoids explanation; the stories usually have a single emotion or impression, often set in one scene. The plot is simple and the action takes place in a short amount of time. Every character in a short story is essential, and the story has one strong effect on the reader, not many. The first paragraph arouses and holds the attention and usually tells you whether the story is primarily about character or action or setting—not all three. The end likely will contain a twist or a surprise that delights the reader. There's a great deal to explore in this category that offers delicious bites of reading to busy people.

Wendell Berry's *Fidelity* contains stories so poignant that I want to stop the nearest person and read aloud to her. Few can spin a spell quite like Berry, whose economy of words conveys so much. Each story in this collection comments on a dimension of faithfulness and reveals the connectedness of families to their past and to the landscape. *Remembering* by Berry is either a short novel (124 pages) or a long short story about a farmer's journey from wounded alienation to healed community. *Booklist* called Berry "one of our finest, keenest-eyed, sharpest-eared" writers. For crisp, clean, good writing, read Wendell Berry.

If you want your heart twisted a bit, or if you love things Irish, by all means read *The Hill Bachelors* by William Trevor. Trevor ranks among the greatest living writers in English. His tight, perfected short stories—each an astonishing tale with acute psychological insights—are reminiscent of Thomas Hardy's writing. Each of the stories is about men and women and their missed opportunities.

A collection of short stories is a good addition for your library because it allows you to pull down the book for a single story and have a first-rate reading experience. Wallace and Margy Stegner edited *Great American Short Stories*, a collection of twenty-six classic stories by writers like Washington Irving, Herman Melville, Mark Twain, William Faulkner, John Steinbeck, Eudora Welty, and other notables. Robert Penn Warren and Albert Erskine have put together a fine collection called *Short Story Masterpieces. The Collected Stories of Wallace Stegner* makes excellent reading. I like my edition of *The Oxford Book of English Short Stories*, containing over thirty short stories by authors from Graham Greene to T. H. White. Southern writers have interesting collections of short stories. Try *Acts of Faith* edited by Jane Mead and Reid Sherline, or *New Stories from the South* edited by Anne Tyler.

Flannery O'Connor, a Southern writer and a devout Catholic, is considered one the great writers of short stories. I find experienced readers like her stories best. Her characters are usually bizarre, a device she uses to help readers understand total depravity and other theological truths. In *Parker's Back*, a man named Parker has the word *Jesus* tattooed in large letters on his back to prove to his wife that he is spiritual. O'Connor's world does not feature your usual kind of reality, but she uses the extreme to shock the reader into noticing. Her stories almost cry out for discussion because you have a suspicion you might be missing the point. Her use of humor is disarming, but she wants the reader to join in her laughter at the comical side of the universe. Look for *Flannery O'Connor: The Complete Stories*.

My favorite novels and classics, plus the allure of short stories, make quite a reading list. Do read some of my favorites if they are new to you. I hope some of my enthusiasm for the classics has rubbed off on you, too, so that you will decide to try at least one, and perhaps discipline yourself to do one a year. You'll feel richer on the inside if you do. But you've only just begun; *read on!*

I am trying to claim for fiction both the taste of sherbet
and the importance of steak.

HENRY ZYLSTRA

Chapter 4

Something for Everyone:
Genre Fiction

You think your pain and your heartbreak are unprecedented in the history of the world, but then you read. It was books that taught me that the things that tormented me most were the very things that connected me with all the people who were alive, or who had ever been alive.

JAMES BALDWIN

*O*f the making of books there is no end! Even in ancient days this was true, according to the writer of Ecclesiastes. One friend told me that he loved books until he worked in a used bookstore where he began to feel besieged by the sheer quantity of unread books that surrounded him. It was too much to contemplate.

Within the genre of novels are many subgenres, and it's this variety that brings such pleasure to the reader. A purist would be hesitant to link mystery stories and Western adventures with any discussion of literature, but a good story still qualifies. Whatever the genre, there is always the challenge of good, better, and best.

Women Writers

Among contemporary novelists, women writers are numerous, and they are turning out good stuff. I'm reminded of an amusing quote

from Mark Twain: "She warn't particular, she could write about anything you choose to give her to write about, just so it was sadful."
That's the stereotype often given women writers—sentimental
thoughts dripping tears everywhere—but these writers don't quite
fit that description. Not that there is anything wrong with "sadful"
writing, since reality can be pretty sad. What we are really talking
about is sentiment, emotional content. However, *sentiment* and *sentimentality* are not the same thing. Sentimentality is a manipulative
device that exists for its own sake. Sentiment is the healthy part of
fiction. It is earned through the skillful use of language and authentic characters who struggle with the real stuff of life. It's a good thing.

Getting to know authors is a key way to find good books, so here
are some women writers you may want to investigate. Some of these
writers' success has meant that editors keep urging them toward
"another book," and in some instances this has led to a repeat of
themes and less significant plot development than in the earliest
books.

Maeve Binchy places her stories in the Ireland she knows so well.
Her characters are authentic, like people you know, often not saintly,
but always very Irish. In the end, those who break the rules do not
prosper. Look for *The Glass Lake, Circle of Friends*, and *Evening Class*,
among others.

Anne Tyler, whose characters are always a little quirky, helps us
get beyond labels and stereotypes that keep us from seeing people
made in the image of God. In *Dinner at the Homesick Restaurant*, one
brother in a family of self-destructive individuals struggles repeatedly
to gather his family for dinner at his restaurant, hoping to create the
kind of family he wishes he had. Also read *If Morning Ever Comes,
Breathing Lessons, Saint Maybe*, and *Back When We Were Grownups*.

Belva Plain's *Secrecy* is a story of sin and lies as one family tries
to cover up the violent behavior of a son. Ultimately it is a story of
redemption, the kind that grows when someone dares to tell the
truth. Plain's books often reveal the chaos that accompanies lies and
deceit in her characters' lives. Also see *Blessings, Tapestry*, and *Homecoming*.

Amy Tan is best known for *The Joy Luck Club*, in which four
young Chinese-American women and their immigrant mothers struggle to understand each other. Tan's *The Kitchen God's Wife* and *The
Bonesetter's Daughter* continue the theme of intergenerational struggle, obviously something Amy Tan knows about from experience.

I like Anna Quindlen's writing style. In *One True Thing* she recounts a daughter's sacrifice in leaving her own life behind to care for her dying mother, only to be accused of euthanasia at her death. *Black and Blue* is a realistic and poignant story of an abused wife's terror and courage. Quindlen, a columnist for the *New York Times*, also wrote *How Reading Changed My Life* (nonfiction).

Gail Godwin explores issues of faith in *Father Melancholy's Daughter* and its sequel *Evensong*. The first is a story about a daughter's devotion to her father, rector of a small Virginia church, and the grown-up role forced upon her at age six when her mother departs. *Evensong* continues that daughter's life as she becomes an Episcopal minister herself. Look also for *A Mother and Two Daughters, A Southern Family,* and *The Good Husband*. There's a compelling flavor to her writing.

Book-sharing friends recommend Rosamunde Pilcher's books, especially *The Shell Seekers* and its sequel *September*. Set in the Cotswold country of England, both are stories of the complications of family life. Other friends recommend another English author, Susan Howatch, who has written a series of novels *(Glamorous Powers, Glittering Images, Ultimate Prizes)* that interweave issues of faith and the Church of England, with clergy infidelities and doubts about faith and the psychological inquiry to figure it all out. Pilcher is on my list of authors to read. I have not read all of Howatch's books. I include them for your investigation.

The next three authors belong in the gifted writer's list, even though these women are no longer living. Barbara Pym wrote *Excellent Women* in 1952. That this "high comedy" is still in print comments on its quality. It's a tale of a thirtyish English spinster, Mildred Lathbury, one of those "excellent women" whose ordinary life allows her to get involved in the life of everyone else in the parish. You will find yourself loving the character and smiling as you read. See also her *Quartet in Autumn*, a poignant story of four single people who work in the same office. Delightful and very British.

Angela Thirkell writes about small-town life in Britain in a similar vein. Look for *Never Too Late,* a comedy of manners with wit and insight to make you laugh and have you looking for her *A Double Affair, Enter Sir Robert,* and *County Chronicle*. Books that make you smile all the way through are hard to find.

Harriet Doerr is known for *Stones for Ibarra*, a moving story of an American woman who returns with her husband to his native town in central Mexico in the mid 1900s to reclaim a crumbling homestead and an inactive copper mine. They went to "find out if it was true, the width of sky, the depth of stars, the air like new wine, the harsh noons and long, slow dusks. To weave chance and hope into a fabric that would clothe them as long as they lived." Harriet Doerr received her bachelor's degree at age sixty-seven and published this, her first book, a year later.

I Capture the Castle by Dodie Smith is back in print! It's the amusing story of Cassandra and her eccentric family who live in not-so-genteel poverty in a ramshackle old castle. Wanting to be a writer, Cassandra chronicles the family's distress and her encounters with the new American landlord in her journal. It's a survival story and a love story. By the time she pens her final entry she has "captured the castle" and one of the American landlords.

Mystery

The British seem to have a corner on mysteries, making it into a popular genre with millions of avid fans. The biography *Agatha Christie: The Woman and Her Mysteries* by Gillian Gill tells of Christie's leadership in making this a British "industry." New mystery writers are breaking into this trade every year. Obviously, as with all books, some are better than others, but the creation of a really good mystery story is no small feat; it takes a certain kind of genius to pull it off. While some of the stories may never be considered great literature, others are already classics and extremely well written.

Detective fiction, as we know it, was born in Paris, where Edgar Allan Poe set "The Purloined Letter." And it was reared in London where Arthur Conan Doyle placed almost all his adventures of Sherlock Holmes. (*The Hound of the Baskervilles*, his best-known, is an exception and is set in desolate Dartmoor.) Early mystery writers used urban settings almost exclusively. Poe is credited as America's first mystery writer, publishing *Tales of Mystery and Imagination* in 1845. O. Henry followed in 1903 with *A Retrieved Reformation*. In 1905 Willa Cather wrote *Paul's Case*. Melville Davisson Post's *Uncle Abner* mysteries, considered some of the finest ever written, are set in rural nineteenth-century Virginia. A comparison of the leisurely pace in the stories of these early writers with the brisk pace of today's stories is worth noting, as well as the freedom to set stories in purely fictional towns and villages.

Why do people read mysteries? Mysteries, whodunits, or whatever you want to call them, are great escape literature. Frequent flyers eat up long waits and thousands of miles absorbed in a crime-solver. Interestingly, theological professors are avid readers of this genre. Something about following the twist in the story, figuring it out before the last chapter—or whatever—attracts that kind of philosophical mind. How can thrillers be relaxing? Read one and find out.

Here are some of my favorites. Josephine Tey, who was really Elizabeth Mackintosh from Britain, wrote delightful mysteries in the first half of the 1900s, still in print. Start with *The Daughter of Time,* her sleuth Inspector Grant, who has his own peculiarities, lies in a hospital bed trying to solve the murder of the nephews of Richard III hundreds of years after the event. Look also for *The Franchise Affair, Brat Farrar,* and anything else she has written.

Dorothy Sayers's detectives are the elegant Lord Peter Wimsey and his compatriot, Harriet Vane. Her mysteries are on the classics list—very British and all, don't you know. Try Sayers's *The Nine Tailors.* Then read the rest of them.

P. D. James writes mysteries as literature. Her novels have more substance, more investment in characters, and more of a multilayered plot line than most other mysteries. *Death in Holy Orders* is James's fifteenth novel. Her detective Adam Dalgliesh goes to St. Anselm's theological college to investigate the murder of Archdeacon Crampton. *A Taste for Death* or *Death of an Expert Witness* provide a good introduction to P. D. James. (A new autobiography by P. D. James called *A Time to be Earnest* will delight her readers.) Try to define her basic values about life and faith as you read.

Martha Grimes gives some of her mysteries the names of British pubs and challenges you to find the culprit with great twists of plot. Try her *The Man with a Load of Mischief, The Old Fox Deceived,* and *The Five Bells and Bladebone.* Not all her books have pub settings; look for *Hotel Paradise,* one of her best.

Ellis Peters's Brother Cadfael mysteries are set in an abbey in the twelfth century. The "detective," a placid, savvy monk, provides us with a series of interesting stories. Cadfael's knowledge of herbs plays a large role in his crime detection. Do read her *Sanctuary Sparrow,* it's one of my favorites. Also *One Corpse Too Many, Monk's Hood,* and *A Morbid Taste for Bones.*

British writer Jeffrey Archer spins a mighty good tale. He sat as a member of Parliament, doubtless using the duller speeches as occasion to dream up a new plot. I've enjoyed all his mysteries, but am especially fond of *Kane and Abel,* a wondrously complex page-turner weaving the past and present together. Look also for *The Eleventh Commandment, Shall We Tell the President, First among Equals, A Matter of Honour,* and *The Fourth Estate*—all riveting readings.

For light reading and smiles, you will be delighted with Dorothy Gilman's Mrs. Pollifax series. Mrs. Pollifax may look like the senior citizen living next door, but she's bored with her life. Imagine the shock of the CIA director who takes her application for a job, sends her overseas as a courier, and finds this innocent-looking lady a clever crime-solver.

Tony Hillerman writes regional mysteries set in the Navajo and Hopi cultures of Arizona and New Mexico. His crime solvers—Joe Leaphorn and Jim Chee—are complex and memorable, torn by the tension between their Native American heritage and contemporary culture, yet finding their background essential in solving crimes. Begin with *The Blessing Way* and then read on.

I like to read Dick Francis's thrillers because the first paragraph tumbles me into his story, and I'm hooked. Francis's protagonists, never the same person, usually tell the story in first person, always taking the moral high ground (except sometimes in romantic relationships). The villains inevitably beat up the good guy, but the complexities get worked out satisfactorily in the end. Engaging and fast-paced, the stories involve horses and racetracks—since Dick Francis was once a jockey. His titles capture the tone of his writing: *Nerve, Straight, Decider,* and others.

John Grisham, a master of legal thrillers, has had a loyal following ever since he wrote *The Firm.* I recommend his *The Testament* as a starter because it has a different tone. A missionary woman ministering to a remote tribal group in the Amazon basin refuses an enormous inheritance. A dissolute young lawyer, sent to track her down, is disarmed by her faith and sacrificial lifestyle, an encounter that profoundly changes him.

Many mystery stories are better known for their detectives than their authors. Hercule Poirot, Agatha Christie's sleuth, has a life of his own. William Buckley's detective is Blackford Oates (how is that for an elitist name?). G. K. Chesterton's mysteries are known as the Father Brown mysteries, with the priest as his crime solver. Harry Kemelman has Rabbi David Small as the genius who figures it all out. His best-known titles begin with the days of the week. Ngaio Marsh writes about crime solver Roderick Alleyn. Margaret Allingham has Albert Campion as her detective.

Most famous of all is Nero Wolfe, Rex Stout's detective. Stout says, "My theory is that people who don't like detective stories are anarchists"—which tells you something about Stout. His enormous detective's many neuroses add to the tale. Mystery pundits consider Stout's *Too Many Cooks* a classic; it is out of print, but available at the library. Diehard mystery fans get to know some of these detectives so well that it is like greeting an old friend in an English pub.

Women make up the wave of new mystery writers—like Sara Paretsky, Sue Grafton, and Patricia Cornwell—who have liberal-minded sleuths (V. I. Warshawski, Kinsey Milhone, and Kate Scarpetti) bearing the lifestyle distinctives of the sixties. Grafton sends out Christmas cards signing fictional Kinsey's name along with her own—that's how real these people become to their readers. Anne Perry, who writes Victorian mysteries set in England, has two protagonists—one is Monk, who suffers from amnesia with hints that he himself may have been arrested for criminal behavior. Apparently Perry's own past is similar to the one she gives Monk in her stories.

Mystery writers endow their crime solvers with peculiarities that identify them—like quirky habits or fears or occupations. P. D. James's Adam Dalgliesh writes poetry. Josephine Tey's Inspector Grant is claustrophobic. Stout's Nero Wolfe, an enormous man, is a food connoisseur. Diane Mott Davidson's unofficial sleuth is a food caterer, making it almost impossible to read her books without feeling hungry. She scatters her recipes throughout books that bear titles like *Prime Cut, Dying for Chocolate,* and *Killer Pancake.*

Here are some quick entries for your own sleuthing of good mysteries: Look for Nancy

A Religious Detective

Faye Kellerman is my favorite new mystery writer. The wife of mystery writer Jonathan Kellerman (whose work I haven't read), her stories are good mysteries if you already like detective novels. What I find really interesting is that the detective Peter Decker's romantic interest (in later books: his wife) is a devout Orthodox Jew. Her religious beliefs get a lot of attention in the books—observances she keeps, why and what they symbolize, the importance of faith, and her sometimes frustration with the "rules" of her religion. In the first books when the detective is dating her, she refuses sexual involvement because of her religious belief in chastity outside of marriage. (Quite an anomaly in today's fiction!) Her beliefs add interest to the books.

(Interested readers: check on *Unholy Orders: Mystery Stories with a Religious Twist,* edited by Serita Stevens.)

RECOMMENDED BY MARIA BERGSTROM, LITERATURE PH.D. AND FULL-TIME MOM

Pickard's *The Whole Truth;* Laurie King's *The Beekeeper's Apprentice;* Kate Charles's *A Deadly Drink of Wine;* Ross MacDonald's *The Chill.* And while you are looking you might be interested in getting *100 Favorite Mysteries of the Century*—an excellent listing of titles with annotations by Jim Huang—or pick up the handy pocket-sized *Detecting Women Pocket Guides* (there's one for "Detecting Males" too) for lists of mysteries to read. Tony Hillerman has collected *The Best American Mystery Stories of the Century,* which includes mystery stories from 1903 to the end of the century. A great book for quick but substantial reading.

Why I Read Mysteries

My lifelong love of mysteries began when I was ten years old and Nancy Drew and I solved *The Secret of the Old Clock.* Since then I have found no substitute for a dark and stormy night, a fog-bound street, or a creaking staircase.

What makes the mystery so appealing to me? It is the puzzle. The satisfaction of spotting clues, ignoring red herrings, and trying to solve the crime before the detective. It is the comfort of following a favorite detective through a series from one case to the next. It is the atmosphere, the psychological suspense, and the impact of the past on the present—the inevitable consequences of secrets that will not remain buried. And it is that which lies beneath, the skull beneath the skin. For truly the mystery grapples with the great moral dilemmas, the dark secrets of the heart, and the desire for order and justice in a chaotic, vicious, and unjust world. In the more violent or "hardboiled" novels, the detective battles the darkness, often in the midst of battling his or her own darkness. Even the "cozy" or the "Golden Age of mystery" writers never underrate the power of evil. Agatha Christie's Miss Marple, that gray-haired sleuth in orthopedic shoes, knows that even the smallest village harbors all the deadly sins. Yet, as P. D. James, says, "Crime writers are among the few who are still able to tell a story . . . that affirms the sanctity of individual life."

I read mysteries for all of these reasons . . . and because, when all is said and done, there is nothing like curling up with a good murder story. The first sentence of Charles Williams's *War in Heaven* says it all: "The telephone bell was ringing wildly, but without result, since there was no one in the room but the corpse."

CONTRIBUTED BY JUDITH E. MARKHAM, EDITOR

A Selected List of Mysteries

For a mystery lover, it is impossible to choose a limited list of favorites, but here are some I have enjoyed. I have tried to include a variety of writing styles and categories within the genre. Many of the books below are one in a series by the author, so look for the rest. Check out some of the mystery Web sites, including *www.deadlypassions.com.*

Kate Charles, *A Deadly Drink of Wine*

Deborah Crombie, *A Share in Death*

John Dunning, *Booked to Die*

Aaron Elkins, *The Dark Place*

Peter Dickinson, *The Yellow Room Conspiracy*

Terence Faherty, *The Lost Keats*

Martha Grimes, *Hotel Paradise*

Teri Holbrook, *A Far and Deadly Cry; The Grass Widow*

Wendy Hornsby, *Telling Lies*

Laurie King, *The Beekeeper's Apprentice*

Ross MacDonald, *The Galton Case*

Francine Mathews, *Death in a Mood Indigo*

Anne Perry, *The Cater Street Hangman*

Elizabeth Peters, *Crocodile on the Sandbank*

Peter Robinson, *In a Dry Season*

Mabel Seeley, *The Listening House*

Minette Walters, *The Ice House*

RECOMMENDED BY
JUDITH E. MARKHAM, EDITOR

Historical Novels

Gone with the Wind by Margaret Mitchell tells a good story while at the same time giving readers information about the Civil War. It is a prime example of a historical novel. Mitchell's book is also a great love story, and if I had a romance category it could well be listed there. Many novels overlap categories. However, if the writer sets the story in the past and does careful research, weaving a story around a historical event, the book qualifies as a historical novel. The chief value of putting books in a genre is that it helps the reader know what to look for and how to read it.

Novels That Helped Me Understand History

The Covenant by James Michener:
about South Africa

Trinity by Leon Uris: about Ireland

Byzantium by Stephen R. Lawhead:
about Europe in the 900s

Dynasty by Roberts Elegant:
about Hong Kong

Tanamera by Noel Barber:
about Singapore

The Far Pavilions by M. M. Kaye:
about India

Spring Moon by Bette Bao Lord:
about China

The Flame Trees of Thika
by Elsbeth Huxley: about Kenya

Pillars of the Earth by Ken Follett:
about building a cathedral in England

Remembrances and *Winds of War*
by Herman Wouk: about World War II

Stones from the River by Ursula Hegi:
about Germany during the World
Wars

The Fatal Shore by Robert Hughes:
about the beginnings of Australia

Nicholas and Alexandra and *Peter the
Great* by Robert K. Massie:
about Russia

RECOMMENDED BY THEA VANHALSEMA,
RETIRED DEAN OF STUDENTS AND COLUMNIST

The Agony and the Ecstasy by Irving Stone is the fictionalized story of Michelangelo and his passion for painting and sculpture, for his city, and for God. The story brings a whole era of the fifteenth- and sixteenth-century Renaissance—its wars, popes, and power figures—into focus, as well as the trials and challenges of painting the Sistine Chapel ceiling and sculpting his famous David.

Kenneth Roberts's fine accounts of Revolutionary days deserve good readings. His *Northwest Passage* and its characters on their westward exploration into New York and Michigan make history come alive. His other books *Arundel* and *Rabble in Arms* give an informed look at Aaron Burr and the haphazard bravery of the Continental Army at the time of our separation from Britain. Our family found them great read-alouds. Roberts's *Oliver Wiswell*, the story of the Revolutionary War from the viewpoint of a loyalist, challenged me to consider whether I would have been a revolutionary or a loyalist had I lived in those days

If you are interested in the Middle East, James Michener's *The Source* will add greatly to your understanding of the history of that region. Through the ruse of archaeological digs, Michener takes the bones of the past and creates a history of the land, reconstructing the bones into people whose story he tells—including histories of the three faiths that have dominated the area. Don't stop there. Michener's well-researched and interesting novels about other parts of the world make good reading: *Hawaii* (1948 Pulitzer Prize), *Alaska*, *Mexico*, *Chesapeake*, and others.

Exodus by Leon Uris weaves a story around the migration of a suffering, hopeful people to the newly created nation of Israel in 1948. The story of his Jewish characters puts a face on history that allows us to understand the passion for the land. Other stories connect us with history in different ways: *A Tale of Two Cities* by Charles Dickens chronicles the French Revolution; Alexander Solzhenitsyn's *One Day in the Life of Ivan Denisovich* impresses the reader with historical realities about living under communism.

I find John Hersey's accounts of historical events, peopled with characters he devises to tell the story, a means of absorbing history in the best possible way. *The Wall* is the story of Jews forced to relocate in the Warsaw ghetto in 1939, a prelude to their destruction. *Hiroshima* gives a face to the statistics of the dropping of the atom bomb during World War II. *A Bell for Adano* (Pulitzer Prize 1945) tells the story of the American liberation that brought humanity to a small village in Italy.

Nevil Shute wrote *A Town Like Alice*, a gripping novel based on the true story of a young British secretary and an Australian soldier, both made prisoners of war by the Japanese in Malaysia. She is marched 1,200 miles around the jungle and he endures a mock crucifixion for stealing food for her. They seek each other out after the war, and settle in the Australian outback.

Recently a friend gave us a copy of *Gone for Soldiers* by Jeff Shaara, a novel about the American-Mexican War, about which I knew nothing. Shaara researched the letters and the extensive diaries of two principals in the war: Captain Robert E. Lee and General Winfield Scott. He tells the story of the war through the thoughts and voices of the characters themselves. It was a page-turner for me—and I am not a reader of war chronicles. I liked Shaara's writing style so much I immediately ordered his other books—*Gods and Generals* and *The Last Full Measure*—for our library. His father Michael Shaara won the Pulitzer Prize for *The Killer Angels*, his classic on the battle at Gettysburg. I have since read that to my profit. Reading tastes differ, but at this point in my life I found myself ready to learn from these two authors.

A much gentler wartime book is *All Quiet on the Western Front* by Erich Maria Remarque, a beautifully written story about a German soldier during World War I. Remarque ranks as the best novelist of World War I, despite the fact that from our point of view he was on the "wrong" side. His book is an expression of the terror and tedium felt by men on the front, no matter which way they were facing.

Jean Plaidy (who also writes romantic suspense novels under the name of Victoria Holt) has written historical novels about English,

Scottish, and French monarchies. Her writing is accessible and enjoyable. Look for *Madame DuBarry*; *The Lady in the Tower* (part of the Queens of England series); *Katherine, the Virgin Widow*; and *Passionate Enemies*.

If you are curious about the Middle Ages I recommend a book about a tremendously gifted woman who ignored the boundaries placed on women. Read *Scarlet Music by* Joan Ohanneson. It is a story about Hildegard of Bingen. Hildegard, a Benedictine abbess, was the composer of some seventy-seven liturgical songs and the author of the first morality play and a book on healing arts—in short, an amazing woman. Barbara Lachman has done a credible work of historical imagination in another book that tells her story, *The Journal of Hildegard of Bingen*.

A Beacon at Alexandria by Gillian Bradshaw is the story of a girl who flees Ephesus disguised as a boy to go to Alexandria to study

Books about Life During World War II

Number the Stars by Lois Lowry

Annemarie Johansen is ten years old in 1943 when Nazi soldiers march into her town. Life is now filled with food shortages, prejudice, and danger. When Annemarie's Jewish best friend and her family escape to Sweden, she must find the strength and courage necessary to save their lives.

Kinderlager: An Oral History of Young Holocaust Survivors by Milton J. Nieuwsma

Three compiled accounts of Jewish children who survived the Holocaust give us frightening stories of the horror of war through the eyes of youth. The impact of life in concentration camps and the slaughter of their people has had a lasting effect on these three witnesses.

The Ark by Margot Benary-Isbert

A delightful German family discovers an enchanting woman and her peaceful farm in the aftermath of World War II. Postwar hardships challenge this lovable family as they wait for their physician father to return from the battlefield. In the meantime their four children find all sorts of adventure and new friendships as they begin this new phase in their lives. (Sequels include *Rowan Farm* and *The Long Way Home*.)

RECOMMENDED BY PAT FELDHAKE AND SARAH JOY, MOTHER/DAUGHTER READERS medicine. She is accepted as an apprentice by an old Jewish doctor who teaches her both medicine and compassion. The historical setting is the decline of the Roman Empire. Another Bradshaw book set in this same time period is *The Bearkeeper's Daughter.*

Teenagers may know Sonia Levitin's book *Journey to America,* the story of a courageous Jewish family fleeing Germany through Switzerland. Levitin's *The Return* tells the story of an Ethiopian Jewish teenage girl who was airlifted from Sudan to Israel during the 1984 Operation Moses. These are great stories to read with an adolescent daughter. A more recent book by Levitin is *The Cure,* a powerful historical/science fiction novel, about Gem who is sent back to fourteenth-century Strasbourg to become Jacob, the son of a Jewish moneylender.

Carry on, Mr. Bowditch by Jean Lee Latham is a fictionalized biography, but a ripping good tale to read alone or aloud with your family. In the late 1700s Nat Bowditch was sold to Ship Chandler as an indentured servant for nine years. Read how his courage, hard work, and pluck saved more than his own life.

You will find historical novels covering nearly every important event of the past. Keep looking; I have given you only a few ideas to set you on your way.

Western Stories

The American West is storybook country; there's a romance to frontiers. The rough living, the crudely erected towns, the gun battles, the staking out the land—these and more have become the stuff of legends. It's *big* country, requiring courage and endurance. You can still feel it when you visit those states that comprise the backbone of the Rocky Mountains.

Louis L'Amour is the foremost storyteller of the American West. At least one of his books is a must for an American reader. Maybe one of the Sackett Family series is a good place to begin—a Sackett leaves England for the new world, the next generation pushes inland, his progeny find trails that lead through Appalachia, and every generation has its own adventures pushing through to the Rocky Mountains. Each book in the series is about the next generation of the Sackett family. What's in it for a woman reader? Don't think "Cowboys and Indians." Think exploration, adventure, romance, great writing. His *Last of the Breed* has a different setting: a Native American Air Force

Books You Will Love

The [Educa]tion of Little Tree
  by Forrest Carter
    Little Tree, orphaned at age five, goes
to live with loving Native-American
grandparents who teach him the ways
of the Cherokees. A moving semi-
autobiographical story.

Jim the Boy by Tony Earley
    A small gem you won't be able to put
down. The story is pitch-perfect, told from
the point of view of a ten-year-old boy
raised by a widowed mother and three
bachelor uncles. It's the story of Jim discovering the world. Please don't miss this
superb story.

Last of the Breed by Louis L'Amour
    What a good tale he tells!

The Trees and *The Fields*
  by Conrad Richter
    These two books are part of a trilogy
of a strong heroine Sayward Luckett, who
with her family does more than survive
the rigors of settling out "West" in Ohio.
Not only are the characters memorable,
but Richter's descriptions of the life and
setting of the story are unforgettable.

*The Long Walk: The True Story of a Trek
to Freedom* by Slavomir Rawicz
    An epic true story of survival against
all—and I do mean *all*—odds. It is a tale
of tragedy and triumph that almost defies
retelling. The trek is from Siberia over the
Himalayas to India.

RECOMMENDED BY JAN KARON, AUTHOR

major shot down in Russia escapes across the Bering Straits, using his
Indian background and savvy to accomplish an amazing feat. L'Amour
is the best! Look for *Dark Canyon, Crossfire Trail*, and others.

Edna Ferber's *Cimarron* and *Giant* both chronicle Western life.
Cimarron introduces you to Yancey Cravat, a pioneer newspaper editor and lawyer, and his clever wife, Sabra, who live in a small town in
Oklahoma in 1889. The story is told through Sabra's eyes as she sees
the violent frontier collide with the resentful Indian population. *Giant*
spins the lore of Texas. An Eastern girl's marriage to a Texas cattle
rancher provides the fodder for this powerful story, giving good
insights into Texas history and the changes that came with the discovery of oil. Ferber is a great storyteller.

Shane, by Jack Schaefer, is considered one of the best Westerns
ever written—a classic. "Call me Shane," says the mysterious gunman,
who turns out to be the white knight that saves the situation in the

conflict between the homesteaders and the powerful Wyoming cat-
tleman who had originally cleared the land. It's more than a cattle
land conflict; it is a story about choices and their consequences.

The Virginian by Owen Wister is on my English professor-friend's
"must-read" list, and I agree. The hero takes his new bride on a camp-
ing trip to a remote mountain stream, a place that has been his alone,
for their honeymoon. Who knew cowboys could be so romantic? The
story, set in Wyoming territory, handles the tensions between the
romantic idea of freedom and the need for community.

The Sea of Grass by Conrad Richter is set in New Mexico in the
late nineteenth century. Jim Brewton, his unstable Eastern wife, Lutie,
and the ambitious Bruce Chamberlain provide the character-soil for
this mix between pioneering free-range ranchers and settlers. Look
for other novels by Richter.

A. B. Guthrie's *The Big Sky* is the story of Boone Caudhill, a true
mountain man, driven by a longing for the blue sky and brown earth
in big, wild places. The story takes place in Montana in the 1830s and
is character-driven, with awesome descriptions of nature. Guthrie is
a fine writer; look for his other books if you enjoy this one.

One year when traveling in Arizona we bought a couple of Zane
Grey Westerns, *Riders of the Purple Sage* and *30,000 on the Hoof*, and
the area came alive for us. Grey wrote over one hundred Westerns,
and reading his books is a sure way to enhance any visit to the West.
Don't let anyone spoil these books for you with remarks like "cowboy
books, eh?" because Grey is really a good adventure writer.

Fantasy

Fantasy is a huge category of fiction. To read fantasy is to take a holiday from everyday life. Most of us had our first encounter with this
genre in fairy tales. Fantasy creates another world or a parallel world
with its own kind of people. Good fantasy tells the truth; it is truth
from a different angle, and that is its benefit. C. S. Lewis said that a
person does not despise real woods because he has read of enchanted
woods: the reading makes the real woods all the more enchanted.
Reading fantasy keeps us from growing old from the inside out.

My all-time favorite fantasies are the Narnia Chronicles by C. S.
Lewis. Going through the back of the wardrobe, passing the lamp-
post and entering Narnia to meet *The Lion, the Witch, and the
Wardrobe* will always be one of my favorite journeys. Imagine living

in a land where it is always winter and never gets to Christmas, until news that Aslan, the golden-maned lion, is on the move and begins to tangle with the White Witch, whose actions teach me more about temptation than I could possibly learn another way. Then add to my expanding world all the other characters like Prince Caspian, Puddleglum, and Reepicheep, and let me travel on the *The Voyage of the Dawn Treader*—well, no reader could ever be the same. Thank you Clive Staples Lewis for conceiving of this world and making it possible for Lucy, Edmund, Susan, Peter—and me—to get there! All seven books are worthy of many readings.

(If you have read these books, or read them because of this recommendation, you will appreciate my dismay when a church librarian told me she did not recommend these books because Christ is pictured as an animal. An animal indeed! I had the same reaction when someone described Tolkien's stories as animal stories.)

I find *Til We Have Faces* by Lewis a book I want to discuss with someone. Many think this is Lewis's best. The story is the Cupid and Psyche myth from the perspective of Psyche's ugly and adoring sister Orual. Its parallels to the Christian gospel are profound. Lewis's *Great Divorce* is a memorable, complaining trip with a busload of visitors from hell who get to the edge of heaven's shores and give their reactions.

J. R. R. Tolkien's *The Hobbit* and The Lord of the Rings trilogy took fifteen years to write; one can hardly say enough about their excellence. Frodo, a simple hobbit creature, is tortured by the terrible burden of The Ring (which symbolizes the evil in the world). He struggles onward through battles, despair, and seeming defeat to the mountain where it must be destroyed. Readers will not forget Gandalf at the Bridge of Moria, the horrors of Mordor, the final confrontation with the enemy—and then the last bittersweet final chapter. The ordinariness, the bravery, the persistence for right: what noble creatures all! It's enough to break the reader's heart. And the use of language! Some passages we have read over and over simply to let the beauty of the words wash over us. Lewis said about his friend's work, "Here are beauties which pierce like swords or burn like cold iron." The best of the twentieth century.

George MacDonald's *At the Back of the North Wind* is the story of Diamond, a young stable boy who is given a magical journey with a beautiful woman, known as the North Wind, who takes him to far places. Generally considered a magical favorite children's book, the primary theme is adult and explores the place of death in life. *The*

Princess & the Goblin and *The Princess & Curdie* are a pair. In the first book Princess Irene and her good friend Curdie protect the kingdom from evil goblins; in the second, a more grown-up Curdie is given a gift of insight and uses it to save the kingdom from greed and selfishness. But the story is more—much more—than that simple plotline. *The Light Princess*, cursed by a wicked witch, has no gravity and therefore cannot enjoy what life offers until she is rescued at the last minute by a prince who loves her enough to die for her. MacDonald's fantasies profoundly influenced C. S. Lewis. They are simple enough for children, but rich enough to reward an adult reading.

John White, a Canadian author, has written a set of five in the Narnia vein: *The Sword Bearer, Gaal the Conqueror, The Tower of Geburah, The Iron Scepter*, and *Quest for the King*. In White's story children enter a parallel world through a television screen and take their part in combating evil on behalf of Gaal, the Conqueror. For fantasy-loving families these are good read-aloud stories.

Walter Wangerin's *The Book of the Dun Cow* takes the reader into the barnyard to recognize people you know—in all their mixture of grace and waywardness. This adult story is the age-old struggle between good and evil embodied in Chaunticleer the Rooster and the wicked Wyrm. And look for Wangerin's *Ragman and Other Cries of Faith*, also fantasy.

If you are avid about fantasy, explore the mystical works of Charles Williams, who was a member of the famous Inklings along with Lewis and Tolkien. His books, filled with images and allusions, profit from group discussion. In Williams's *Descent into Hell*, hell turns out to be historian Wentworth's daily choice to cheat on the truth, which leads him into terrifying isolation. Heaven, by contrast, is inhabited by Pauline Anstruther, who faces her fears and loves the truth exactly as it is. That's a simple plotline, but reading the book will keep you pondering the underlying details. Other Williams titles are *The Place of*

Journey to Other Worlds

The Dragonriders of Pern series by Anne McCaffrey

In this science-fiction/fantasy series of at least eleven books, McCaffrey creates a complex world on a distant planet where some colonists from earth bond empathically with intelligent dragons and fight the dreaded Thread that falls like silver rain, consuming living things.

The Chronicles of Thomas Covenant the Unbeliever series by Stephen Donaldson

Donaldson's fantasy books explore deep issues of faith, love, and suffering. His wordsmithing is unsurpassed when it comes to original images and figures of speech.

RECOMMENDED BY LINNEA BOESE, LINGUIST AND BIBLE TRANSLATOR

the Lion, Many Dimensions, Shadows of Ecstasy, War in Heaven, All
Hallow's Eve, and The Greater Trumps. Thomas T. Howard's The Novels of Charles Williams helped me relish these symbol-laden books.

Honoring the one-hundredth anniversary of Saint Exupery's birth,
an old favorite has a fine new English translation from the French. *The
Little Prince* by Antoine de Saint-Exupery is said to be second only to the
Bible as the most widely read book in the world. It is, in fact, translated
into ninety-five different languages. A downed pilot in the Sahara Desert
meets a little prince who takes him on a journey from planet to planet.
The scenes are metaphors for dimensions of everyone's life. Whether you
are an old fan or a new one, this is a whimsical, delightful book.

Watership Down by Richard Adams, a rabbit-centered epic that
can be read on many different levels, went straight to the best-seller
list when it was first published. The Berkshire rabbits must flee to
escape destruction of their homeland by a developer. The engrossing,
page-turning story deals with issues of freedom, ethics, human nature,
and lots more to discuss with another reader.

Joan Aiken's *The Stolen Lake* follows in the train of her Wolves
Chronicles. (The English-born Aiken is the author of the children's
book *The Wolves of Willoughby Chase*.) This story takes the heroine
Dido Twite on a voyage to Cumbria, a mysterious country in the
South American Andes where a neighboring king has stolen a queen's
lake. The tale has revolving palaces, apocalyptic volcanoes, and a curious lack of female children. More fantastical than most.

Adults and teens wait patiently each year for Brian Jacques's stories about Redwall. Jacques, a first-class fantasy writer, develops the
history and the creature-heroes who inhabit the medieval red-walled
Abbey of Mossflower Woods. The stories capture youth and adults
alike, and are great books for teenage birthdays. Our grandson first
introduced us to *Redwall*, saying, "Here is a book I think you will both
enjoy." We did, and since then have given the books in the series to
many young friends. One of my young friends even got specific with
his gift request, saying to me, "Hardcovers, only, for my library, please.
I have already read the one you gave me three times."

Science Fiction

Science fiction has a close tie-in with fantasy, which sometimes blurs
the distinctions. Science fiction may attract more male readers than
female ones. If you are a fan, see the latest edition of *Annual World's*

Best Science Fiction, edited by Donald A. Wollheim. Some of its most popular authors are Arthur C. Clarke, Ursula LeGuin, Ray Bradbury, George Orwell, Jules Verne, and many others. Note the sidebar praising Orson Scott Card. I have had several recommendations for his writing from women readers.

Out of the Silent Planet, Perelandra, and *That Hideous Strength* by C. S. Lewis (especially the last in the series) are generally classified as

Science Fiction for the Rest of Us: Orson Scott Card

Ender's Game

Andrew or "Ender" is selected for the elite Space Battle School, where children are trained in readiness for the coming war with an alien species. The novel is less about the battle itself and more about the lives of the gifted children as they are thrown into this challenging environment. Card captures much of the turmoil of children: alternating self-doubt and exuberant confidence, the oppression and support from peers, and the first inklings that adults may not be infallible. My brother, once labeled a "gifted child" himself, got me to read this book by declaring it his absolute favorite novel.

Speaker for the Dead

In my opinion, this is the best of the trilogy, but read them all in order to get the most out of the story. An adult Ender travels to a planet where humans are making their first attempts to study a living alien species. Orson Card is Mormon, and his stories resonate with difficult moral questions. Card makes us think about how hard it is to get outside our own point of view and how often we interpret the world strictly according to our own perspective.

Xenocide

Probably the weakest novel of the three, but by the time I got to this point I had to keep reading to find out what happens to these characters. Here Ender deals with personal guilt as he tries to reestablish an extinct alien species. One storyline features a planet where a genetic disorder has been interpreted as a spiritual gift. Card raises moral questions about the right to knowledge versus the cultural disruptions such knowledge can bring, and about the "right to life" of different species when that life entails risk or sacrifice on the part of others. This is a "thinker" series as well as a "thriller" series. (Coarse language)

RECOMMENDED BY MARIA BERGSTROM, LITERATURE PH.D. AND A FULL-TIME MOM science fiction. In both *Out of the Silent Planet* and *Perelandra* Lewis creates an extraterrestrial world to not only engage us in an adventure, but to parallel our own world with unavoidable significance. *Perelandra* is a metaphor of the fall in Eden. Both these books are rich in allusions, and I will be content to let you categorize them.

Religious Fiction

Literary fiction has not been the strength of most religious publishing houses in past years. Part of the reason for this has been readers' fear of stories. Publishers produce what people want to buy because religious bookstores exist to sell books. Experience has made them cautious about accusations of unorthodoxy if anything falls outside the boundaries of a reader's expectations. The complaint of one reader about something offensive can set a bookstore manager to boxing up all copies of the book to send them back to the publisher. It is a kind of catch-22. Sadly, as a result, much of the fiction produced tends toward simple narratives, touching on ideas and situations that make the reader feel comfortable.

Prejudice works both ways. In response to the negative stereotype of these books, other readers form strong opinions against any fiction that comes from a religious publishing house. Understandably some fine Christian writers do not want to be caught in this crunch and so proceed to find secular publishers. However unfortunate this may be, it is an accurate portrayal of past history.

The good news is that publishing houses are wrestling with this problem and working at raising standards for fiction that will compete in any market. Over the years the insistence on higher standards has helped to raise the literary level of religious novels, and you will find the best of these in Barnes & Noble, Borders, and other large book chains. In the spring of 1999 a group of publishers launched the Christy Award to recognize novelists and novels of excellence in several genres. For this to produce higher standards demands that readers raise their own level of literacy so that they do not require everything spelled out for them. Reading is meant to widen one's world and understanding of reality. Remember, all good fiction is about what is true.

Religious fiction can often fit into one of the other genre fiction categories, such as historical, mystery, or romance. Christian bookstores, however, tend to shelve all fiction together without separating the categories, so you may have to hunt a bit to find a new author in a genre you enjoy. For your convenience, I've attempted to place books into three categories: classics, contemporary fiction, and historical fiction.

Classics

I begin my list with some of the tried-and-true that have been around a long time and still excite readers. A minister wrote me an

Catherine Marshall Wrote for Women

Christy. The story of a young mountain schoolteacher who grows in faith and wisdom through the lessons of life, death, and love taught by the people of her small village and the remarkable Miss Alice. If you have never read this lovely story, do get it and enrich your life.

Julie. Equally compelling, and said to be her autobiographical novel. Set in Johnstown, Pennsylvania, *Julie* deals with a young woman's desire to be a newspaper writer and ends with a vivid description of the Johnstown flood.

A Man Called Peter. The true story of a remarkable young minister with a Scottish background whose profound preaching led him to be chaplain of the Senate of the United States before his premature death.

Something More. As Catherine Marshall's life ran down, she discovered her spiritual life accelerating. She writes about spiritual maturity as a lifelong process.

First Easter. This book weaves the dramatic narrative of Easter with some of Peter Marshall's (her husband) memorable sermons.

Adventures in Prayer. Catherine Marshall shares her personal discovery about how down-to-earth God wants our prayers to be, and answers many questions about prayer.

The Collected Works of Catherine Marshall contains two of her popular books: *To Live Again,* a powerful recollection of her early widowhood, and *Beyond Ourselves,* which recounts her spiritual journey in search of a meaningful life and a practical faith.

RECOMMENDED BY KRISTY MOTZ,
LIBRARIAN AND STORYTELLER

enthusiastic letter telling me about his discovery of the novels of Elizabeth Goudge, wondering if I knew about her books—and this more than fifty years after they were first published. Elizabeth Goudge, an English author, wrote such critically acclaimed novels as *The Bird in the Tree*, *Pilgrim's Inn*, *The Heart of the Family*, *Green Dolphin Street*, *The Scent of Water*, and *The Child from the Sea*. Set in the English countryside, these books are a series, best read in order even though each stands on its own. The English publisher allowed these books to go out of print; but other publishers here have printed new editions. When you look for them you may find some title confusion, since some titles were Americanized; forget about titles, just get her books. My favorite is her prize-winning book *The Dean's Watch*, set in a mid-nineteenth century English town; it is the story of Isaac Peabody, an obscure watchmaker, and Adam Ayscough, the brilliant dean of the cathedral. Inspiring and memorable, this book gives a taste of Goudge's skill in linking the importance of place in the lives of people. Her other books are family sagas, involving truth in relationships, values, and the importance of place. And oh, how I loved her *Little White Horse*. It's back in print! Look for Elizabeth Goudge in a bookstore, the library, or in a used bookstore.

Michael Phillips is responsible for putting into modern English the novels of George MacDonald, editing out the Scottish dialect for easier reading. If you like used bookstores, look for single copies of *The Fisherman's Lady*, *The Marquis' Secret*, *The Baronet's Song*, *The Shepherd's Castle*, *Sir Gibbie*, and others—about a dozen in all. In print today are two compilations of novels. One is called *The Parish Papers: Three Complete Novels* of George MacDonald, which includes *A Quiet Neighborhood*, *The Seaboard Parish*, and *The Vicar's Daughter*, likely new titles to old books. The second collection edited by Michael Phillips is called *The Scottish Collection: The Maiden's Bequest*, *The Minister's Restoration*, and *The Laird's Inheritance*. Some single titles are also in print. The stories in these books are set in small towns and contain the ingredients of life: romance, honor, integrity, guilt, grace, and doubt. MacDonald tells a good story well; all the stories are peppered with wisdom that will warm your heart. In short, you confront your own self and your own life when you read them, even though they were written in the nineteenth century. What a legacy this poor Scottish parson George MacDonald left behind!

If you have access to a good library or a used bookstore, look for the writings of Canadian Grace Irwin, who published in the 1960s.

Her *Servant of Slaves*, a fictionalized life of John Newton, is a winner. The story of this profane sailor, slave trader, and later devoted Christian minister who wrote "Amazing Grace" and hundreds of other well-known hymns is a model for biographical novels. Other books by Irwin worthy of note: *Least of All Saints, Andrew Connington,* and *In Little Place*. Irwin's books may be hard to find, but they are exceptionally good. One of my friends found them all by haunting used bookstores—a satisfying hobby for a book lover.

Contemporary Fiction

Philip Gulley's *Home to Harmony*, a Christy Award winner, is the story of Sam Gardner, who goes back to his hometown of Harmony to pastor Harmony Friends Meeting House. Harmony is a town on the map right where the staple is, so it is hard to see. Each chapter contains anecdotal accounts of grace, forgiveness, and love. This book is a delightful read; I laughed all the way through it.

Robert Whitlow writes thrillers of the John Grisham ilk, and there is a good likelihood that readers may like him even better. *The Trial* was a co-winning Christy Award book, the story of attorney Kent "Mac" MacClain who, almost suicidal after the loss of his wife and two sons in an accident, is called back to reality by defending the life of Pete Thomason. Is Thomason a victim or an ingenious psychopath? Another Whitlow page-turner is *The List*, a story of good and evil that comes from the terms of the will left by Renny Jacobson's father.

T. J. Davis has written a number of books for readers to investigate. *The Great Divide* is the award-winning story of a once-legendary lawyer who investigates a young woman's disappearance overseas. Also look for *The Quilt, The Presence,* and *The Book of Hours,* this last book a mystery set in England.

Velma Still Cooks at Leeway by Vinita Hampton Wright is the story of ordinary people in a Kansas small town who tell their stories to Velma at the restaurant she runs. She listens, journals her thoughts, and keeps on cooking her way through the town's problems. Velma's recipes are scattered throughout, as is the theme of forgiveness so needed in this complicated story that charts a new course in novels from religious publishing houses. Wright also wrote *Grace at Bender Springs*.

I found *Some Wildflower in My Heart* by Jamie Langston Turner a winsome book. Margaret, the protagonist, is crusty and controlling, shutting everyone out of her life because of the pain in her past. Birdie

Freeman works for Margaret in the school cafeteria and is everyone's stereotype of a too-nice, exuberant Christian. Yet she is the one who emotionally disarms Margaret so that authentic changes begin. Readers see stirrings of new freedom in Margaret. Without being maudlin, this book covers the real stuff of life and does not end with all the knots tied up neatly.

Augusta Trobaugh, a Southern writer, has two books that explore relationships in the Southern culture of the 1940s. *Resting in the Bosom of the Lamb* has an eccentric cast of characters. Four elderly women share a house, a past, and a long-buried secret. We sit on the front porch and listen to their stories, getting to know these women and gasp at the eventual revelation of the secret. Trobaugh's first book is *Praise Jerusalem*, the story of three Southern women who learn lessons about letting go, growing, forgiving, and loving in Jerusalem, Georgia. Good writing style.

James Calvin Schaap's *Romey's Place* is the story of the friendship of two teenagers in a small Midwest town—one from a devoutly religious home, the other from a thoroughly irreligious family without rules or much peace. The story is thoughtful, not fast-paced, and the theme centers on how the two boys influence each other, especially in the area of beliefs. A well-written novel with some profound ideas to discuss with another book lover or in a reading group.

John Fischer has a good touch in *Saint Ben*. Ben is a small town pastor's son, and possesses an extraordinary ability to live without pretention. He also receives incredible perceptions about people and God. No one who ever meets Ben is quite the same, according to his friend Jonathan, who tells the story. What begins as an easy read soon explodes into action and significance.

Passing by Samaria by Sharon Ewell Foster moves into the African American community, chronicling young Alena's 1919 move from the south to Chicago, amidst riots, misplaced love, and the confusion of growing up. It's a story of betrayal and forgiveness, confronting racism and its pain. Her second novel set in North Carolina, *Ain't No River*, gives us strong characters and action in the story of slick GooGoo Walker, a suspected opportunist, and Meemaw, the grandmother about to be conned. Both novels are a welcome breaking of ground for black evangelical Christians.

In Lisa Sampson's *The Church Ladies* you will find yourself and others you know sitting in the pew. You will laugh and cry and relate to Sampson's story. I especially liked *Eve's Daughters* by Lynn Austin, a story about the effect of choices that reach down through four generations of women. Penelope J. Stokes wrote *The Blue Bottle Club*, the story of four friends who seal up their dreams for the future in a cobalt blue bottle—and then go their separate ways. The story line traces what happens to each woman in the years that transpire as they make their choices in life.

If you like futuristic fiction, look for *Father Elijah* by Michael O'Brien, the story of a Jewish convert, a Holocaust survivor who has become a Carmelite priest, now called out of twenty years of seclusion to ferret out the antichrist. This is both a literate and spiritually profound novel. Also look for *The Transgression* by Randall Ingermanson, a thriller novel in which a female Messianic Jewish archaeology student and an Israeli physicist encounter Dr. Damien, who holds Christianity responsible for all the ills in the world.

Historical Fiction

Francine Rivers is a favorite writer of historical novels based on biblical characters. Her newest series is called The Lineage of Grace. The first of these is *Unveiled*, the story of Tamar's life; the second *Unashamed*, the story of Rahab, won the Christy Award in the historical novel category. Others are *Unshaken*, the story of Ruth; *Unspoken*, David and Bathsheba's story, told in Bathsheba's voice, and *Unafraid*, about Mary.

Bodie and Brock Thoene have produced several historical series that have won acclaim. The Zion Chronicles and The Zion Legacy place strong characters, imaginative plots, and strong themes of redemption and reconciliation in Jerusalem centering around the time when Israel became an independent nation. The stories are without stereotypes of the varied peoples of the Middle East, and include the lives of Christians, Muslims, and Jews. To their readers' delight they are researching more stories about the Middle East. The

The Ultimate Love Story

Redeeming Love by Francine Rivers

This retelling of the biblical story of Hosea and Gomer is set in the California Gold Rush days. Sold into prostitution, Angel has never believed in love—nor trusted anyone else for her survival. When Michael Hosea obeys God's call to marry Angel and to love her unconditionally, he is discouraged at not being able to convince her of his devotion. Unable to cast off the demons of her past, Angel flees his overwhelming kindness and love and searches for the truth she cannot deny. Her final healing will not come from the man she loves, but from the Almighty, the One who will never let her go. This is a life-changing story for any woman who feels she can never do enough or be good enough to deserve the love of God.

RECOMMENDED BY SUE BROWER,
MARKETING DIRECTOR

Galway Chronicles, a series about nineteenth-century Ireland, are actually based on stories Bodie Thoene's grandmother told her when she was young.

Michael Phillips spent so much time in George MacDonald's novels and became so familiar with Scotland that he began telling his own stories. Look for *Legend of the Celtic Stone, An Ancient Strife, The Secrets of Heathersleigh Hall,* and *The Stonewycke Legacy* (with Judith Pella) and others. These stories are family sagas, with four or five books in each series.

Recommending books from religious publishing houses is sometimes hindered by how quickly some of them go out of print, but these books will likely be around for a while and give you hours of enjoyable reading.

Humor

Humor is the hardest genre of books to recommend. What is funny to one person may leave another cold. You can almost hear the person to whom you gave the book saying, "What's so funny about that?" E. B. White, a funny writer himself, once compared analyzing humor to dissecting a frog, in that the thing tends to die in the process.

Comedy or a comic plot is usually U-shaped: it begins in prosperity, confronts problems, and manages to end happily. The comedy comes with the obstacles that must be overcome for the happy ending. That's true in silly, simple stories that make us belly-laugh, as it were, or in something as serious as Dante's *Divine Comedy* or as lighthearted as Shakespeare's *Midsummer Night's Dream*.

Humor in writing depends on the author's ability to portray the ridiculous, to take what should be ordinary and turn it upside down. At our house we laugh at James Thurber's funny stories. If you can read *The Night the Bed Fell In* without laughing, I want to meet you. We have read aloud his *The Thirteen Clocks* every Halloween, just for fun. His works are included in short story collections and in *The Thurber Carnival*. His writings often have equally quaint line drawings, a fact that is especially interesting because Thurber was blind. He was a favorite writer for the *New Yorker Magazine* during his lifetime.

P. G. Wodehouse is the favorite writer of more writers than any other writer, or so I read. The quantity of his writings is certainly impressive, and maybe that alone impressed his peers. His work can be measured in tonnage. He began writing when he was twenty-three and finished when he was ninety-three, and was in the middle of another story when he died. He appears to have written ninety-four books, at least six movies, sixteen plays, the lyrics for twenty-eight musical comedies, and more than three hundred short stories. He is considered the most successful comic novelist in history, but his stuff is very British. Where to begin? Try *Right Ho, Jeeves* or *The Code of the Woosters* or *Pigs Have Wings*. Wodehouse called his novels "musical comedies without the music." Find one and see if it tickles your funny bone.

A Year in Provence by Peter Mayle is a terribly funny tale of an English couple who decide they like the sunshine of Provence better

Books That Made Me Laugh

Traveling Mercies by Anne Lamott
Lamott tells of her journey to faith in words like you never heard in church, but she is so honest and grace-filled we are reminded that God can find anyone anywhere. We laugh and recognize ourselves. (Language)

Will Mrs. Major Go to Hell?
by Aloise Buckley Heath
A collection of essays. Heath, mother of ten children, hated to write but every Christmas she delivered, under duress, one essay to the *National Review*—funny, tender, or satirical. When she tragically died, her youngest child (five) declared they would never have fun again.

84 Charing Cross Road by Helene Hanff
For twenty years Hanff corresponds with a London bookshop. This is a record of sheer delight in words and books. Written with a rare sense of humor.

The World of Mr. Mulliner
by P. G. Wodehouse
A collection of short stories. One tale begins: "If men were dominoes, Osbert would have been a double blank." Start anywhere and be prepared to keep reading and laughing.

Lake Wobegone Days by Garrison Keillor
Fictional Lake Wobegone, Minnesota, "the little town that time forgot and the years cannot improve." As Keillor says, "These are my people." They are ours too, which is why we love them and laugh so deeply at their foibles.

RECOMMENDED BY MARGIE HAACK,
WRITER AND COLUMNIST

than the rains of England. They buy a dilapidated villa and have hilarious adventures in making it livable and coping with all their guests.

While they defy classification, it's hard to beat veterinarian James Herriot's *All Things Bright and Beautiful* and *All Things Wise and Wonderful* for a good evening of reading. They wear well through multiple readings. We first read his antics aloud in bed while staying in a bed and breakfast in Wales and were almost expelled for our hilarity.

You will love the Mapp and Lucia books by E. F. Benson. They are hilarious stories of 1930s manner and pecking order. Lucia rents the home of Elizabeth Mapp in an English village. Together they make their life interesting by meddling and spying on the neighbors. Look for *Miss Mapp, Queen Lucia, Lucia's Progress,* and others.

The Situation in Flushing by Edmund Love is a nostalgic novel set in Flushing, Michigan. It's the story of a young boy's love affair with steam engines in the early 1900s. In school, he frequently pretends to need the outhouse so he can run down to the train station to see his favorite trains. Eventually he is sent to the doctor to have his bladder checked! The book keeps you smiling all the way through.

Some humorous books claim to be nonfiction, written about real people, but so much fiction is woven into the story to make it funny that it becomes fiction. Robert Benchley's wit seems almost effortless. He seems like a good-natured man who is bewildered by the world. Look for his *My Ten Years in a Quandary* and *The Benchley Roundup* for good laughs. His books caused Thurber to comment, "One of the greatest fears of the humorous writer is that he has spent three weeks writing something done faster and better by Benchley in 1919."

In *Life with Father* Clarence Day tells the story of his father and his family in 1880 when his father took responsibility for everything from world peace to a good economy. Thyra Ferre Bjorn's *Papa's Wife* tells the story of a Norwegian family's life—another family to laugh at, along with the family in *Cheaper by the Dozen* by Frank and Ernestine Gilbreth. Having twelve children with a father that believes a family should be run like a factory offers lots of material for laughs. A more contemporary writer who takes her life and embroiders it for laughs is Erma Bombeck, popular columnist, now deceased, whose best pieces are collected in *Forever Erma.*

Babe, the Gallant Pig by Dick King-Smith is a great book to read aloud. King-Smith has numerous stories about animals of one kind or another. There's more: Richard Armour's *It All Started with Colum-*

bus; Harry Golden's *For Two Cents Plain;* Jean Kerr's *Please Don't Eat the Daisies.*

Pick a category and get started and you will suddenly discover new authors, new titles, and many hours of good reading. We've only begun to explore the world of good books!

The most influential books, and the truest in their influence,
are works of fiction. They repeat, they rearrange, they clarify
the lessons of life; they disengage us from ourselves;
they constrain us to the acquaintance of others; and they
show us the web of experience so we can see it for ourselves.

ROBERT LOUIS STEVENSON

Chapter 5

The World and People Around Us: Nonfiction

Reading is an opportunity, a privilege to meet people you've never seen in places you've never been before.

ERMA BOMBECK

Stories of China have always fascinated me. Once, when Mao Tse-tung was in power, our family stood at the closely guarded border crossing, feeling fear and darkness as we looked across into China. Our entry was barred. We have never had a return visit. The land, the people, its history still seem mysterious to me, even after considerable reading that goes back to Pearl Buck's *The Good Earth*. Over the years news of the Cultural Revolution, the Red Guard, and the persecution of Christians within China shocked my American sensibilities. How could this happen?

When a friend gave me a copy of *Wild Swans: Three Daughters of China* by Jung Chang I attached myself to the lives of three generations of Chinese women and became thoroughly engrossed in China's more recent history. Jung Chang, the third-generation daughter, recounts her grandmother's life and the events that led to the welcoming of Chiang Kai-shek. Her father and mother, both intellectuals, were attracted to Mao, and I got new insights into why people followed him. Jung Chang's own life and education suffered from the Red Guard era and all its deprivations. I couldn't get away from these people; they filled my dreams, and I couldn't read fast enough to take it all in.

What a book! It is not fiction; the story is true. I look at my widened world and am reminded afresh that we read for two reasons: for pleasure and to gain information. The person who reads for only one reason is a reading cripple. No one has been everywhere or done everything or knows all the nuances of human experience. Reading nonfiction is part of expanding our worldview.

Books That Stretch Me for Cross-Cultural Living

The Call by John Hersey

Hersey traces the fictional missionary career of David Treadup in China from the early 1900s through World War II as his parochial North American faith encounters a culture thousands of years old. Hersey, born in China, writes with a deep love of the country and faces issues that are very real.

The Covenant by James Michener

In his usual style of tracing the history of a region through the lives of successive generations, Michener brings alive the struggles of South Africa. Settled by a profoundly religious people who based their domination of other races on the Bible, this country raises again and again questions about what true faith looks like. One wishes that Michener could add another chapter about the emerging democracy.

Letters Never Sent by Ruth Van Reken

As an adult and a missionary herself, Ruth expresses in letters things she had been afraid to say as a child in a missionary boarding school and as a young adult left behind in North America for college.

The Third Culture Kid Experience: Growing Up among Worlds by David Pollock and Ruth E. Van Reken

This nonfiction book examines both the advantages and challenges of being raised in a culture different from one's parents. Every adult who has lived overseas will identify with the feeling of no longer belonging in the North American suburban context and the pain of frequent separations.

No Graven Image by Elisabeth Elliot

The discouragements and frustrations of missionary life come through in this fictionalized account of Elisabeth's ministry the year before she married Jim Elliot. Now out of print, look for it in a church library or used bookstore. Excellent.

RECOMMENDED BY LEANNE HARDY,
LIBRARIAN AND MISSIONS WRITER

Reading Nonfiction

More people read nonfiction than fiction—which may surprise readers of fiction; the ratio is about sixty percent nonfiction to forty percent fiction. Nonfiction is the broadest category of writing, covering a wide range of subjects. It encompasses biographies, autobiographies, travel adventures, historical events, nature books, true experiences, political movements, and other interests. The list goes on to include any writing that centers on real events or issues, instead of imaginative ones. Some readers say that they read nonfiction because they want to read about reality—real people, real events—instead of something made up by the author.

Nonfiction has this strong appeal. But the level of imagination can be very high in a work of nonfiction. We still need to ask *Is this true?* All authors write about a world seen through their own lens; the author's voice informs every page. This led editor Clare Booth Luce to caution readers that all autobiographies are alibi-ographies. *All* is too broad a statement, but obviously a writer presents life and events from a personal point of view. Who has sufficient self-awareness and judgment to get even her own life right? With the slipping away of time, memories tend to be selective. I think of this when my brother and I share unmatched memories of events of our growing-up years. Is his version right? Or is mine? Or does it matter? Maybe both are true—just different perspectives on the same event.

Autobiography comes from the person's own pen and offers us unique access into the inner life of an individual. In contrast, biographies are written by observers who interpret the life, values, attitudes, and successes of another person's life. How this turns out depends on whether the writer is cynical or has a jaundiced view of his subject or whether he writes to magnify the virtues of his subject. Selective truth or slanted truth is not uncommon, as anyone who reads the newspapers already knows. Contemporary biography seems bent on exposing the unworthiness of the life examined. Someone called it "pathography as biography." It seems a coup of some sort to find moral flaws in our heroes. Writers can make a political tract out of almost anything, if they have a mind to do so.

Academic studies are not immune to the truthfulness problem. If a scholar begins with a given hypothesis, that scholar may face the charge of making research match the hypothesis. It's too simplistic to say, "I read it in a book." I heard a National Public Radio interview in which a scientist said that one famous and enormous redwood tree has now been proven to be only slightly over a thousand years old, not the several thousand years originally published. When asked why this information had not been corrected sooner, the scientist pondered and said he didn't know, but he supposed it was because people liked linking monumental size and age. Errors like this mean that history and information books have to be corrected and rewritten every few years.

Or suppose the writer believes that matter is eternal; with that presupposition he will not likely question whether there is a God; he collects his data accordingly. This should not discourage reading nonfiction, but only to emphasize that *whatever* you read must be done thoughtfully and with an eye out for truth. There's only one Book to stake your life on!

So how does one read nonfiction? With an eye for truth as the first principle. Beyond that, nonfiction simply asks the reader to be aware of the category of the book. This may be complicated by overlap in subject. Some books are both biographical and historical. Others are opinions, personal experiences, theories, or observations. Some require heightened openness of mind and spirit to receive what the writer says; other books allow you to be an observer; still others take you with them on an adventure. Reading nonfiction requires you to be in sync with the writer.

Autobiography

"O, Lord, you were turning me around to look at myself. You were setting me before my own eyes." So wrote Augustine about his conversion experience. Knowing of his mother's diligent prayers for him and acknowledging his wayward life, Augustine (A.D. 430) sat in his garden one day with some troubled thoughts. Suddenly he heard a child's voice chanting, "Take and read. Take and read!" He received that as a spiritual word that he was to *read*, and opened his Bible to Romans. That reading led to the changed life that Augustine tells about in *Confessions*, recounting his life up to his conversion to Christianity.

His *Confessions* gave birth to autobiography as a separate genre from all that had been written before. His is a spiritual autobiography. Aside from St. Paul none of the early Christians left us a record of their conversion. Many have since written their own stories, but at this point in time a self-reflection of this sort was unique to Augustine. *Confessions* is now considered a "founding document" to all auto-biography, whether spiritual or secular. It is not a polemic; it is a revelation of self.

In one sense, all autobiographies have a spiritual dimension because they reflect the values of the person writing, even when the person is a blatant atheist. What we look for in reading an autobiography is not a detailed narrative of life's events (there are some things we could care less about!) so much as a look at its significance. What made this person unique? What contribution does the writer's life make to mine? We are not looking for ego-trips or excruciating details of failures. We look for understanding, and bookshelves are heavy with autobiographies that enlighten and instruct. You will find the choices are many.

Check out the personal spiritual stories of three well-known contemporary leaders: William Buckley, Billy Graham, and Charles Colson. In his inimitable prose, William F. Buckley Jr. wrote *Nearer, My God: An Autobiography of Faith,* sharing without apology not only his deeply held religious convictions as a Catholic but the impact of these beliefs on his larger family, all of whom are prominent in literary circles. In quite another style Billy Graham's *Just As I Am* tells the story of his early years that led to his worldwide preaching ministry, of the decisions made in his youth, of his lifestyle commitments, of the response to his crusades. Reading it I realized that, after hearing of the Great Awakening in our country before the American Revolution, I had lived through another Great Awakening in Graham's incredibly far-reaching ministry. Charles Colson, imprisoned as a result of his involvement in the Watergate scandal during Richard Nixon's presidency, recounts his own life-changing conversion in *Born Again*, telling how reading a book (C. S. Lewis's *Mere Christianity*) led him to faith. Reading of his subsequent concern for the prison system, which has led to the effective Prison Fellowship ministry, reminds one again that God doesn't waste any of our experiences.

C. S. Lewis's *Surprised by Joy* (that title is the best!) tells of his own journey to faith as an academic at Oxford University. Surveying the Lewis books on my shelves and the incredible influence of his writing makes me glad that he was one day surprised by joy. It comes through in all that he writes.

Kathleen Norris, writer and poet, left New York City to claim the inheritance of her grandmother's home in South Dakota. As she struggled with adjustment to life in a small town, she wrote her first book *Dakota*. And as she began her own inward journey to discover her true self and faith in God, one of her survival resources was a community of Benedictine monks. In *Cloister Walk* she shares not only how this community affected her spiritual journey, but also what she learned about God, the Bible, meditative prayer, and quietude in this isolated place. It's an uplifting spiritual biography. Her book *Amazing Grace* takes on theological words and the meaning of biblical concepts—less an autobiography than a definition, but still representing her very personal discoveries.

Anne Lamott, a disarmingly honest contemporary author, writes still another kind of spiritual autobiography in *Traveling Mercies: Some Thoughts on Faith*. What she writes reflects growing up in the 1960s. Anne's self-effacing humor and ruthless honesty allow her to describe her not-so-perfect moments perfectly. Her language and lifestyle may shock you, but you will find yourself attracted to her kind of honest self-appraisal.

Herman Wouk, a noted contemporary writer and playwright, wrote *This Is My God: The Jewish Way of Life* some years ago. It remains a favorite of mine. Wouk, as a practicing Jew, tells us what his faith means to him. One of my favorite passages from this book recounts how he feels about leaving the hassles of theater life on Friday afternoon and coming home to the peace and meaning of Shabbat. More recently he wrote *The Will to Live On*, a blend of personal reflections and anecdotes about his Jewish heritage and faith.

Alfred Kazin's *A Walker in the City* takes the reader to his old neighborhood in Brownsville in east Brooklyn, a neighborhood populated by Jewish immigrants, and lets you smell the shops along the streets, see the old synagogue, sense life in his mother's kitchen, and follow Kazin's attempts to envision life beyond the block he lives on. It is an extraordinary reading experience.

From others we want a more detailed story. How could we ever know what life was like for South Africa's Nelson Mandela without his own voice giving us *Long Walk to Freedom*? How does a person experience imprisonment, abuse, and prejudice and emerge from the experience with a gentleness and humility that writes on the world's history? This book tells us.

Or compare abolitionist Frederick Douglass's account of being beaten and mobbed for his insistence on freedom for black people in the mid-1800s in *Narrative of the Life of Frederick Douglass*. Douglass movingly tells us how he learned to read:

The frequent hearing of my mistress reading the Bible aloud . . .
awakened my curiosity in respect to this mystery of reading, and
roused in me the desire to learn. Up to this time I had known
nothing whatever of this wonderful art, and my ignorance and
inexperience of what it could do for me, as well as my confidence
in my mistress, emboldened me to ask her to teach me to read. . . .
I used to carry almost constantly a copy of Webster's Spelling
Book in my pocket and when play time allowed me, I would step
aside . . . and take a lesson in spelling. And as I read, behold! Light
penetrated the moral dungeon where I had lain.

The Color of Water by James McBride, a black man's tribute to his
white mother, is an account of an abused rabbi's daughter who con-
verts to Christianity, marries a black man, and raises twelve children,
putting them all through college, even though poverty stalked her life.
Only two things mattered: school and church. Often confused by how
different his family was as he grew up, McBride's memoir is a convincing story of persistence against all odds.

Ben Carson grew up in the inner city of Detroit, parented by a
mother who had a third-grade education and worked two, sometimes
three, jobs to support her two sons. She did more than put bread on
the table; she made certain the boys knew how to read. Every week
Ben and his brother went to the library, where each chose two books
to read so that they could give their mother the required book
report. Today both men are university graduates, and Ben Carson is
a world-renowned neurological surgeon at Johns Hopkins Hospital.
He tells his inspiring story in *Gifted Hands: The Story of Ben Carson.*
Read this wonderful book and share his story with a teenager you
know.

The Autobiography of Malcolm X as told to Alex Haley comes out
of the American Civil Rights struggle and is a must-read if you want
to more fully understand issues from the point of view of a black man.
It is testimony to a turnaround in the life of an enraged man.

The Hiding Place by Corrie ten Boom has been named by many
as the most influential autobiography of the twentieth century. The
courage of ten Boom's Dutch family and their story of hiding Jews in
their home during the German occupation in World War II makes this
book a page-turner and a great family read-aloud book. It's hard to
imagine seeing various family members sent away to death camps. Corrie ten Boom, a remarkable Christian woman, survived Ravensbruck

camp and later had a significant worldwide ministry in sharing the faith that brought her through this ordeal.

Joni, another story of amazing faith and courage, gives new perspective to your own life. Joni Eareckson, a beautiful young woman who became a quadriplegic as the result of a diving accident, realistically shares her pain and struggle as she begins to make a meaningful life out of her tragic experience. This book has encouraged people for over twenty-five years. Its inspiring spirit makes it worth reading again, and if you missed it, it's a new book to you! Joni has many other books, some of which are devotional books that will be listed in a later chapter on spiritual growth.

Well-known authors have done reminiscences of growing-up days. Look for Annie Dillard's *An American Childhood* and Russell Baker's *Growing Up*. Former President Jimmy Carter recorded his own boyhood memories in *An Hour before Daylight*. This kind of focused autobiography takes the reader on more than a nostalgia journey. It is a highly readable way to understand the history and values of another generation.

The Land Remembers by journalist Ben Logan greatly warmed my heart. He recounts his boyhood world on a lonely ridge farm in southwest Wisconsin growing up in the 1920s and 1930s. The pace of his life—the family gathering under the maple tree in the front yard on hot summer evenings, the wisdom and fairness of his father in daily life, the unclutteredness of living—makes good reading. Logan has a naturalist's eye for detail—the kind of "noticing" that enriches a reader's life. He describes winter on the farm: "The shrinking down of the farmhouses as the cold set in and the land outside grew vaster."

Walter Cronkite's autobiography has all the interest and spice of *A Reporter's Life*, recounting events and people with fascinating detail—the inside scoop. Englishman Alistair Cooke, host for *Masterpiece Theater* for many years, interviewed many of the most influential men and women of the twentieth century, and recorded the interviews in his book *Memories of the Great and the Good*. These men take readers inside a different world.

I like Beryl Markham's fine-tuned prose. I found a delightful paperback entitled *The Splendid Outcast*, containing eight beautifully crafted short accounts of life in colonial Africa, where Markham grew up as a white expatriate. In 1930 she became a bush pilot. Her celebrated autobiography, *West with the Night*, contains her story of crossing the Atlantic, east to west. This is more than a pilot's memoir, however. It is full of wise, funny, and adventurous explorations of life.

Out of Africa recounts Isak Dinesen's (aka Karen Blixen) love affair with Africa. For twenty years Dinesen ran a coffee plantation in Kenya, and this is a memoir of her experiences. The reader is quickly swept away by her imagery so that the continent and life in colonial Africa gets under the skin.

Many collections of short autobiographies are in print. If you are into Southern writers, look for *Southern Selves: From Mark Twain and Eudora Welty to Maya Angelou and Kaye Gibbons: A Collection of Autobiographical Writing* edited by James Watkin. If you have a favorite historical person or a favorite author, look in the library to find an autobiography or a biography, perhaps one included in a collection, and learn from that person's life.

Published diaries and letters are another kind of autobiography and bring the reader inside a person's life without much comment, letting the reader form his own opinions. Lest this sound dull to you, let me assure you that it is not. I was surprised at how much I have enjoyed this kind of reading. I began with *The Habit of Being, the Letters of Flannery O'Connor* and came to "know her" in the way you do if reading someone's letters. Her world took shape for me, and when she wrote a friend that she was mailing her only readable copy of a novel to her by post, having retained only carbons with blurred erasures, I was conscious of two things: the wonder of copy machines and the reliability of the postal service in days of yore.

I later read *The Letters of J. R. R. Tolkien*, and was fascinated by how real his created world was to him. He wrote to his son and other interested friends about the problems he faced in his imagined world with as much concern as if he were planning a world summit. As I read I began to think of him as an old friend, and it heightened my enjoyment of his fantasy books.

Years ago I read Anne Morrow Lindbergh's *Gift from the Sea*, a sensitive exploration of her personal life and its meaning as she retreated for a time alone by the sea. I found myself wishing she lived next door! I followed that book with the more detailed story of her life and marriage to Charles A. Lindbergh in her diaries. *Bring Me a Unicorn: 1922–38* covers her early life and marriage. Together Charles and Anne flew a historic exploratory trip by air, pilot and navigator in a single-engine plane, a story later chronicled in *North to the Orient*. The joyful birth of their baby boy and the terror of his subsequent abduction and murder is recorded from her diaries in *Hours of Gold, Hours of Lead: 1929–32*. When the pressure of news reporters and camera men proved too much, they moved abroad to France and England, and Anne recorded their life there in *Locked Rooms and Open Doors: 1933–35* and *The Flower and the Nettle: 1936–39*. During this time Charles Lindbergh became increasingly involved as a spokesman for conciliation with an aggressive Germany, a position that caused him to fall out of favor with the American public. Those years are storied in *War Within and Without: 1939–44*. Anne Morrow Lindbergh is an exceptionally gifted writer, expressing feelings and insights that only another woman can appreciate. I found myself copying her thoughts into a notebook.

Many readers familiar with Madeleine L'Engle's novels, poetry, and children's books will enjoy The Crosswick Journals (named after her country home). In this series of three books, L'Engle gives an intimate look at her life, her writing, and her thoughts. Look for *A Circle of Quiet*, *The Summer of the Great Grandmother*, and *The Irrational Season*.

On a visit to Virginia I picked up a small volume called *A Southern Woman's Story: Life in Confederate Richmond* by Phoebe Yale Pender, her diary of life as the matron of a Confederate hospital during the Civil War. It is fascinating! Whenever we travel to a new part of the country I look for regional authors who are writing about the landscape and its history. Here are some other good accounts: *A Black Woman's Civil War Memoir* by Susie King Taylor; *Army Letters from an Officer's Wife* by Francis M. A. Roe; *The Civil War Diary of a Southern Woman* by Sarah Morgan; and *Letters of a Woman Homesteader* by Elinore Pruitt. These women have opened history we would never know apart from their journals and letters.

One of my delights was to happen upon an amazing book by Joy Buel and Richard Buel Jr. called *The Way of Duty*. This book classifies as biography, but I am putting it here because it is the result of journals and letters of a woman named Mary Fish. We have few such intimate pictures of life in the 1700s, but because this Connecticut woman Mary, in the course of a long life, produced a large amount of written material, preserved with unusual care by the generations of her family, we have this amazing story. Few women of Mary's day knew how to read and write. The Buels were amazed to find in the Yale University Archives this record of her life. It is an irresistible story that has been made into a television movie, "Mary Silliman's War."

The stress the War of Independence brought to the lives of citizens, and the impact of grass-roots politics cannot be imagined without a book like this, but I liked it for its look at everyday life in the 1700s.

An Interrupted Life: The Diaries of Etty Hillesum 1941–43 are wartime diaries of a young Dutch Jew who reads and is drawn to the New Testament before dying in Auschwitz. The *New York Times Book Review* called this "a story of spiritual growth such as I have seldom seen anywhere."

Letters and Papers from Prison by Dietrich Bonhoeffer is a collection of notes and correspondence covering the period from Bonhoeffer's arrest in 1943 to his execution by the Gestapo in 1945, put together by his friend Ebehard Bethage. Bonhoeffer's writings (which include *The Cost of Discipleship* and *Life Together*) have been called "fragments of incomparable genius"—writings of such enduring quality and depth of insight that urging you to read them is a pleasure. What a man for such a time in history!

The word *memoir* is a fancy and currently popular name for an autobiography. A memoir usually focuses on one theme or time frame of the writer's life. Memoirs are usually shorter, less detailed, more engaging than some autobiographies, but the label does not always mean anything specific. However, it sounds chic, and I am not inclined to judge which is a memoir and which is an autobiography unless the author says so. (Not all memoirs are true memoirs, however. *Memoirs of a Geisha* is written as if dictated by a geisha, but the author is Arthur Golden, who interviewed many geishas to get his information. It's fiction; a good book, incidentally.)

Angela's Ashes: A Memoir by Frank McCourt is a story of unmitigated misery growing up in Ireland. The dysfunctional lifestyle of McCourt's parents is relieved only by the kind of humor that makes poverty and survival a miracle. It isn't pretty reading, but it wasn't pretty living either. It is *good* reading, winning a Pulitzer Prize, and places the reader into another reality.

Jill Ker Conway's *The Road from Coorain* tells of her childhood in New South Wales, Australia with such good use of language and vivid descriptions of the Australian Outback that John Kenneth Galbraith remarked, "I've been several times to Australia; this book was the most rewarding journey of all." Conway has since been the president of Smith College.

Tuesdays with Morrie by Mitch Albom, on the nonfiction bestseller list for so long that it almost seems permanent, is the story of

Morrie Schwartz, college professor and mentor of journalist Mitch Albom. Just months before Morrie's death from Lou Gehrig's disease, Albom reconnected with Morrie and visited him every Tuesday, recording his wisdom, memories, and feelings about dying. Something sweet and caring in this book captures readers and leads to good discussions about life and death.

Frederick Buechner has written a beautiful book called *The Eyes of the Heart—A Memoir of the Lost and Found*. Buechner takes us into his library, which he calls the Magic Kingdom, and uses the treasures he finds there as a gateway to his heart and mind. As he recollects details in his life, he draws the reader into his contemplations of the meaning of his various relationships. He has also written *The Sacred Journey* and *Now and Then*, both exceptionally enriching spiritual memoirs. Buechner advises the reader, "Listen to your life; see it for the fathomless mystery that it is. In the boredom and pain of it no less than in the excitement and gladness: touch, taste, smell your way to the holy and hidden heart of it, because in the last analysis, all moments are key moments, and life itself is grace."

Elie Wiesel's *Night* is near the head of the list of books everyone needs to read. With an economy of words, Wiesel takes us with him into the Jewish nightmare of the Holocaust. Suffering in a concentration camp, he tries to care for his aging father until he dies. It is a small book, but it is the best of reading on this historical tragedy. Wiesel's use of language is something to linger over—such an intense experience in so brief a reading. Follow up with his two-volume memoir: *All Rivers Run to the Sea* and *And the Sea Is Never Full*.

Biography

Since I sing the merits of reading the writings of C. S. Lewis and J. R. R. Tolkien, I have devoured Humphrey Carpenter's *The Inklings: C. S. Lewis, J. R. R. Tolkien, Charles Williams, and Their Friends*. Carpenter has also written an excellent book on the life of Tolkien. How I would have enjoyed eavesdropping in The Eagle and Child Pub to listen to the discussions of the Inklings! It's amazing how reading biographies gives you the illusion of knowing the people involved.

Dorothy Clark Wilson wrote an enlightening biography of missionary doctor Paul Brand and his work with lepers in India, called *Ten Fingers for God*. It's a fascinating account of a man of God whose attention to detail changed the world for lepers. A new edition is in

Puritans and Reformers Who Got Me through Dark Times

Five English Reformers by J. C. Ryle

In the 1550s, while Queen Mary was on the English throne, many Protestants were burned for their faith. There is something about reading of these men's convictions, their faith, and their suffering—not just from the fire, but from their own sorrow at leaving families and flocks behind—that helps bring our own griefs into perspective. Beneath all their lives is a foundation of unquenchable hope and joy in the God we love.

Charles Simeon: Pastor of a Generation by Handley Moule

Charles Simeon (1759–1836) ministered at Holy Trinity Church, Cambridge, for fifty-four years. A man who suffered great opposition to his ministry, he was yet regarded as one of England's greatest and most influential preachers. The words of his sermons and diaries still have the power to make a heart cry out in recognition: "This man *knows* me."

The Mystery of Providence by John Flavel

This book was first published in 1678 and I read it in 1997, the darkest year of my life—the year our daughter was raped by a stranger and became pregnant as a result. Word by word, page by page, this man taught me the beauty of the providence and sovereignty of God. Not all my questions were answered, but when I finished with this dense book, I knew and loved God in a way I never had before. In heaven, I am going to find John and give him a holy kiss.

The Valley of Vision: A Collection of Puritan Prayers edited by Arthur Bennet

The Puritans' prayers are marked by a spiritual devotion, balance, and beauty that are thoroughly missing in the missiles I send heavenward. And yet there is a practicality and poignancy that would surprise those who don't know the Puritans. I often pray them because they give perfect voice to my heart's deepest desires.

Here I Stand: A Life of Martin Luther by Roland H. Bainton

"I cannot . . . I will not recant! Here I stand" were the words spoken by Martin Luther in 1520. Accused of heresy and threatened with excommunication and death, Luther boldly continued his fight for the reformation of the church. His prescription for depression: shoveling manure. His unshakable faith in God helped shatter the corrupt structure of the medieval church.

Letters of John Calvin, Selected from the Bonnet Edition

Calvin's letters reveal a humble man who was not only involved with historical matters of church and state, but who was compassionately involved in the personal lives of others. A man who suffered exquisitely from all kinds of troubles, he is, as are all the Reformers and Puritans, a reminder that as Christians in the twenty-first century we stand in a stream of people stretching back across peoples, continents, and time. We are not alone.

RECOMMENDED BY MARGIE HAACK, WRITER AND COLUMNIST

print, with an addendum written by Philip Yancey about the life of Dr. Brand. I feel an excitement just writing about these kinds of books, to say nothing of reading them.

Wisdom and Innocence: A Life of G. K. Chesterton by Joseph Pearce should capture the eye of all Chesterton lovers. What a wise and joyful man Chesterton was! Certainly he is among the most quotable. An English journalist, apologist, and orator of the early 1900s, he became famous on both sides of the Atlantic for his potent prose. As a convert to Catholicism, he defended Christian beliefs with vigor. He wrote a stirring description of the church as a heavenly chariot, "thundering through the ages, the dull heresies sprawling and prostrate, the wild truth reeling but erect." His best-known works are *Orthodoxy* and *The Man Who Was Thursday.* If you are a Chesterton fan, or wish you knew more about him, log on to *www.chesterton.org.*

David McCasland's well-crafted biography *Oswald Chambers: Abandoned to God* is an inspiration, especially meaningful for those who know the classic devotional guide *My Utmost for His Highest.* Chambers, a young English clergyman, was known internationally as an outstanding devotional speaker and teacher as well as a prolific writer. (His books have never been out of print!) During World War I he served as chaplain for the British Commonwealth soldiers in Egypt, where he died in 1917 at the age of forty-three. I was amazed at all this zealous man accomplished in a very short life. David McCasland proves himself a fine biographer again in writing about the life of Eric Liddell, the young Scottish missionary, whose Olympic race story was heralded in the film *Chariots of Fire.* Liddell's life is the story of heroics in the ordinary. His biography is *Eric Liddell: Pure Gold.*

John Pollock, a gifted researcher and credible biographer, has penned fascinating and very readable biographies of Christian leaders: *John Wesley, Dwight L. Moody, The Apostle: A Life of Paul, Billy Graham, Hudson [Taylor] and Maria, Wilberforce,* and others. You will not be disappointed in any of them, but I especially liked the story of Dwight L. Moody's life—such a rough-hewn man so filled with grace and vision and so convinced about his message.

One of my favorite biographies, written by Miriam Rockness, is *A Passion for the Impossible: The Life of Lilias Trotter.* It's the story of a talented aristocratic English woman, proclaimed by John Ruskin to be the most promising woman artist of the nineteenth century, who left her career behind to pioneer a Christian mission among the Muslims in North Africa. Lilias Trotter is a poet, artist, visionary—an extraordinary woman—revealed in this well-written book that also contains some of her sensitive drawings and her parables.

Amma: The Life and Words of Amy Carmichael by Elizabeth Skoglund introduces you not only to the ministry of Amy Carmichael, but also to her fine writings and poetry. Born in 1867, this courageous

Breathtaking True Stories

When the Snow Comes, They Will Take You Away by Eric Newby

Newby, now an author of descriptive world travel books, writes with breathtaking reality of the summer he spent hiding in a small northern Italian town after he and his partner were shot down during World War II. In a part of Europe often missed in stories of the war, the villagers put themselves at risk to hide the airmen through the summer, knowing cold weather would eventually force them into shelter and bring them to capture.

The Scarlet Pimpernel of the Vatican by J. P. Gallagher

Approximately the same time frame as Newby's book, this is the amazing story of Hugh O'Flaherty, a Vatican cardinal who risks his career and life, challenging the Vatican's neutrality as he involves himself in the Italian Underground Movement, under the nose of the Nazis.

A Thousand Miles Up the Nile by Amelia B. Edwards

In the late 1800s a remarkable and intrepid English spinster hired an Egyptian dahabeeyah and traveled up the Nile from Cairo to Nubia, describing the sights in vivid word pictures, accompanied by charming sketches of the Egypt she encountered. Keep a book about modern Egypt close by to compare her sketches to the color pictures available today, and note the accuracy of her drawings.

My American Adventure: 50 States, 50 Weeks by Amy Burritt

In the mid 1990s, leaving behind home, friends, and family dog, fifteen-year-old Amy and her family take a motorhome tour of the United States to learn more about America by visiting every governor of every state. The story is remarkably suspenseful as Amy battles loneliness, the frustration of close quarters, and the tensions of bureaucracy in attempting to reach her goal. There are heroes, villains, and last-minute rescues for this family. This is a great read-aloud family book.

RECOMMENDED BY KRISTY MOTZ,
LIBRARIAN

woman went to India in 1901 as a missionary. She boldly began a rescue operation for unwanted children given away to the Hindu temple. Called Amma by the children, she set up the Dohnavur Family and began to write letters to people in England soliciting prayer and support for these little girls, as well as devotional tracts and poetry. Elisabeth Elliot also wrote an earlier book about her in *A Chance to Die: The Life and Legacy of Amy Carmichael.*

Those who love Catherine Marshall's writings will enjoy reading *Catherine Marshall* by Kathy McReynolds. Catherine Marshall is heralded in other parts of this book for her novels and her devotional writing.

Hundreds of biographies record the lives of famous historical figures. Instead of being dry and dull, as some might think, they are alive with interest. Take David Hackett Fischer's *Paul Revere's Ride,* for example. This book is not just about Revere's epic ride to warn the colonists, but transports the reader back to all that was happening in the new world when Revere rode into that dark night and into history. In 1942 Esther Forbes received a Pulitzer Prize for her book *Paul Revere and the World He Lived In,* which has been reissued in 1999. Her story of that same era is presented from the point of view of Paul Revere, the rider.

William Manchester has written a number of readable, important biographies. *The Last Lion* places Winston Churchill—a giant in intellect, courage, and leadership in England—in his historical setting and reveals a man with an uncanny grasp of the issues at stake on the political scene and in World War II. Manchester's title fits the importance of this man on the stage of history.

Manchester also wrote *American Caesar: Douglas MacArthur,* the story of the American general who dominated the outcome of the war in the Pacific. A brilliant strategist in winning the war, he also played an amazing role in the reconstruction of Japan following World War II. During the Korean War his strong-minded military strategy led him to openly disagree with President Harry Truman, his Commander-in-Chief. He was relieved of his command, but his significant role in our history will never be forgotten.

More books have been written about Abraham Lincoln than any other person save Jesus and Shakespeare, or so it has been said. I didn't do a count. Carl Sandburg's *The Prairie Years and the War Years* paints Lincoln with broad, beautiful strokes, depicting his life and his times. His writing helps the reader understand the magnitude of Lincoln's moment in history. Sandburg is both historian and poet in writing this book, and may be the only person to receive a Pulitzer Prize in both categories. This is not a book for the faint-hearted reader. Its preface begins, "There is no new thing to be said about Lincoln. There is no new thing to be said of the mountains or of the sea or the stars." It ends with "He was a star in steadfast purity and service. And he abides." Stephen B. Oates has written another shorter biography of Lincoln, *With Malice Toward None: A Life of Abraham Lincoln*. His biography tells of Lincoln's "majestic control of the English language, his raw humor, and his undeniable heroism."

David McCullough's *Mornings on Horseback* is a first-class biography of young Theodore Roosevelt Jr., who was seriously handicapped as a child with almost fatal asthma. This colorful account focuses largely on his family—the larger Roosevelt clan—but primarily on the influence of his father and mother in shaping and molding this great leader. Theodore Roosevelt became president when William McKinley was shot in 1901. The book's title comes from his morning rides under the blue skies of the Badlands when he was young. McCullough's writing is lucid and readable; it makes you want to read more.

As for other presidents, McCullough's *Truman* is a thick, intimidating book that you won't be able to put down. It will soon be 2:00 A.M. and you will hardly care. Truman proves a man of rock-solid American values who becomes president almost accidentally after the death of Franklin Roosevelt twelve weeks into his final term. A Pulitzer Prize winner too good to miss. In fact, McCullough is too good to miss. He has written *Reagan: An American Story, John Adams,* and others; other writings are historical accounts like *The Johnstown Flood.*

Every president has an autobiography and probably several biographies, generally good and informative reading. I recently read the first volume of Robert Caro's book *The Years of Lyndon Johnson: The Path to Power.* Caro's dogged research into the titanic personality of the president known as LBJ lays bare the roots of Johnson's duplicity and tragic failures, as well as his achievements. His research airs details that seem an outrage in a democracy.

How much do you know about another man who left his mark on history—Martin Luther King? If you read Stephen B. Oates's book *Let the Trumpet Sound: The Life of Martin Luther King* you will come to know the real King and be inspired by his vision—as well as his perseverance. His bravery, his triumphs, his vision, and his doubts are portrayed without undue sentiment in this recommended book.

Philip Yancey's *Soul Survivor* is a cross between an autobiography and a biography and chiefly tells how the lives of twelve other people have profoundly influenced his own life. The subtitle tells Yancey's story: *How My Faith Survived the Church*. Twelve chapters, each containing a compelling look at the life and thought of people like Martin Luther King Jr., G. K. Chesterton, Robert Coles, Dr. Paul Brand, and others from our list of recommended reading, underscore the value of reading biography. This may well be Yancey's best and most enriching book.

Enjoying History

Stephen Ambrose has taken many readers along on the explorations of Lewis and Clark in their journey to the Northwest in his book *Undaunted Courage*, a book that is popular with both men and women. This difficult charting of uncharted territory and the people who went along often seem guided by angels seen and unseen. Ambrose has also written the nearly incredible story of those who built the transcontinental railroad, *Nothing Like It in the World*.

Interested in the Civil War or don't know enough about it? Try reading one of Bruce Catton's wonderfully written accounts: *A Stillness at Appomattox*, *This Hallowed Ground*, or *Mr. Lincoln's Army*.

Blood Brothers by Elias Chacour fits the category of autobiography, but there is a historical significance to Chacour's content that leads me to place it here. With the Mideast continuing to be a hot spot, this book proves enlightening from the point of view of the Arab world. Chacour is a Palestinian Christian with a deep love for both Jews and Palestinians.

Travel to New Places

I find myself attracted to people who are curious about the world, about the people in it, about places they have never been. Their conversations inspire me to be more alive, more curious and adventuresome. Of all people in the world, those who have an investment in eternal things ought also to give wide attention to temporal things—to be on the cutting edge of life. No one can ever know everything, but good stewardship of our years ought to mean we push ourselves beyond the smallness of our life into the largeness of the world God created.

Books That Help Me Understand Our World

A World Lit Only by Fire: The Medieval Mind and the Renaissance
by William Manchester

  Manchester, a distinguished historian, a skilled and readable writer, depicts Magellan as the greatest hero of his era. Reading this book, it seems none-too-grandiose a tribute to Magellan's memory to have the Magellanic Clouds, "two luminous galaxies . . . some twenty-five degrees from the south celestial pole."

The Great Explorers: The European Discover of America
by Samuel Eliot Morison

  This is an abridgement of a multi-volume series I listened to on tape. It covers some of the same period as Manchester's book. Morison, another great historian, personally retraced the great voyages of discovery and accompanies his text with maps and photos.

Black Lamb and Grey Falcon
by Rebecca West

  Written in 1937, this is an in-depth (2 volume) look at the Balkans—its tumul-tuous history and religious and ethnic animosities. Dame West, an accomplished, if somewhat verbose writer, illuminates the root causes of both World Wars.

Let Us Talk of Many Things
by William F. Buckley

  While not exactly history, this is a collection of the author's speeches over the last fifty years, each one a vivid reminder of a significant event. Buckley's intellect and political vision even as a very young man are remarkable in the extreme. Even those who do not share his views acknowledge him as the founding father of the conservative movement as we know it today.

Witness by Whittaker Chambers

  Although this book deals with events of the Cold War and is, therefore, historical, it is a chronicle of Chamber's metamorphosis from an active member of the communist party to his ultimate rejection of totalitarianism and finally his conversion to Christianity. It is surely a work that shows goodness and truth and the price that is exacted from those who fight evil with truth.

RECOMMENDED BY MARILYN BAKER,
COMMUNITY LEADER, READER

Reading travel books is an excellent way to expand your view of the world. I've been reading John Muir's *Travels in Alaska* with great pleasure. Muir, a wide-eyed searcher for the wonders of America, embarked in May 1879 on his Alaskan adventure. His descriptions of what he saw pull me into the country. One night in a heavy rainstorm outside of the small village of Wrangell he climbed a hill to see how

Alaskan trees behave in storms. He writes, "It was wonderful . . . the trees glowing against the jet background, the colors of the mossy, lichened trunks with sparkling streams pouring down the furrows of the bark and the gray-bearded old patriarchs bowing low and chanting in passionate worship!" John McPhee, another fine chronicler of his adventures, gives another good look at Alaska in *Coming into the Country*—especially for Alaska-lovers or would-be travelers. I like the way McPhee writes.

Baghdad without a Map: And Other Misadventures in Arabia by Tony Horowitz is a hair-raising and fun read as this journalist with a Jewish name and looks to match works his way through Arab countries. He introduced me to some of the people he met, shared his conversations with me, and took me places I would never dare go.

Engaging the Natural World

Gerald Durrell is a slightly "crazy" Englishman who travels far and wide in his search for wildlife. His books allow you to travel with him and expose yourself to the antics that someone will endure to photograph an endangered species. Try his *Two in the Bush*, which may lead you to other adventures with him, including *Birds, Beasts, and Relatives* and *My Family and Other Animals*.

Farley Mowat, a Canadian author, has written two golden oldies still in print: *The Dog Who Wouldn't Be* and *The Boat That Wouldn't Float*. Our family read them aloud years ago and it is time for a reread. It isn't hard to picture the ridiculous scenes Mowat wrote about, and sometimes we had to stop reading because we couldn't stop laughing.

If you are a nature lover, have you tried Annie Dillard's *Pilgrim at Tinker Creek*? Dillard is not an easy read; her sentences all have the same intensity, but she does help her readers see her Virginia landscape with new eyes. She writes vividly, but I found I needed to read in small sections with lots of time to absorb.

Every once in a while a reader finds an author and meets a friend who shares life in a way that makes you better and bigger on the inside. Linda Hasselstrom is such a person for me. My daughter (in-law) discovered her first book on a trip west when she bought *Windbreak: A Woman Rancher on the Northern Plains*. She ended up ordering everything this woman had written. The author lives and works on a cattle ranch in South Dakota. She shares her life—the fencing, the birthing, the winds and storms, the harvests—so simply and intimately, we both felt like we had worked alongside her. When

Looking for Eden: Books That Explore Garden and Home

Tottering in my Garden: A Gardener's Memoir by Midge Ellis Keeble

A delightful romp through forty years of gardening with real problems, failures, and successes. She has practical suggestions for soil, pests, weeds, and species.

Under the Tuscan Sun by Frances Mayes

A beautiful memoir about reclaiming an abandoned Italian villa with its vineyards and gardens. I was utterly captured by this life in Tuscany.

A Country Year: Living the Questions by Sue Hubbell

A woman whose husband has left and whose children are grown moves to a cabin in the Ozarks where she begins a new life alone as a bee-keeper. The writing is rich and alive.

Assault on Eden: A Memoir of Communal Life in the Early 70s by Virginia Stem Owens

Fascinating account of the struggle to find the ideal by living off the land in northern New Mexico. Their failed quest became a catalyst for conversion to Christianity.

The Not So Big House by Sarah Susanka

Susanka, an architect, favors quality over quantity. She believes home is about the need for human dimensions that reflect warmth, beauty, intimacy, and even spiritual space for quiet reflection.

RECOMMENDED BY MARGIE HAACK,
WRITER AND COLUMNIST

her second book *Going Over East: Reflections of a Woman Rancher* arrived in the mail I had a tearful telephone call with the sad news that Hasselstrom's husband had died. We felt her loss as keenly as if she lived down the road from us. I love it when books make you feel that way; it's like caring for an extended family. Hasselstrom's *Land Circle: Writings Collected from the Land,* explains so much about loving the land, about death, about being a woman. Her poetry is of the finest. Some have called her the most deeply attuned nature writer the West has.

Women in the Wind, a collection of short essays and poetry about friendship and women in the sagebrush west, contains delightful, nourishing pieces about putting down roots, facing hardships, taming the land, and being neighbors. Linda Hasselstrom, Gaydell Collier, and Nancy Curtis compiled the writings by a variety of authors.

It's hard to know just where to place Kathleen Norris, author of *Dakota*. A successful New York writer and poet, Norris moved to South Dakota when she inherited her grandmother's farm. It is her noticing that most pulls at my heart as she describes the geography of the plains, its feel, its smell, and its people. She writes with first-time eyes about sunsets and the vastness of the land and analyzes what the geography of the land does to the people who live there. Her other writings are listed as autobiographies, but *Dakota* is about the land and its people.

True Tales of Adventure and the Will to Survive

Polar Dream by Helen Thayer
    The story of a solo trip to the North Pole by a fifty-four-year-old woman.

The Brendan Voyage by Tim Severin
    An enthralling story of two men crossing the North Atlantic in an open leather boat, demonstrating that a sixth-century monk, St. Brendan, could have crossed the Atlantic in a similar craft and that Irish monks may have been the first Europeans to set foot in North America.

We Die Alone by David Howarth
    The story of the many ordinary Norwegians who put their lives on the line to save an injured resistance fighter in World War II.

The Seamstress by Sara Tuvel Bernstein
    An appealing memoir of a spunky Jewish girl's survival growing up in anti-Semitic pre-war Romania, culminating in Ravensbruck concentration camp and her rescue and emigration to the United States.

O *Rugged Land of Gold* and *Home in the Bear's Domain* by Martha Martin
    An intensely moving story of unquenchable courage. Martha, terribly injured and stranded in the frozen wasteland of Alaska, learns how to survive and bears a child alone before she is rescued. The second book is a sequel.

The Long Walk by Slavomir Rawicz
    An incredible story of escape from a Siberian labor camp and a four-thousand-mile trek to freedom crossing the Gobi Desert and the Himalayas, without map or compass, but with a fierce determination to survive.

RECOMMENDED BY DAPHNE DRURY,
HOMEMAKER

Courage and Hardship

On the Missionary Trail: A Journey Through Polynesia, Asia and Africa with the London Missionary Society by Tom Hiney is a fascinating account of an extraordinary odyssey two men take in 1821 to fulfill an assignment to visit the mission stations of the Society, a journey that lasts eight years. The homespun sense of wonder of those on the journey, plus their remarkable fortitude, can't help but absorb the reader. And what you learn about the world makes you wide-eyed.

Lest Innocent Blood Be Shed by Philip Hallie has been called a miracle of goodness. Under the leadership of Pastor Trochme and Pastor Theis, the whole town conspires to save thousands of Jews in the small French Huguenot village of Le Chambon. The book examines how such goodness could happen in a world where evil is rampant.

Killing Fields, Living Fields by Don Cormack will have you gasping over man's inhumanity to mankind in Cambodia. This is not an easy book to read. What can I say about such heroism, such uncompromising faithfulness in the middle of such senseless destruction? The story is both heart-warming and heart-wrenching. It prompts tears, praises, prayers, and hopes. It is poignant reading, but it has the potential to change petty concerns about our own lives.

Parenting

Books have made a difference in parenting, of that there is little doubt. Reading a parenting book is like having a counselor who gives you ideas and suggestions when you feel stuck. For over thirty years *Honey for a Child's Heart* by Gladys Hunt has been encouraging parents to read to their children and helping them find the best books available. A new revised edition containing all the best books, new and old, will help make a reader out of your child. See also the new edition of *Honey for a Teenager's Heart*.

Parenting in the Pew by Robbie Castleman contains words of wisdom for guiding your children into the joy of worship. It's full of practical ideas, such as "let your children know you are going to worship, instead of going to church."

Grace Ketterman is a mother and a pediatrician. Together with Pat Holt, she has written the practical *Don't Give In; Give Choices* and *When You Feel Like Screaming*. Dr. Ketterman is the author of numerous books, among them *The Complete Book of Baby and Child Care*.

Books That Helped Me as a Mother

A Mother's Heart by Jean Fleming

An inspiring look at values, vision, and character for the Christian mother, full of motivation and practical advice on how to raise our children in a godly way and inject humor and fun into our homes.

And Then I Had Kids
by Susan Alexander Yates

An encouragement for mothers of young children. For me, it has been the most encouraging, empathetic, and human book I have read on the subject, all the more credible because it is a book written by a mother (of five children) to mothers. The most memorable aspect of the book was the reminder that the years pass quickly, with enormous implications for the future of my family.

Susanna by Arnold Dallimore

A biography of the mother of Charles and John Wesley, a highly intelligent and capable woman who passed on to her children a rich spiritual heritage in the face of severe hardship, poverty, constant childbearing, lack of support from her husband, and numerous tragedies, including the loss of many of her babies. Susanna lived at a time when opportunities for women were few; I find her an inspirational character.

Parenting Isn't for Cowards; Dare to Discipline; Hide or Seek; Preparing for Adolescents; and *Living on the Edge*
by James Dobson

I wouldn't be without these books. Dobson's views are garnered from over three decades of counseling children and their parents. His style is gracious and his methods are sensible, practical, and have stood the test of time.

Teaching Your Child How to Pray
by Rick Osborne

This was a recent godsend for me at a time when I felt particularly despondent about how to encourage my small children to pray for more than just a generous supply of sweets every day. A good wake-up call for my own prayer life too!

RECOMMENDED BY ROSEMARY MOORE,
ATTORNEY AND MOTHER

Books on parenting are not in scarce supply; some are more helpful than others. But in the best and worst scenarios it's important to remember that successful child-rearing is a grace-filled business. In times of deep pain it is helpful to remember that God is often disappointed with his children too. John White's *Parents in Pain* is full of grace and wisdom.

Mothers of daughters profit from reading Mary Pipher's *Reviving Ophelia: Saving the Selves of Adolescent Girls*—a treatise on raising daughters in contemporary culture. It would be a good book for a discussion group. What cultural agendas keep girls from becoming all they could be?

A Potpourri of Interests

What are you looking for? What are your interests? There is a book to fit that part of your life. They can't all be listed, but friendly librarians and bookstore owners will help you if you can't find what you want from the recommendations in this book.

Maybe you always wondered about Greek mythology and never quite got it straight. Then get for your bookshelf a copy of *The Golden*

I Love Books about Gardening

These books are good reading and good viewing. The pictures pull you into the world of the gardener-writer.

Tasha Tudor's Garden by Tovah Martin
　　Tasha Tudor is a children's book writer and illustrator. Her gardens are filled with flowers and fantasy. This book follows a year in her Vermont garden.

Caring for Perennials by Janet Macunovich
　　This is a no-nonsense book about "what to do and when to do it." It is filled with great ideas.

The Art of the Kitchen Garden by Jan and Michael Gertley
　　If you thought vegetable gardens were boring, this book will change your mind

forever. It is a feast for your eyes as the authors cleverly show you how to design your garden in patterns that are pleasing and bountiful. If you love quilts and gardening, read this book!

Herbs in the Garden and *Herbs in Pots* by Rob Proctor and David Macke
　　The authors share their own herb gardens as well as the many gardens of their friends. Their experiences so enthused me that I have been growing potted herb plants on my three porches, in my gardens, and in the house. I love the fragrance!

RECOMMENDED BY MARIAN HUNT,
ONCOLOGY NURSE AND GARDENER

Fleece, and the Heroes Who Lived Before Achilles by Padraic Colum. It was a 1921 Newbery, a marvelous resource book, but a delight just to read.

This one defies category: Three men died on November 22, 1963: C. S. Lewis, Aldous Huxley, and John F. Kennedy. In *Between Heaven and Hell*, Peter Kreeft conducts a dialogue in purgatory between these three, as they discuss their beliefs. Kreeft also wrote *Socrates Meets Jesus*.

Dorothy Sayers, best known for her detective fiction, was also a gifted medievalist and translated Dante's works. She wrote a famous play-cycle for broadcasting on the BBC, based on the gospels, called *The Man Born to Be King*. It makes good reading about Easter time each year.

And yet there is more!

Always read stuff that will make you look good
if you die in the middle of it.

P. J. O'ROURKE

Chapter 6

Piping Down the Valleys Wild: Poetry

Piping down the valleys wild
Piping songs of pleasant glee . . .
"Piper, sit thee down and write
In a book that all may read."

WILLIAM BLAKE

$\mathscr{I}$t had been snowing through the night and all morning in western Michigan. We stood together at the window, my neighbor and I, looking out at a beautiful white world. Then I said, remembering what I had once memorized:

The snow had begun in the gloaming,
And busily all the night
Had been heaping field and highway
With a silence deep and white.
Every pine and fir and hemlock
Wore ermine too dear for an earl,
And the poorest twig on the elm-tree
Was ridged inch deep with pearl.
I stood and watched by the window
The noiseless work of the sky . . .

And then I stopped because I couldn't remember anymore. She said, "What is that from? That's exactly the wonder I feel looking at this. Say it again." A simple James Russell Lowell poem caught the moment. Poetry had not been part of her life—no memorization in school, no reading at home—and yet it was getting at her heart. It had been stored in mine, and it came out in a timely way to name what we were feeling. The part of the poem I had never memorized goes on to lament the small burial mound under the snow, a child's death being common in the mid-1800s, when Russell penned this poem.

It's a pity we don't make poetry more a part of our reading life. It's in our bones, but we have stifled it. We worry that we won't understand it; we don't take time to let the meanings sink into our hearts; its different form—all those unusual line breaks—scares us away. In short, we don't give ourselves a chance to enjoy this wonderful sustenance of the inner life.

A major part of the Bible is written in poetic form. The special language of poetry with its metaphors and similes is found everywhere in the Scriptures. In fact, most of the poetry the average person reads likely comes from the Bible. People have remained loyal to the King James Version of the Bible because of its poetic rhythm and its musical use of language. Most early writing was done as poetry, including dramatic performances. We've all read of the minstrels who wandered from castle to castle putting on plays in rhyme form.

Poetry is rich in images. It is fresh and clean because word choices are critical in making a poem. The words are concrete and vivid. They convey emotion, never simply information. Sound counts, so does rhythm. Listen to Shakespeare, the immortal bard, tell us what to see and hear:

> *When icicles hang by the hall*
> *And Dick the shepherd blows his nail*
> *And Tom bears logs into the hall,*
> *And milk comes frozen home in pail*
> *And Marian's nose looks red and raw . . .*

You know it is unmistakably winter. Each word counts.

A minimum of words, a maximum of detail; that is poetry. Alfred Lord Tennyson writes about the eagle:

He clasps the crag with crooked hands;
Close to the sun in lonely lands,
Ringed with the azure world, he stands.
The wrinkled sea beneath him crawls;
He watches from his mountain walls,
And like a thunderbolt he falls.

Samuel Coleridge observed that prose is words in their best order. But poetry is the best words in the best order. You could call poetry *heightened speech*. Word choices paint the picture and give the rhythm. It matters that the eagle *clasps* the crags, rather than *grabs* the crags. It matters that the sea is *wrinkled*, rather than *wavy*, *rough*, or *roiled*. A student could write a two-page essay describing this scene with the eagle, so fine-tuned are its words.

Poetry is not a way of decorating speech with fancy words or finding a nice way to say things. It is a way of seeing; it is awareness so that what is real is seen in a new way and said in a fresh way. It's not easy to describe; that's why we read poems to feel them rather than to understand them. Sometimes a poem tells us what cannot be said, or tells us what ideas feel like. Robert Frost once said that a poem is never a put-up job. "It begins as a lump in the throat, a sense of wrong, a homesickness, a love sickness. It is never a thought to begin with." No, it is a feeling put concretely into words.

"A poem is a thousand times closer to the concerto or a painting than it is to the sermon or the speech. . . . In common vernacular, 'A poem is a trip,'" Rod Jellema writes in *Realms of Gold*.

The Color of Metaphors

The poet thinks in images. Actually we all do. We use metaphors daily in our speech and hardly recognize what we are doing. Metaphors spice up language; they give it color. A person says, "He's as homely as a fencepost." She doesn't mean that the man and the fencepost are identical. She means they share a similarity; they are related. One of my friends commented on a very dark night, "It's black as homemade sin." That was a new phrase to me, but I knew what he meant. I don't know which it made the darker—the night or homemade sin.

We speak of a "ship plowing through the sea" and understand the likeness between a ship dividing the water and a plow moving through the soil and turning it over in a wake-like furrow. We sing

"A Mighty Fortress Is Our God" and know exactly what we mean; we do not mean that God is a pile of stones made into a defense tower. Job comments in his miserable state, "God has unstrung my bow and afflicted me," and we know he is not talking about archery. That device in language is a *metaphor*. A simile, another poetic device, takes this form: "The sun made the water *like* liquid gold" or "The rain was *like* pellets stinging my skin." Both metaphors and similes say *this* is like *that* in different ways.

"It is the nature of things to appear in images—royalty in lions and kings, strength in bulls and heroes, industriousness in ants and beavers . . . terror in oceans and thunder," Thomas Howard says in *Chance or the Dance. This* suggests *that!* And so we say that he has "the heart of a lion" or a person is an "eager beaver" or he "thundered out in rage" and behold! we have used metaphors or similes and didn't even know it.

The word *poet* means *maker*. God, the first maker, was also the first poet, and it is he who sets his seal of approval not only on creating but on expressing truths in imagery. He reasons with us and says, "Though your sins are like scarlet, they shall be white as snow; though they are red as crimson, they shall be like wool" (Isaiah 2:18). I, for one, am glad for his use of metaphor. Though my sins have stained me, he sees me as pure, by his grace. He says, "With joy you will draw water from the wells of salvation" (Isaiah 12:3), and because God uses that imagery or metaphor I see the "well of salvation," not as a one-time drink, but as a continual supply for my daily needs.

The Bible is a treasure store of metaphors. If you become aware of this, you will find them everywhere. Look, for example, at Psalm 19:

> *The heavens declare the glory of God;*
> *the skies proclaim the work of his hands.*
> *Day after day they pour forth speech;*
> *Night after night they display knowledge.*

The next lines tell us that the heavens have a "voice" and "speech." Have you heard the heavens shouting? What is the speech the day pours forth? The psalm goes on.

> *In the heavens he has pitched a tent for the sun,*
> *which is like a bridegroom coming forth from his pavilion,*
> *like a champion rejoicing to run his course.*

Genuine Poetry Communicates Before It Is Understood

House of Light by Mary Oliver
(Pulitzer Prize 1983)

This poet helps you to see deeply, summoning your full attention to nature, to experience beauty in all of life's pangs. *New and Selected Poems* teems with images like this one from "Egret," "Look! Look!/ What is this dark death/ that opens/ like a white door."

The Father by Sharon Olds

This is healing ointment for anyone who has been abused or preyed upon. Her excavations of the darkest actions of betrayal, abuse, and violence are stunning. From, "I Wanted to Be There When My Father Died," "because I hated him. Oh, I loved him,/. . . but I had feared him so, his lying as if dead on the/ flowered couch had pummeled me,/ his silence had mauled me, I was an Eve/ he took and pressed back into clay . . ."

Carnival Evening, New and Selected Poems 1968–1998 by Linda Pasten

Her poetry, rich in biblical and historical imagery, can provide new sight and open doors to your own imagination. In "The Almanac of Last Things," "but I choose the Song of Songs/ because the flesh/ of those pomegranates/ has survived/ all the frost of dogma."

What We Carry by Dorianne Laux
(Pushcart Prize)

Laux's poems, full of song, usher the reader to a new interior space with vivid images and musical words. From "As It Is," "his voice strung along the wires outside my window/. . . even in the farthest future, in the most/ distant universe, I would have recognized/ this voice, refracted, as it would be, like light/ from some small, uncharted star."

Stars and Songs by Gwendolyn Carr

Carr is virtually unknown and self-published, but she is not to be missed. Tucked away in a New England coastal town she crafts short works that are lyrically full. From "First Frost," "One spiteful stroke/ upon their heads,/ the keenest of my marigolds/ lie rumpled in October beds." Carr's poetry is available by writing: BOOKS, P.O. Box 5538, Magnolia, MA, 01930-0007.

Don't miss these female poets:

Jane Kenyon, Marilyn Nelson, Jane Hirshfield, and Meg Campbell.

Nor these fine male poets:

Edward Hirsch, T. Crunk, Stephen Dunn, Billy Collins, and Li-Young Lee.

RECOMMENDED BY ALYCE T. REIMER,
POET

The sun is compared to a bridegroom, a champion running its course.

What an amazing picture comes to mind with these words! *This is like that* . . . and we understand something bigger than we knew before. You don't need so much to define a metaphor or a simile as to experience it.

The last half of the psalm is about the Word of the Lord. The psalmist is not content to simply say, "God's Word is good!" No, he uses wonderful figures of speech to tell us how good!

> *They are sweeter than honey,*
> *than honey from the comb.*

No marvel that the Jewish Rabbi would put a drop of honey on the page of the Torah to show the sweetness of God's law.

In *The Mind of the Maker* Dorothy Sayers writes, "The Jews forbade the representation of the Person of God in graven images. Nevertheless, human nature and the nature of human language defeated them. No legislation could prevent the making of verbal pictures: God walks in the garden, He stretches out His arm, His voice shakes the cedars . . . to forbid the making of pictures about God would be to forbid thinking about God at all, for we are so made that we have no way to think, except in word pictures."

Luci Shaw, favorite poet of many women, says that she sees all life as a metaphor. *This* is like *that.* Our life is like the seasons. Our life is clear shining after rain. Our life is like a tree in blossom that later bears fruit. Psalm 92 says that the righteous are like palm trees planted in the court of the Lord. When I say Luci is a "tree person in the house of the Lord," you know what I mean. One Christmas she sent out this poem, "Stars in Apple Cores."

> *You*
> *are the One who put*
> *stars*
> *in apple cores.*
> *God*
> *of all stars and symbols*
> *and all grace,*
> *You have reshaped*
> *the empty space*

deep in my apple heart
into a core of light
a star to shine
like Bethlehem's far
to-near Night Sign:
bright announcement
of Your
Day Star.

I like to cut my apples crossways to see the star and recite part
of this poem. My life is enriched by what poets notice. You will find
this poem in *Polishing the Petoskey Stone.*

Poems are not necessarily full of metaphors and images. Sometimes they simply catch an insight that makes the difference. Here
are two poems from Luci Shaw—both with insights—on two different subjects. The first, published in *The Secret Trees*, is called "Man
Cannot Name Himself."

Man cannot
name himself
He waits for God
or Satan
to tell him
who he is.

The second, from *Listen to the Green*, is called "Forecast."

Planting
seeds
inevitably
changes my
feelings
about
rain.

Look for Luci Shaw's poetry books: *Polishing the Petoskey Stone,*
Postcard from the Shore, Angles of Light, and *Writing the River.* There are
many "versifiers" and rhymers, but fewer real poets. Luci Shaw is one
of the real ones. Much of her poetry is longer and deeper than what
I have quoted here, and for that you should have her books on your
shelves.

Personification

Personification is another poetic device. Poetry uses images—metaphors (implies a comparison), similes (is a comparison: *as, like*), and symbols or *personification*. Notice how the lamb becomes the symbol or personification of gentleness in these stanzas from William Blake's poem:

> Little Lamb, who made thee?
> Dost thou know who made thee?
> Gave thee life, and bid thee feed
> By the stream and o'er the mead
> Gave thee clothing of delight,
> Softest clothing, wooly, bright;
> Gave thee such a tender voice,
> Making all the vales rejoice?
> Little lamb, who made thee?
> Dost thou know who made thee?
> Little lamb, I'll tell thee,
> Little lamb, I'll tell thee:
> He is called by thy name,
> For he calls himself a lamb,
> He is meek, and he is mild,
> He became a little child.
> I a child and thou a lamb,
> We are called by his name.
> Little Lamb, God bless thee!
> Little Lamb, God bless thee!

Poetry That Delights the Heart

Psalms of Lament by Ann Weems
   This book speaks powerfully to a grieving heart with tender and insightful poetry.

Poems 1968–1972 by Denise Levertov
   The style is sharp and poignant; the poems read almost like "sound bites," but she offers insight into the ways of the human heart.

Otherwise by Jane Kenyon
   These poems include short, brooding poems about rural life and the moody interiors of New Englanders.

Guerillas of Grace by Ted Loder
   A collection of contemporary prayer poems filled with honesty and humor.

RECOMMENDED BY
DARCY LENZGRINDEN, WRITER

The difference between poets and the rest of us is that the poet uses figurative language more self-consciously. They are God's gift to us.

Let These Words Sing to You

You may well know more poetry than you think you do. Poetry is best left just sitting around on a table, waiting for someone to pick it up. A good anthology of poetry on your shelf could enrich your household. It will have most of your favorites. Let me remind you of some stanzas you've probably heard before but need to hear again to inspire you.

Sara Teasdale wrote in "Barter":

> *Life has a loveliness to sell—*
> *All beautiful and splendid things,*
> *Blue waves whitened on a cliff,*
> *Climbing fire that sways and sings,*
> *And children's faces looking up*
> *Holding wonder like a cup.*

If you remember Robert Frost from high school days, get *The Poetry of Robert Frost.* Do you remember the first and last stanzas of Robert Frost's "Stopping by Woods on a Snowy Evening"?

> *Whose woods these are I think I know.*
> *His house is in the village, though;*
> *He will not see me stopping here*
> *To watch his woods fill up with snow.*
> *The woods are lovely, dark, and deep*
> *But I have promises to keep,*
> *And miles to go before I sleep,*
> *And miles to go before I sleep.*

Nature Poems to Help Us See

As a nature lover I have taken joy from the poetry of English poet Gerard Manley Hopkins. It's a simply wonderful feeling to go out of doors on a golden autumn day and say aloud these words from "God's Grandeur." Read it aloud to feel it.

> *The world is charged with the grandeur of God*
> *It will flame out, like shining from shook foil;*
> *It gathers a greatness, like the ooze of oil*
> *Crushed. Why do men then now not reck his rod?*
> *Generations have trod, have trod, have trod;*
> *And all is seared with trade; bleared, smeared with toil;*
> *And wears man's smudge and shares man's smell: the soil*
> *Is bare now, nor can foot feel, being shod.*
> *And for all this, nature is never spent;*
> *There lives the dearest freshness deep down things;*
> *And though the last lights off the black West went*
> *Oh, morning, at the brown brink eastward, springs—*
> *Because the Holy Ghost over the bent*
> *World broods with warm breast and with ah! bright wing.*

Can you picture yourself standing on a pier overlooking the lake and then feel the wetness and see the mist in Carl Sandburg's "Fog"?

> *The fog comes*
> *on little cat feet.*
> *It sits looking*
> *over harbor and city*
> *on silent haunches*
> *and then moves on.*

Edna St. Vincent Millay's "God's World" expresses the same wonder:

> *O world, I cannot hold thee close enough!*
> *Thy winds, thy wide gray skies!*
> *Thy mists that roll and rise!*
> *Thy woods, this autumn day, that ache and sing*
> *And all but cry with color!*

Reading Poetry Aloud

Poetry is best when read aloud. But where are those who will listen? You could always read it at the dinner table. That's been done many times in our house. My husband's father did it fairly regularly, and my husband caught the joy of it. Especially if you have small children or have any influence on children, make part of your reading time something from poetry. Children love the rhythm of a poem well read. It's like singing to them, and you are building good things into their memory.

We stood on the dock off Lake Huron one summer day watching preparations for the sailing regatta at a student training center. The wind was picking up; we heard the snap of the sails, the gradually fading voices—and then a small voice from the group on the wharf, a young boy saying the first lines from John Masefield's "Sea Fever," quite spontaneously. Somehow it stuck there when nobody thought he was listening.

> *I must go down to the seas again, to the lonely sea and the sky,*
> *And all I ask is a tall ship and a star to steer her by;*
> *And the wheel's kick and the wind's song and the white sail's shaking,*
> *And a gray mist on the sea's face, and a gray dawn breaking.*

One of my favorite memories is the morning our eight-year-old grandson came into our bedroom carrying a book, climbed into our bed between my husband and me, settled back on a pillow, opened Nancy Larrick's *Piping Down the Valleys Wild*, and began to read poetry. He had only just learned how to make his voice reflect the beat of the poem, and he wanted to try it out on us. He had a ready-made audience who were delighted.

Some poetry tells wonderful stories. Longfellow's "Paul Revere's Ride" is a favorite of children and adults alike. Poetry is very inter-generational. This poem demands that it be read aloud! Listen to the first stanza:

> *Listen my children, and you shall hear*
> *Of the midnight ride of Paul Revere,*
> *On the eighteenth of April, in Seventy-five;*
> *Hardly a man is now alive*
> *Who remember that famous day and year.*

We've read again and again Ernest Thayer's ballad of "Casey at the Bat" when "there was no joy in Mudville 'cause mighty Casey had struck out."

Longfellow's story poems of "Hiawatha" and "Evangeline" are ageless. The reader feels almost mesmerized by the beat as "Evangeline" begins.

> *This is the forest primeval. The murmuring pines and the hemlocks,*
> *Bearded with moss, and in garments green, indistinct in the twilight,*
> *Stand like Druids of eld, with voices sad and prophetic,*
> *Stand like harpers hoar, with beards that rest on their bosoms.*
> *Loud from its rocky caverns, the deep-voiced neighboring ocean*
> *Speaks, and in accents disconsolate answers the wail of the forest.*

It would be hard to describe what the forest looks like; it is a feeling, not a description.

In 1927 James Weldon Johnson penned *God's Trombones: Seven Negro Sermons in Verse*. Johnson captures the rhythms of Southern black preachers. Still in print, his poems are best as read-alouds—a great way to try out your own histrionics. Here's the first verse of "The Creation":

> *And God stepped out on space,*
> *And he looked around and said:*

> *I'm lonely*
> *I'll make me a world.*
> *And far as the eye of God could see*
> *Darkness covered everything,*
> *Blacker than a hundred midnights*
> *Down in the cypress swamp.*
> *And then God smiled,*
> *And the light broke,*
> *And the darkness rolled up on one side,*
> *And the light stood shining on the other,*
> *And God said: that's good!*

Look for *Selected Poems of Langston Hughes,* another stellar black poet. I like this one called "Dreams":

> *Hold fast to dreams*
> *For if dreams die*
> *Life is a broken-winged bird*
> *That cannot fly.*
> *Hold fast to dreams*
> *For when dreams go*
> *Life is a barren field*
> *Frozen with snow.*

Laughing Verse

When the poet captures the ridiculous for us, the lines sing with laughter and paint a vivid picture for us. British friend Evangeline Patterson, a poet with an eye for such things, wrote a poem called "Miss Peewit" that has stuck in my head and always makes me smile. (She would not call it her best poem, nor would I, but I like reading it.)

> *Lord, forgive Miss Peewit*
> *For the hat that she wears on Sunday.*
> *Forgive her its shape*
> *(Which is an outrage)*
> *And forgive her its colour*
> *(Which is like mud)*
> *And forgive its intention*
> *Which is to garb Miss Peewit*
> *Suitably for a creation*
> *That is somehow not yours.*

She has never admitted
To her heart the small and transient
And quite unnecessary violet;
She has barred her shutters
Against the sense-stealing, dangerous
Breath of the rose;
And if she could see the deliciously
Frivolous scented puffball
Flower of mimosa
She would think you had played a joke
In very poor taste.

Lord, forgive Miss Peewit
And prepare her gently for heaven
Where some day she is going
To have to live
And meantime, Lord, look not
On the hat she chooses to wear
Twice weekly to your house
In your honour.

Evangeline Patterson herself has since gone to heaven, where her style and flair will convert any Miss Peewits she finds there.

We read Ogden Nash because his "doggerel" has so many smiles in it. For example:

Some primal termite knocked on wood.
And tasted it and found it good;
And that is why your Cousin May
Fell through the parlor floor today.

Edwin Lear has delighted generations with his nonsensical verse and his limericks:

There was an Old Man with a beard,
Who said, "It is just as I feared!
Two owls and a hen,
Four larks and a wren,
Have all built their nests in my beard."

Here's part of the Hilaire Belloc poem "Matilda":

Matilda told such dreadful lies,
It made one gasp and stretch one's eyes;

Her aunt, who, from her earliest youth,
Had kept a strict regard for truth,
Attempted to believe Matilda:
The effort very nearly killed her,
And would have done so, had not she
Discovered this infirmity.

The poem goes on to tell of Matilda's calling the fire brigade one night when she was bored, and then a disastrous third verse about her doing so when the house was really on fire!

George Herbert: Startled into Submission

The Temple by George Herbert

Herbert, an Anglican priest, lived from 1593–1633. He struggled with being a poet: how could he be sure his poems would cause people to worship God, not admire the poet? He struggled with his inconstancy, his rebellion. Again and again his poems end with his being startled into submission and worship by the sweet familiar voice of the Lord. My heart is flushed with joy remembering his lines.

Any bookstore should have short collections of his poetry. Start reading individual poems: "The Collar," "The Flower," "The Elixir," and "Love (III)." Join C. S. Lewis as a lover of Herbert's poetry.

RECOMMENDED BY LOIS WESTERLUND,
RETIRED ENGLISH PROFESSOR

Feeling the Truth in Poetry

A friend sent me a couplet from English clergyman George Herbert, who penned these words in the seventeenth century. Each time I read this couplet I am filled with reverence and awe. I feel and sense truth in dimensions that I haven't yet fully explored.

Love is that liquor sweet and most divine,
Which my God feels as blood; but I as wine.

Recently I quoted Emily Dickinson to a friend as we talked about the confusion that comes after a sudden death. The small details that seem so unimportant in the face of loss, and yet—

The bustle in a house
The morning after death
Is solemnest of industries
Enacted upon earth,—
The sweeping up the heart,
And putting love away
We shall not want to use again
Until eternity.

Two contemporary poets grab at my heart in this same way. If you are serious about poetry, get a copy of *Otherwise* by Jane Kenyon. She writes so poignantly of relationships and nature and death (her own life was taken by cancer). I feel a greater sensitivity to life when I read what she has written. I am there, feeling and learning in these poems.

> *I saw him leaving the hospital*
> *with a woman's coat over his arm.*
> *Clearly she would not need it.*
> *The sunglasses he wore could not*
> *conceal his wet face, his bafflement.*
>
> *As if in mockery the day was fair,*
> *and the air mild for December. All the same*
> *he had zipped his own coat and tied*
> *the hood under his chin, preparing*
> *for irremediable cold.*

I became a fan of Wendell Berry when I first discovered him a few years ago. His love of language and its music, whether in novels or poetry, communicates his thought and values with profound clarity. About twenty some years ago he gave up the literary life in New York to seek a deeper bond with his ancestral home on a hillside in Kentucky. His life is connected to the soil; family and marriage are sacred to him. His poems shine with gentle wisdom, as do his novels and short stories. Look for *Collected Poems* by Wendell Berry. Here is one:

> *To go in the dark with a light is to know the light.*
> *To know the dark, go dark. Go without sight,*
> *and find that the dark, too, blooms and sings,*
> *and is traveled by dark feet and dark wings.*

Calvin Miller's *The Singer* tells the world's Great Story in poetry— wonderful to read aloud. It is rich in metaphor and imagery, and because you already know the story it will enrich your understanding of it. I recommend it as accessible and worthy of space on your shelf.

Poetry books on your bookshelves make it easier for you to pull down a book and enjoy a poem or two, according to your mood. Here are some ideas of what to look for in a bookstore: *When We Were Very Young* by A. A. Milne (for when you feel Pooh-ish); *The Family Book of Verse* edited by Lewis Gannett; *Classic Poems to Read Aloud* edited by James Berry; *Weather of the Heart* by Madeleine L'Engle; *A Hundred White Daffodils* by Jane Kenyon; and the classic Norton's anthologies, which cover almost everything!

Lest this chapter become an anthology, I will stop. I hope, however, that you find your appetite whetted as you hear the music of words. Poetry says what the heart needs to hear.

On the morning after God took one of my elderly aunts to heaven, I went to visit her sister—ninety-four-year-old Aunt Ann, the last of this God-blessed family. Instead of greeting me with a lament or a reminder that she was outlasting everyone in her family, she said, "Oh, honey, I'm so glad you came. I've been wanting to share this poem with someone. It is so wonderful!" Then she read to me a fine poem about the grace of our Lord who provides all we need, giving us his righteousness, taking us to be with him. The poem painted a picture, a feeling, a hope, a joy in the best of words. Such a moment of sharing was given us by poetry. Thank God for words, for poets, and for fresh looks at reality.

Poetry and Hums aren't things which you get,
they're things which get you. And all you can do
is to go where they can find you.

THE HOUSE AT POOH CORNER, A. A. MILNE

Chapter 7

Honey from the Rock:
Reading the Bible

You would be fed with the finest of wheat;
with honey from the rock I would satisfy you.

PSALM 81:16

This is the Word of the Lord. Public readings from the Bible often end with these words. Christians believe this is what the Bible is: *the Word of the Lord.* Such startling words can be said about no other book recommended in *this* book.

One of the gifts of knowing how to read is knowing what is best to read. If God speaks through a book, then this is the best of all books to read. *The Word of the Lord.* The Bible makes that claim for itself. You don't need to hold this point of view about the Bible to find it worth reading. But it helps in reading it if you know that this is the Christian perspective.

The Significance of This Book

God speaks to us in the Bible. Maybe from the parts that you have read you are inclined to think that he isn't speaking as clearly as he might. It's confusing, you say. Even if you are loyal to the Bible and believe all the "right" things about it, you may still have unspoken feelings that resonate with this attitude. If you expect an outline from God to answer all the questions in the universe, you will be disappointed.

When God worked through human beings to put the Bible together, he gave us a piece of literature. The Bible is literature. It is sixty-six books put together in two testaments. It is history. It is poetry. It is prophecy. It is story. It is teaching. It is revelation. The various parts of the Bible must be read for what they are. You read poetry differently than history. Prophecy takes another kind of reading. What do you hear from the stories? The previous chapters of this book have been about learning how to read literature; the same principles in those chapters apply in reading and understanding the Bible. The Bible is a good book!

When we say that the Bible is literature, or that it is imaginative, we are not saying that it is fictional rather than historical and factual. To say that it is literature is to say that *it needs to be read*. Taking bits and pieces from the Bible and thinking we have the whole is an enormous affront to this timeless book. You probably won't understand everything in the Bible. When you stumble over something you can't understand, lay it aside like you do a bone at a fish dinner. There's a good chance that things will fall into place with further study.

The sum total of the content of this Book of books is to reveal who God is and how we as his creatures can be rightly related to him as the Creator. That's a pretty simplistic summary, because woven through the story is a bigger Story with incredible explosions of truth and understanding.

It's no exaggeration to say that this Book in comparative terms is the only significant book in the world. It holds the key to life. The message, however, is not given on the first page; it unfolds. We read carefully; we look for the big picture and begin to understand maybe a little—not so much as to make us arrogant—of who God is and how he regards those he made in his image.

Some people have a bad habit of piecemeal Bible reading—a verse here and a verse there. We don't read any other book that way. Poetry may be read a poem at a time, and the Psalms can be read as poetry. We need the context of the whole if we are to understand what we read; we don't take a stanza out of a poem or a psalm without reading the rest of the piece. Treating individual verses of the Bible as a magic talisman of truth without reading a whole book has always seemed to me a poor way to do Bible reading. It does not show respect for the text.

The first testament (the Old Testament) is about God creating what is good and man choosing what is not good. It is the story of

God's plan to redeem the situation by choosing a people (the Hebrews) and giving them a history with himself. We read their story and see our story. We read what they learn and are instructed ourselves. The pages are many, but the story's theme is the utter reliability of God. (Look at the big picture—the whole of what it says. Don't be put off by wars and violence. Look for the kindness and love of God in its pages. It's there!)

The second testament (the New Testament) tells of the culmination of God's great plan as Jesus is born, the very likeness of God in human flesh, to show humanity what God is like and then to rescue them from their fallen condition. Martin Luther called it the Great Exchange: In dying Jesus takes the sins of mankind; in exchange he pardons those who trust him. When God raised Jesus from the dead he confirmed the exchange. After Jesus ascends into heaven, God sends his Spirit into the world to sweetly woo the listening ones. The Holy Spirit also gets believers ready for the last big thing God has in mind in this book: namely, to take them into his presence.

If this book tells us all this—and more besides—is it a significant book? How carefully should you read it? What more will it tell you? Like all good writing, this book is multilayered in its theme. You have to read carefully. If you take it seriously you won't be content with book reviews. You will want to read the whole thing.

Too many people are content to be first-graders in the subject of God. They let other people tell them what the Bible says. They have access to a book that makes these claims and has this great storyline, yet they aren't really sure what it says. Often people are curious, but slightly intimidated by the Bible. Others think

My Invitations to Grow Spiritually

Holy Invitations: Exploring Spiritual Direction by Jeannette A. Bakke

The most accessible book on the topic, written for anyone unfamiliar with the discipline of spiritual direction. Reflection questions at the end of the chapters give readers a guided experience of spiritual direction. Soon to be a classic.

The Joy of Listening to God
by Joyce Huggett

One of the best books on prayer I have found!

The Critical Journey
by Janet O. Hagberg
and Robert A. Guelich

This book explores the different stages of adult spiritual development and experience. One of a kind.

*Disciplines of the Holy Spirit:
How to Connect to the Spirit's Power
and Presence* by Siang-Yang Tan
and Douglas H. Gregg

Immensely practical and easy to read, a guided journey into the practice of spiritual disciplines.

The Waiting Father by Helmut Thielicke

Sixteen parables of Jesus. There is so much wisdom in this book it almost hurts. Warm and easy to read.

RECOMMENDED BY JENNIFER H. DISNEY, WRITER, EDITOR, AND COUNSELOR they know what it says and are content with that. Even those who claim to believe it from cover to cover sometimes treat it shabbily.

In 1350 John Wycliffe risked his life to translate the text from Latin into English so the common people could read the Bible. Later other people, like William Tyndale, zealous to share this book, were martyred for doing so. Wycliffe and Tyndale believed this Word of the Lord was for everyone. Why did some people not want the Bible translated and circulated? It was an issue of control; they wanted the teaching filtered through their power structure. From the way you treat the Bible, whose side would you likely be on in the controversy?

This chapter is not a guilt trip about reading the Bible. You will have to make the decision to read the Bible yourself. But it will tell you what the Bible can do for you and give you some clues about how to read it.

The Benefits of Reading the Bible

Readers must benefit from Bible reading, probably in more ways than we can recount, because it has been on the bestseller list ever since it was first printed.

The Bible comforts us in hard times by connecting us to God. George Hamlin Fitch, columnist for the *San Francisco Chronicle*, wrote an essay about his grief at the death of his son. "Who," he wrote, "turns in time of affliction to the magazines or to those books of clever short stories which so amuse us when the mind is at peace and all goes well? No literary skill can bind up the brokenhearted; no beauty of phrase can satisfy the soul that is torn by grief. No, when our house is in mourning, we turn to the Bible first—that font of wisdom and comfort which never fails him who comes to it with clean hands and a contrite heart. It is the medicine of life." Over the centuries people have found this book meeting their deepest needs.

The Bible's truths relate to everything around us. You can hardly read any other book without coming upon some allusion to biblical texts. Our western civilization is built on its code of ethics, its teaching, and, most noticeably, its Savior. We date every year *anno domini*, "in the year of our Lord." The artistic craftsmanship of the Bible tells us something important about its Source. It is literature, but it is more than that. It presents human experience accurately; it also presents the only answer to our human problem. It tells the truth.

The Bible changes our perspective, and indeed, our very lives. It is not a theological outline with proof texts attached. It contains theological truth that changes people's lives. It needs to be read regularly for that reason alone. It is not "my idea of God" that matters; it is God's revelation of who he is that matters. It is not a search for the historical Jesus that teases us intellectually; it is meeting him in the pages of the gospels and listening to what he says.

The Bible points to a Savior. Dorothy Sayers wrote in the dedication for one of her books, "In the name of the One who assuredly never bored anyone in the thirty-three years He passed through the world like a flame." What did she know about Jesus that caused her to say this? The story needs to be read from the New Testament.

The Bible is literature worth reading. Wonderful stories are found in the pages of the Bible, memorable characters, a revelation of the human heart, the importance of choices—it's all there in well-chosen words, words and ideas that demand more than a moment's contemplation. How much of the biblical story or setting can you reconstruct from the lines given below? What pictures come to your mind?

> Moses went to Pharaoh and said, "This is what the Lord says,
> 'Let my people go.'"
> And she tied a scarlet cord in the window.
> And Goliath said, "Am I a dog, that you should come at me
> with sticks?"
> "O my son Absalom! O Absalom, my son, my son!"
> The king called in an anguished voice, "Daniel, has your God,
> the living God, been able to rescue you from the lions?"
> There was a man who had two sons . . .
> A farmer went out to sow his seed . . .
> Then they led him out to crucify him . . .

Besides the power of its stories, the Bible should also be read for the sheer beauty of its language—an economy of words, so well chosen that your heart swells. It's a masterpiece, containing phrases so beautiful, so rich, so melodic—like these from Isaiah 40:

> *Who has measured the waters in the hollow of his hand,*
> *or with the breadth of his hand marked off the heavens?*
> *Who has held the dust of the earth in a basket,*
> *or weighed the mountains on the scales and the hills in a balance?*
> *Who has understood the mind of the LORD,*
> *or instructed him as his counselor?*
> *. . .To whom will you compare me?*
> *Or who is my equal? says the Holy One.*

The Bible lights the paths in our life. The Bible is more than stories or a record of events; it claims to affect our personal lives. More than once it reminds us that human beings "do not live by bread alone." The Word of the Lord is a lamp to our feet and a light to our path, the text declares. Personally, I need that divine light on my daily journey; I have found that the words of the Bible give me this. I can tell the difference when I haven't been listening to the God who speaks in the Bible. God's words shape me up; they give me heaven's point of view about the details of my life. It clarifies my vision to see the big picture: I see people through his eyes, not my own. The psalmist said this kind of "heavenly food" is sweeter than honey from the honeycomb; I have found it so.

The Bible always surprises me, and I have been reading it for years. It says what I need to hear. I think I know what it says, and then find it speaking with a fresh voice when I read it again. I tend to think that anyone who seriously reads it is in for a surprise. Christians don't worship the Bible; they worship God, but they have found the words of eternal life in this book. It's well worth reading if you are new to the book. And for those who claim to believe it but never open its pages, maybe you need to ask why you don't read it.

Getting the Most Out of the Bible

One of the best gifts in my life was attending a large state university where I joined the InterVarsity Christian Fellowship student group that met on campus. At the university I learned several things, mostly about myself; I learned I had been "christianized," taking on the veneer of my family background. Anything I knew about God or the Bible was a result of my believing what someone had told me. Since it's impossible to inherit faith, I needed to make those beliefs my own. Fortunately I had a university professor who helped me do this by asking me all the hard questions and raising many doubts as to whether what I had learned was even true. His questions made me look at my belief structure with new eyes. In my InterVarsity group I learned something even more important: I was taught how to study the Bible. I was taught how to ask questions, questions that would illuminate and open up the biblical text. Learning how to do inductive Bible study has been the single most identifiable and important skill I gained during those years. I became a diligent reader of the Bible.

It is important to me to find out what the text says. I underline and mark the other books I read; I mark this book too. I read it with a pencil and a notebook. If the Bible is what it claims to be, I feel I need to give it the attention it deserves.

Whenever you read anything, it's appropriate to ask questions. The first one should always be *What does it say?* Understanding what the words are really saying is critical to understanding any text— whether history, literature, or the Bible. What the text says is the most important thing about it—not *How do I feel or think about this?*

The second question to ask is *What does it mean?* I must take the facts and try to interpret their meaning in the context in which it is written. I ask *Why?* or *How?* How do I make sense out of what the words are saying?

Because the Bible is no ordinary book and because of what it claims for itself, my third question is *What does it mean to me? Is there a personal application to make? What can I learn?*

Asking these three questions helps me get the most out of my reading. Put another way, it's simply *observe; interpret; apply.* To make this less academic, I want to share the notes from one of my Bible-reading sessions on the temptation of Eve in Genesis chapter 3. First I read the biblical text, recorded for you here.

> Now the serpent was more crafty than any of the wild ani-mals the LORD God had made. He said to the woman, "Did God really say, 'You must not eat from any tree in the garden'?"
>
> The woman said to the serpent, "We may eat fruit from the trees in the garden, but God did say, 'You must not eat fruit from the tree that is in the middle of the garden, and you must not touch it, or you will die.'"
>
> "You will not surely die," the serpent said to the woman. "For God knows that when you eat of it your eyes will be opened, and you will be like God, knowing good and evil."
>
> When the woman saw that the fruit of the tree was good for food and pleasing to the eye, and also desirable for gaining wis-dom, she took some and ate it. She also gave some to her hus-band, who was with her, and he ate it. Then the eyes of both of them were opened, and they realized they were naked; so they sewed fig leaves together and made coverings for themselves.
>
> Then the man and his wife heard the sound of the LORD God as he was walking in the garden in the cool of the day, and they hid from the LORD God among the trees of the garden. But the LORD God called to the man, "Where are you?"

My first step is go back over what I read. Then I recorded these notes in my journal. (You go back over the Genesis text again yourself and see if I caught all the important points.)

Observations:

The serpent encounters the woman in the garden.

He gets her to question God's instructions.

She ends up eating the forbidden fruit of the tree in the middle of the garden.

Her husband was with her and he ate also.

Something changed in their relationships; they saw their own nakedness.

They made clothes for themselves out of leaves.

They hid from God.

Interpretation Questions:

Who is the serpent? What do I know about him from these verses?

What was the serpent's tactic in approaching the woman?

What doubts does he sow in her mind?

What does he imply about God's character?

What was wrong with the woman's focus after the serpent left her?

Does disobedience always leave a person scared and naked?

Application Notes: (I number these to make sure I get the point!)

1. The evil one still uses the same tactics today—and wins when he gets me to question God's goodness.
2. I need to be certain to focus on God's goodness and be thankful. That will keep me from being enticed by evil.
3. No excuses for wrongdoing or bad choices, no rationalization.
4. My fig-leaf covering for my "nakedness" doesn't cut it with God; it's a flimsy fix.
5. God is incredibly gracious; he doesn't give up on me; he comes looking for me.

Conclusion:

There was only one prohibition; the rest of the garden, full of good things, all belonged freely to the man and the woman. In other words, there was no need for the woman to feel this greed, to want more than God had given. What does that say to me?

This may not seem profound to you, but it is real to me. I didn't write in my journal with the idea of being published; it's personal. But sharing with you the notes from my Bible-reading journal gives you ideas of what you could do. You can see that using a pencil and paper nailed down some specifics for me. I didn't just pass over this account as if it had nothing to say to me. You may decide to do it differently; there is no divine sanction on this method. But if you are serious about reading the Bible you can't use a dilettante's approach.

Bible Translations

I think it is important to have a Bible in modern English. I use the *New International Version* (NIV) because the translation was done by a committee of scholars and it reads well. All Bibles in English are translations from the Hebrew (Old Testament) and the Greek (New Testament). The *New American Standard Bible*, the *New King James Version*, the *New Revised Standard Version*, and the *New Living Bible* are all good committee translations. Paraphrased Bibles are refreshing to read, but are generally a one-person translation and often less accurate, with the focus on fresh use of language and conveying the translator's understanding of the text, rather than a word translation. The *New Revised Standard Version* contains inclusive language, giving careful attention in translating texts to include both men and women where warranted. Many people find the *NIV Study Bible* helpful because the notes give background, definitions, possible meanings, and other references.

Where to Begin Reading

The day after my father's funeral I stopped by the neighbor's house to visit a man who had loved my father and been greatly influenced by him. I found him standing by the bookcase, paging through the

Bible Study Helps

The Bible for Blockheads
by Douglas Connelly
In the kindest way, Connelly helps increase the reader's biblical understanding.

How to Read the Bible for All Its Worth
by Gordon Fee
The title says it all! Practical, easy to understand.

The NIV Study Bible
Contains many helpful notes.

Grasping God's Word
by Scott Duval and Daniel Hays
A basic book on inductive Bible study; easy to understand.

The Zondervan Handbook to the Bible
A helpful resource for the extras you wonder about.

RECOMMENDED BY GLADYS HUNT

yellowed pages of a thick and aged family Bible. He looked up and asked, "Where does a person begin to read in a book like this?"

"That's a good question," I said. And I went out to buy him a modern translation of the Bible—one he could hold in his hand.

Nothing is more likely to kill interest in Bible reading than to start at Genesis and then proceed on through. By the time the average reader hits Numbers, the Bible is back on the shelf. Remember, the Bible is a book of books.

Here's what I suggest if you are just beginning: Read the gospel of Mark; then proceed to the gospel of John. Follow this with Acts. Then read Genesis. That book of beginnings—Genesis—is of critical importance in understanding all beginnings. Then go on to Exodus. Alternate between the Old Testament and the New Testament from then on. The Old Testament gives you history that preceded Jesus' birth; the New Testament will take you to the heart of Jesus' ministry.

Sharing the Bible with Others

If you live in a family, you have a ready-made opportunity to share. There is nothing quite like the fun of reading from the Bible after a meal around a table full of kids. Have each child ask a question about the passage you have just read. All kids like to stump their siblings. Everybody has to ask a question; everyone has to answer a question.

For one thing, you assure that everyone sits up and listens. No one can be sure someone else won't use your question before you get a chance to ask it. And you don't want your turn to pass without being able to answer a question. So listen up! At first children will ask observation questions: *Where was Jesus going? Who was in the boat?* The older children will catch on quickly and begin to ask interpretation questions: *Why did Peter say that? Why was the man afraid?* And parents get to ask the application questions: *What can we learn from this?*

It works. The rules are simple; start with a narrative portion of the Bible and a fairly short reading. The added advantage of gaining Bible knowledge is the study habits that come from this kind of exercise. Children get used to asking questions about what they read.

Large numbers of people are curious about what the Bible says. Just as many have misconceptions about what it does say—misconceptions about God, about Jesus, about what makes a person a Christian. Most have an appalling ignorance of its content—the stories, the historical events, the biblical heroes.

Some of the most stimulating discussions of my life have come when eight or ten new-to-the-Bible women gather to study a book from the Bible—whether in a neighborhood or in a wider circle of friends. It's a specialized book group. It is learning; it is sharing; it becomes a support group. Bookstores carry many different kinds of study guides. I recommend using the study guides from Neighborhood Bible Studies (NBS), located in Dobbs Ferry, New York (1-800-369-0307). Fisherman Study Guides from Waterbrook Press and guides from Zondervan are two other good sources for small group study guides available in your bookstore. Topical guides often catch the eye and look appealing, but I am convinced that book studies (Genesis, Mark, John, and so forth) give better biblical understanding.

The guides recommended above contain discussion questions (not fill-in-the-blanks) based on the text of the book being studied, using observation, interpretation, and application questions like those recommended above. Groups rotate leadership (the leader asks the questions from the guide and moderates the discussion). The answers are found in the biblical text, not in a guidebook. Helps for starting groups and discussion rules are also available from Neighborhood Bible Studies. Bible study groups are my favorite kind of book group because such amazing *ah-ha* moments keep poking through the fabric of the study.

Over the centuries this Book has been preserved for us by diligent scholars and the faithful who believe it to be God's book. It is still being translated into the language of smaller people groups all over the world. A young Congolese man, after reading the Bible in his own language for the first time, said, "This book has made holes in my heart."

It will change your life, too. Read it for all it is worth.

---

*The book that most influenced me was the New Testament,
and in particular the Gospel of Matthew. I believe it
would startle and move any one if they could make a certain
effort of imagination and read it freshly like a book,
not droningly and dully. . . . Anyone would then be able
to see in it those truths which we are all courteously supposed
to know and all modestly refrain from applying.*

ROBERT LOUIS STEVENSON

Chapter 8

Growing Up on the Inside: Spiritual Growth Books

When I have been perplexed, looking for something I could not define to myself, a certain book has turned up, approached me as a friend would. And between its covers carried the questions and the answers I was looking for.

LIV ULLMAN

I don't know about you, but God seems to know just where I am. It's amazing the way just the right book comes into my life at just the right time. These so-called happenstances, which are probably heaven-sent, are often life changers. Sometimes the right books stimulate new devotion, new resolve, new ways to think—and often lead to new books.

I'd like to think that every book mentioned in this volume would help readers become spiritually mature. Complex people that we are, every book or person that touches our life broadens our outlook, gives us a new way of looking at life, helps us see ourselves with fresh eyes, and sharpens our discernment. However, if we are honest about what is going on inside us, we have to admit we can use some help on the specifics. It's not easy to admit that we may have some dragons that need slaying.

This chapter centers on a difficult topic: taking responsibility for the varied facets of our lives. It's not as easy as it sounds. Walter Wangerin reminds us that we "aren't there yet" when he says, "Our spiritual journey is not a noun. We are not in the faith; we are faith-ing." Which is to say that we are in process; we are pilgrims on our way home; we're not there yet. Along the way we have some rough edges in our lives that need attention. They need attention because life is meant for living, not for simply surviving.

Not everyone feels an urge to grow up inside. Some people are lazy or indifferent. Charles Schultz epitomized a kind of embarrassing self-satisfaction in one of his *Peanuts* cartoons. Linus remarks, "Some-times I wonder if God is pleased with me." He asks Lucy, "Do you ever wonder if God is pleased with you?" Lucy, radiating self-confidence, replies, "He's just got to be!"

Some people are so at home with their dragon they don't even know they have one! Nonetheless, books have a way of sticking us in vulnerable areas; it's worth a look to see what is on hand to help us.

What Keeps Us from Growing Up?

Life holds different experiences for different people. No profit comes from looking longingly at someone else's life and whining about our own. Life isn't fair—that's the first thing to get straight. We have to play the hand we are dealt. The good news is that we aren't left to do this on our own. It doesn't take more than a little looking around at the sorrow of others to know that it is a mistake to grab at life. Try-ing to find something or someone to ease our pain—as if we were alone in the game and totally responsible for its outcome—can lead to disaster. Reading books lets us in on the lives of other people who share our life situation or have even worse woes. But comforting as that might be, it still takes some humility to accept the friendship of a heavenly Father who promises to help us, to make "our crooked places straight."

The stickler is that we often don't like the way his divine help comes. Before we know it, we find ourselves telling God what he should do, and when it doesn't turn out exactly as we hoped, we begin to question whether he's in charge. Sometimes I wonder if I have caught the contagious doubting disease of that first woman in the gar-den who began to doubt that God was really good. She turned her concentration away from what *she had* to what *she did not have*, and began to look longingly at the fruit, wondering if she could better life if she chose that way. She got us all into quite a mess, and her prog-eny keep repeating her mistake.

Books from My Spiritual Journey

Healing for Damaged Emotions
   by David Seamonds

   Seamonds gently helps the reader face anger, low self-esteem, and perfectionism. Until I read this book I thought perfectionism was a virtue; then I learned how destructive it was to me, my relationship with God, and with others. No more struggle to be good enough for God.

Knowing God by James I. Packer

   To think really big thoughts about God, read this book! Packer stretches our thinking about who God really is, what he is like, and how that affects your response to him. My daughter said, "Mom, this is a really good book!"

The Bondage Breaker by Neil T. Anderson

   Not a book to avoid because some have overemphasized spiritual warfare. This book and its prequel *(Victory over Darkness)* provide solid teaching about our scriptural identity and position in Christ Jesus—as well as a strategy for breaking free from habitual sins and the enemy's hold.

Prayer: Finding the Heart's True Home
   by Richard Foster

   This is not a how-to-pray manual. Foster focuses on relationship and intimacy with God. This book stirred in me a deep longing for intimacy with God, something I had been afraid of. A delight for those with a contemplative bent.

The Hidden Rift with God
   by William Backus

   Disappointments sometimes cause us to disagree with God's view of what is good for us—and we end up questioning the very nature of God and withdraw from him just when we need him most. I wept as I realized how deeply I had offended God by my attitude. What a relief to find new freedom in loving who God really is.

RECOMMENDED BY
BEVERLY THOMPSON, R.N.

It took me awhile to discover what was happening in the lives of my fiftyish women friends who shared with me the discontent in their lives. Probing and listening to them, I finally boiled it down to a theological issue (it almost always does). These women were victims of the mantra that "God has a wonderful plan for my life." They had been told this as the basic truth, and it seemed easy to believe. They bought into that blank check, but when life began to be not as wonderful as they had hoped, they blamed God. Where was that wonderful plan?

In the end it turned out to be not *God's* wonderful plan, but *their own* wonderful plan that let them down. When life turns bumpy, not nearly as wonderful as expected, it's easy to begin to question God's character. *Where is God in my not-so-wonderful life?*

Actually it was a book a friend shared with me that helped me see what was happening. I read *The Cleavers Don't Live Here Anymore* by Paula Rinehart. Rinehart faces up to her unrealistic expectations, naively thinking that if she did everything right she would never be unhappy and everyone would think she was wonderful! She discovered that God had never signed on to her plan for her own life.

Books for Growth at the Crucial Time

(In the order in which they came into my life.)

Caring Enough to Confront
    by David Augsburger
        This book helped me learn how to deal with conflict honestly and creatively.

Two-Part Invention by Madeleine L'Engle and *God in the Dark* by Luci Shaw
        These two books helped me to feel normal as I worked through my grief after my husband died.

Life Path by Luci Shaw
        I've always been a journal keeper, but this book gave me new ideas and guidance to help me use my journals as a growth tool.

A Long Obedience in the Same Direction by Eugene Peterson
        A study of Psalms 120–134 that gave me focus when life seemed like a very long, slow journey.

Waiting by Ben Patterson
        When I felt stuck with no clear sense of what God wanted me to do next, this book gave comfort and encouragement.

The Body by Chuck Colson
        I needed to feel the strength and courage of the Body in dark places all around the world. My heart was given a new boldness and my love for Jesus and his church worldwide grew.

Breakfast with the Saints
    selected by LaVonne Neff
        It has been good during dry spells to have prayers to read that warm my heart and express my love to God in new ways.

RECOMMENDED BY MARILYN TWINING, ARCHIVES CONSULTANT

Handling Our Disappointments

The enemy has a clever strategy. He has devised an all-too-human way of pushing us down the stairs. Life gives us a *disappointment* on the top step. Something hurts us; we feel let down. If we nurture our pain, disappointment pushes us down another step into *depression*. Depression quickly falls down the steps to *disillusionment*. If the fall is unbroken, we end up in *despair*. It's the pits. I know of only one remedy, and that is to "offer the sacrifice of praise," to discipline ourselves to thankfulness for all that is good in our lives. We can stop the fall at any point by doing this. But it takes a decision, primarily because disappointment makes us hide from God and everyone else. We erect barriers for God to climb over. When I think about it, why would I (or anyone else) allow the devil to kick me down the stairs?

If you have trouble praising God or being thankful, get a hymnbook and keep it handy. It's helpful to read thoughts of praise and faith that have come out of another person's spiritual walk (a good way to absorb poetry too). Singing the words is best of all! There's a wonderful old hymn written by the poet William Cowper that I love to sing:

> *Sometimes a light surprises*
> *The Christian while he sings*
> *It is the Lord who rises*
> *With healing in His wings,*
> *When comforts are declining,*
> *He grants the soul again*
> *A season of clear shining,*
> *To cheer it after rain.*

William Backus wrote *The Hidden Rift with God* from working out struggles in his own life. He hadn't planned on any of the disasters that hit him—an unwanted divorce, the loss of his family life—everything seemed to go wrong. He also ended up with a debilitating anger towards God. He's now a psychologist who has heard many stories like his own and worse. What he gives in this book is not a "ten-steps-to-wholeness" approach, but a chance to discover the root cause of the distress and to work from there. One chapter entitled "Who Does God Think He Is?" reveals the distortions about God that grow in despairing hearts. Backus is honest and convincing about what he sees, and helps the reader profitably look at reality.

William Backus also coauthored with Marie Chapman *Telling Yourself the Truth*, which dismantles false beliefs that are guaranteed to make us miserable. You may be surprised at how many untruths you have bought into. I found *Disappointment with God* by Philip Yancey a helpful think-through on this subject, a larger treatment with no easy answers and lots of reality.

Grief is related to anger and disappointment because of the emptiness it brings. Grief comes from any loss—loss of someone you love, a rupture in a close friendship, betrayal, divorce—even loss of reputation or a position you loved. Grief reaches out for comfort, but also needs to come to terms with God's sovereignty over life.

Some of the hard questions we throw at God are just plain foolishness. I remember a young woman, hysterical about an unfaithful husband, screaming in her outrage, "Why would God do something like this to me!" In my conversation with her I found that she had never paid any attention to God before in her life, but now that she was in a fix, she felt God had let her down. When I asked her what she believed about God, the only answer I got was that he wasn't supposed to let things like this happen.

Choices—our choices—let loose incredible wrong in the world. To say ours is a fallen world is not to exaggerate; in some instances it isn't a strong enough description. What some human beings do to others is mind-boggling, and the further people live from truth, the more complicated life gets. The wrong in the world includes accidents, disease, death, destruction of all kinds. We don't like it. Why does God let it happen? We want to ask *Where is God when it hurts?*

The people who make the effort to get to know who God is, who become increasingly confident of his love and trustworthiness, handle the hard questions the best. It's not glib answers that work, but knowing as best we can who God is. So there is some reading to do on this subject. Gerald Sittser's *A Grace Disguised: How the Soul Grows Through Loss* is one of the finest and most helpful. Sittser came through the terrible personal loss of his mother, wife, and daughter in a tragic car accident, yet later he could write, "The experience of loss does not have to be the defining moment of our lives. Instead, the defining moment can be *our* response to the loss. It is not what happens *to* us that matters so much as what happens *in* us." Such words only point to the grace of God and attract me to investigate Sittser's wisdom.

Learning to Forgive

I find it hard to blame God; I would rather blame others. But this is also a dead-end street, and the blaming turns itself back on the blamer. It becomes a mind-set. Something about *that* person makes my life miserable. Maybe she has done something that is hard to forgive. I am angry, and anger conjures up every offensive thing that person has ever done. I have found that when I make a decision about someone, my contorted mind can usually find evidence to support it. The more I think about it the worse it gets. It's *their* problem, I insist. But it really is *my* problem, because it makes me far more miserable than it does the other person. It hangs on and chafes like a burr under the saddle and will not go away. When this happens to us, we don't even want to hear the word *forgiveness*. It's too hard. It seems like cheap grace.

Some things are hard to forgive. Innocent and helpless people have endured terrible abuse in their lives—the kind of abuse that makes it hard to trust anyone, that causes terrible fears and nightmares long after it has ceased. Some people have been abandoned by death or on purpose or from sheer neglect, never feeling loved, shunted off as unwanted. The deep scars of experiences like these are hard to get over. It's not easy to forgive.

It's all around us in our fallen world. In an interview singer Eartha Kitt recounted how her teenage mother gave her away, the man who fathered her also disappeared, and so, in trying to fill the void as she grew older, she compounded grief and sorrow in her life. When asked if her success and fame had lessened the pain of her past, she gave a disturbingly negative reply, "You never get over it." Probably *without God* it is impossible.

But lack of forgiveness is not compatible with letting God love us. We box ourselves off from the very One who can help. This anger, this lack of forgiveness for the unspeakable, has spoiled many lives. We don't know what to do, and so we let the tragedy keep on happening inside us; there is no end. Professional help can be a beginning, but the solution comes from action we take ourselves. Books that offer insights in such situations include David Augsburger's *The New Freedom of Forgiveness* and Lewis Smedes's *The Art of Forgiving: When You Need to Forgive and Don't Know How*.

We have to forgive ourselves too. Sometimes that is even harder. *Guilt and Grace* by Paul Tournier, a Swiss psychiatrist, has an insightful way of getting down to the basics (look in your library for other books by Paul Tournier). Guilt destroys us and keeps us hiding. *Love, Honor, and Forgive* by Bill and Pam Farrel discusses the varied situations in a marriage where forgiveness and restoration are needed. The right combination of humility, vulnerability, and forgiveness is difficult to achieve, and only a few know the rewards that come from those qualities.

What we are talking about is hurting; no one likes it. Jill Briscoe's *Out of the Storm and Into God's Arms: Shelter in Turbulent Times* offers a balm for hurting people. Dan Allender gives a needed ingredient of encouragement in *Hope When You Are Hurting.*

Loving Across Our Differences by Gerald Sittser doesn't duck the hard issues of life, but presents warm, hopeful instruction about what it means to love. Donald McCullough is helpful in *The Power of Realistic Thinking.* John Townsend and Henry Cloud wrote *Boundaries: When to Say Yes, When to Say No to Take Control of Your Life* and have helped hundreds of people break habits that plague relationships.

A Steady Life

A functional faith works better than a theoretical one, if we would live well. Sad to say, there are many unbelieving believers. And many others who all of a sudden want to be wise and strong when trouble comes but who have invested little time in the regular intake of food that builds muscles of faith. That's why another Sittser book is a positive recommendation: *The Will of God as a Way of Life.* I like the intentionality the title implies. It lines up well with Eugene Peterson's *A Long Obedience in the Same Direction.* Peterson writes that we need an organizing center for our lives with a goal set in place so that currents and fads don't lead us astray. He quotes from Charles Williams's brief drama *Grab and Grace* (which strikes me as a fitting description of a common lifestyle), in which there is a dialogue between Grace and a man who is dabbling in religion, trying out yoga one week, Buddhism the next, spiritualism the next. Grace mentions the Holy Spirit. The man says, "The Holy Spirit? Good. We will ask him to come while I am in the mood, which passes so quickly and then all is so dull." Grace answers: "Sir, purposes last." Intentionality, purpose, is a must if we would grow up on the inside.

An assurance that I am loved by God, that he cares for every part of my life, gives me a sense of incredible stability. In his book *Love Beyond Reason: Moving God's Love from Your Head to Your Heart,* John Ortberg dispels fears and misconceptions about God that keep us from believing that almost-too-awesome truth that God loves us. Does God love me enough to guide me? Try reading M. Blaine Smith's *Knowing God's Will: Finding Guidance for Personal Decisions* for answers to the question of knowing God's will.

The Bible mentions the pain involved in waiting. Probably nothing taxes our assurance that God knows and loves us more than the need to keep on waiting. Ben Patterson's book *Waiting: Finding Hope When God Seems Silent* takes on this issue in ways that quiet our hearts. Patterson has also written *Serving God: The Grand Essentials of*

Books That Propelled Me Forward on My Journey with God

A Testament of Devotion
by Thomas R. Kelley

Kelley, a Quaker, encourages us to live life from the "center," a life of unhurried peace and power, serene and simple. He describes an adequate life as "intuitively grasping the whole nature of things" and refocusing to be in step with God.

The Sacrament of the Present Moment
by Jean-Pierre De Caussade (English translation by Kitty Muggeridge)

How refreshing to affirm that "no moment is trivial." Splendor is encompassed in the ordinary! To meditate on this brings challenge and meaning to the most mundane days of my life. You cannot read this book passively!

The Spirit of the Disciplines: Understanding How God Changes Lives
by Dallas Willard

This book could be subtitled "the secret of the easy yoke." Undisciplined disciples

bear little resemblance to what Jesus had in mind in calling people to follow him. Willard beckons to a lifestyle of disciplines that encourage me to walk in daily step with Jesus.

A Godward Life: Savoring the Supremacy of God in All of Life by John Piper

Each one of Piper's 120 daily readings takes only a few moments to read, but I find myself captivated by the thoughts throughout the day. Piper gives me incentive to consider what it means to live fully, passionately, and relentlessly for God's sake.

The Return of the Prodigal Son: A Story of Homecoming by Henri Nouwen

See description of book on page 165.

RECOMMENDED BY
JOYCE BAILEY SECKINGER,
WOMEN'S MINISTRIES

Work and Worship, which speaks beyond the issues in the title, addressing the universal longing for the future, for something better than we know in seemingly hopeless situations.

Psychologist Larry Crabb has been helping people overcome their hurts for years, holding seminars and speaking publicly, in addition to writing books. He came to the conclusion in *Finding God* that counseling methods only help people face their own realities—a good place to begin. However, the secret to mental health is in finding God.

The Christian's Secret to a Happy Life by Hannah Whithall Smith is a classic, first written in 1870 by a Quaker. She writes with a simplicity aimed at ordinary people who long for God as they struggle for bread. It's a book that refuses to die off. A new edition seems to always appear.

Two habits that hinder a steady life need examination: one is the tendency to get caught up with the urgent and neglect the important. Read Charles Hummel's *Freedom from the Tyranny of the Urgent*. Ordering priorities is a must for a steady life. We talk about it, but often fail to do it. This book highlights ways to get life under control. Second, sexual sin has a stranglehold on many people's lives. Many caught up in the abuse of sex find this addiction an enormous hurdle to overcome in their desire to get close to God. No one handles this better than John White in *Eros Redeemed*—an excellent, readable book about human sexuality with no moralizing, only reality.

Richard Foster's books on spiritual disciplines provide many helpful ideas for developing a steady life. For over twenty years his *Celebration of Discipline: The Path to Spiritual Growth* has brought order to the lives of his readers. More recently, in conjunction with other authors (James Bryan Smith and Emilie Griffin), Foster has put together *Devotional Classics* and *Spiritual Classics* on spiritual disciplines, both with questions to help readers dig out truths from great writings of Christians who have preceded us. These books connect us to our spiritual heritage and put good material within easy reach.

Hungry for God

At some point in our maturing lives we face up to the realization that, no matter what our pain, God's goal for us is to *Get over it!* This is not a demeaning, unsympathetic cultural quip. Rather, God comes to us like he did the paralyzed man by the Pool of Bethesda (John 5) and says, "Do you want to get well? Do you want to get over it?"

Some people don't want to get over it, and that is a great sadness. The people who get over it are those who drink huge drafts of God's love and get to know him. Even then, it takes more than an open mind; it takes an open heart. Getting over it also means understanding what took place in the incarnation of Jesus Christ. My most helpful reading about this was John R. W. Stott's *The Cross of Christ*. It's one thing to wear a cross as a necklace; it's quite another to apprehend what happened on the cross. Nothing helps more to put life in perspective. (And I would add that any of John Stott's books will set the reader well on the way to maturity.)

Two disarming books help readers grasp what God is really like. Philip Yancey's *What's So Amazing About Grace?* takes some pretty awesome truths about God and gives us examples set in contemporary lives. Some of what he writes caused me to think thoughts like, *That's taking advantage of God*, giving God my own small humanness. *The Return of the Prodigal Son: A Story of Homecoming* by Henri Nouwen will break your heart—at least it did mine. Taking Rembrandt's painting of the prodigal son story (and with magnificent illustrations of the painting in the hardcover edition), Nouwen gives a fresh look at the heart of God. Remember the name Henri Nouwen and look for other devotional writings from his pen.

New books coming off the press sometimes deflect us from great older books such as *The Pursuit of God* by A. W. Tozer; the title tells you the tone of the book. It has been a basic book for growing spiritually for over fifty years. E. Stanley Jones's *The Divine Yes* again affirms God's attitudes toward our lives. Mary Ruth Howes has put together a book of devotions called *365 Days with E. Stanley Jones*.

Books That Changed My Thinking about Relating to God

Desiring God: Meditations of a Christian Hedonist by John Piper

Piper asks hard questions in this book—questions about your love for God and your service for him. His fresh and great thesis is that God is most glorified when we are most satisfied with him. Finding joy in God is the wellspring for living a Christian life. The title startled me; then reading the book convinced me that he was absolutely right. This book changed my thinking about my relationship with God in a freeing and exhilarating way.

Bold Love by Dan Allender and Tremper Longman

This book looks at love in action—bold, aggressive love that longs for a person's reconciliation to God. The authors look at the qualifications of love-warriors. Their discussions are rooted in the Bible and illustrated in human situations. Look also for *Cry of the Soul: How Our Emotions Reveal Our Deepest Questions about God*, a book that examines fear, anger, despair, shame, contempt, envy, and desire in the context of the Psalms.

RECOMMENDED BY LOIS WESTERLUND, RETIRED ENGLISH PROFESSOR

Using a book like this will draw you closer to God and make you feel more loved.

James I. Packer's *Knowing God* is on the way to becoming a classic. This shouldn't be read in one sitting or even two; it's too meaty. Read a little; chew a little. I've come to the conclusion that a person ought to read a book about who God is at least once a year. For several years I did an annual reading of Tozer's *The Knowledge of the Holy* for this reason. It's too easy to cast God in our own image.

M. Craig Barnes is a name worth remembering, since he has penned many exceptionally fine books. His book *Sacred Thirst: Meeting God in the Desert of Our Longings* takes Jesus' promise to quench thirst and asks why we are still so thirsty. Barnes is a pastor and an author with keen insights into what people need. Look also for: *When God Interrupts: Finding New Life Through Unwanted Change; Hustling God: Why We Work So Hard for What God Wants to Give;* and *Yearning: Living Between How It Is and How It Ought to Be.*

If you are familiar with Calvin Miller's *The Singer,* which tells the gospel in poetic form, you have already noted his inspired way of dishing out truth. Miller's *Into the Depths of God* is a book about hunger for the inward life—full of uplifting, piercing material, a pleasure to read.

Hungry for God? I am reminded of the C. S. Lewis quote about an inconsolable longing in our hearts that nothing on earth seems to satisfy. Lewis concludes, "Maybe you were meant for another world." Frederick Buechner's book *Longing for Home* points in that direction, with helpful thoughts about our need for a true and lasting home where we feel fully accepted. Look for his other books as well, including *The Magnificent Defeat, The Hungering Dark,* and *The Alphabet of Grace.* Buechner has also written sixteen novels worthy of note. His prose is almost like poetry; his insights provocative.

Talking with God

Dallas Willard wrote a basic book called *Hearing God.* If you are hungry for God you must listen. How do we hear God's voice? People say too glibly "God spoke to me." How do we hear his voice? The answer includes some ideas about guidance.

Listening is one part of life with God. Praying is another. The best way to learn to pray is to pray, not read books about it. Still, we need stimulus in this area. When Rosalind Rinker wrote *Prayer: Conversing with God* she helped generations of students stop making speeches to God and learn instead to talk with him. Her book is a gift to all believers. It's worth looking for in a library or used bookstore, since it is out of print. This book removes all the stained-glass-window tones from prayer. Your prayer life will be revitalized.

More books on prayer? *The God Who Hears* by W. Bingham Hunter answers many questions about prayer: Why pray if God already knows what you need? What about unanswered prayer? Another helpful and motivating book is Bill Hybels's *Too Busy Not to Pray.* Hybels is always practical and on target. Look for *Making Life Work,* which he has written with his wife. The title says it all. *Listening Prayer* by Leanne Payne changes the focus from us to God. How does one listen in prayer?

Ben Patterson's book *Deepening Your Conversation with God* will make you want to pray. Patterson treats prayer, not as a spiritual discipline, but as an anticipated delight.

Giving Meaning to the Word *Christian*

Maybe after all these suggestions for improving your spiritual life you aren't so sure you even know what it means to be a Christian. This word is thrown around freely in conversations, often without definition. The word really means "one of Christ's," and that is its essence. "Being a Christian means setting out on an inner journey—a journey of following Jesus." So writes Mark Harris in his book *Companions for the Spiritual Journey.*

If you've never examined the evidence for believing in Jesus, as God come to earth in the flesh, then *The Case for Christ* by Lee Strobel is for you. Strobel, a seasoned journalist, takes the role of skeptic and chases down what he calls "the biggest story in history." He asks tough, point-blank questions that make riveting reading. It's a good book for an inquirer, a good book for complacent people, a good book to share. Strobel investigates the toughest objections to Christian belief in his follow-up book, *The Case for Faith.* Josh McDowell's book *More Than a Carpenter* is a good apologetic on who Jesus is—a reasoned presentation.

John R. W. Stott, one of the foremost biblical expositors of our time, has written the concise, lucid, and engaging *Evangelical Truth*—a bold statement of the Trinitarian gospel that is at the center of Christianity. It would be hard to find a clearer, more faithful presentation than this. This is one of my favorite gift books because its truths are so essential.

Spiritually Stretching Books

The Cost of Commitment by John White
  White explores suffering and its impact on our spirituality. It's amazing what White has packed into this eighty-nine-page volume to cause one to ponder what commitment to living for Christ truly means according to Scripture.

Between Heaven and Earth by Ken Gire
  A compilation of prayers and reflections that focus on drawing us near to God and deepening our relationship with him. Gire utilizes a rich mix of ancient and modern theologians and laymen to enrich our prayer life.

Here and Now by Henri Nouwen
  Nouwen expounds on the everyday stuff of life to show us the magnificent power of the living God who invades our very selves. An insightful and stimulating read.

Sacred Surprises by Dale Hanson Bourke
  Anyone who has experienced adversity will learn from Bourke's brutally honest account of the heartaches in her personal life. Far from giving pat answers, Bourke explores doubt, anger, and pain in a refreshingly frank way.

The Tapestry by Edith Schaeffer
  An autobiographical account of theologian Francis Schaeffer and his wife, Edith's, spiritual journey. A large volume, it is best read in small sections. It is worth the time invested in exploring God's call on their lives and its effect on their family.

RECOMMENDED BY PAT FELDHAKE,
SCHOOL GUIDANCE COUNSELOR

There are no sacred cows that can't be discussed in Philip Yancey's *Reaching for the Invisible God: What Can We Expect to Find?* Yancey wants to reconcile faith with honesty, to tell it like it seems and then to see how it really is. How can a person have a relationship with the invisible God? Yancey doesn't give you sweet talk; he handles the hard stuff of belief.

Charles Colson takes on a large task in his book *How Now Shall We Live?* which he wrote with Nancy Pearcey. He handles basic subjects that profoundly affect the way we think and live: subjects such as worldview, creation, the fall, redemption, and restoration. A blockbuster of information and inspiration, it's highly readable and full of lively contemporary stories.

If you are tired of reading the Bible and want to see it in a fresh way, either listening to or reading a copy of *The Book of God* by Walter Wangerin can enliven the Bible for you. You will hear biblical stories that are true to the original account, but embroidered with imagination. His book *Paul* brings that same freshness to the apostle's life. Wangerin has a gift for making truth come alive.

Keeping Your Heart on Track

Short devotional readings can make your day! It's no substitute for Bible reading, but a good devotional reading can add some life-applications that will refresh you.

Great Joy and *Great Power* are two thirty-one-day theological stimulating devotional readings taken from writings by James Packer. Ken Gire wrote *Moments with the Savior: A Devotional Life of Christ*. His books are emotional and meditative, and he is a great favorite with many.

I like Kenneth Boa's Face to Face series. One is *Praying the Scriptures for Intimate Worship* and a second is *Praying the Scriptures for Spiritual Growth*. I like these books especially because they use the Scriptures purposefully. The first book, for example, uses Scripture to take the reader into adoration, confession, renewal, petition, intercession, thanksgiving, and a closing prayer. The devotions are brief but substantial, good for those who like spiritual meat.

Ruth Senter's *Longing for Love* begins, "Once upon a time there was a woman who lost her sense of being loved . . ." Thus begins a powerful dialogue between a woman and her compassionate heavenly Father. Six chapters of conversations address all a woman longs for.

Ann Spangler and Jean Syswerda have put together a thoughtful book on *Women of the Bible*—prepared as devotional reading, focusing on fifty-two women in Scripture. Each week the story of one woman is developed for inspiration and practical application.

Tried and true books like *My Utmost for His Highest* by Oswald Chambers or Mrs. Charles Cowman's *Streams in the Desert* help readers today as much as they did when first written nearly a hundred years ago. Both have a combination of spiritual depth and application to life that endear them to readers.

Companions for the Soul by Bob and Shelley Townsend Hudson let the faith of early Christian men and women speak afresh in daily readings. *Daily Readings from Spiritual Classics* compiled by Bernard

Bangley paraphrases the writings of "saints of old" into clear, simple English to make the ideas accessible. We have a rich heritage in the church that needs exploring.

Women of Faith conferences have put out a large number of attractive devotional books—quick reads filled with joy, humor, and truth. Written by the women who speak at the Women of Faith gatherings: Patsy Clairmont, Barbara Johnson, Marilyn Meberg, Luci Swindoll, Sheila Walsh, and Thelma Wells, their titles give you the heartbeat of their work—*Overjoyed, We Brake for Joy,* and *Joy Breaks.*

Books I Read to Grow

The Divine Conspiracy and *The Spirit of the Disciplines* by Dallas Willard

These books, perhaps more than any others, have deepened my understanding of how to live and grow as a citizen of the Kingdom. In Willard's hands, theology becomes the stuff of ordinary but vital life.

The Only Necessary Thing by Henri Nouwen

In this posthumous collection of Nouwen's writings on prayer, every entry has the freshness of one pray-er's real experience and insights. I found it a book to take through the year and reread.

Real Presence: The Glory of Christ with Us and within Us by Leanne Payne

Payne explores the concept of the "incarnational reality" in C. S. Lewis's writings, the fantastic truth that we may each be indwelt by God. In so doing, she clarifies how this reality can be experienced in our lives by practicing the presence of God.

The Unchained Soul: A Devotional Walk on the Journey into Christlikeness from the Great Christian Classics by Calvin Miller

The subtitle summarizes the content. Miller introduces us to truths discovered by ten "saints," giving us access to their God-filled lives.

The Sacred Romance by John Elridge and Brent Curtis

Two men entice us to risk it all and gain everything that matters within the passion of a love relationship with God. Writing out of strong conviction and poignant experience, they cut through the issues that hold us back, and call us to life as it is meant to be.

RECOMMENDED BY LINNEA BOESE, LINGUIST AND BIBLE TRANSLATOR

Joni Eareckson Tada, who has learned to live as a quadriplegic, has much to teach all of us about feeling God's love in hard places. Her devotionals include *Diamonds in the Dust* and *Seeking God: My Journal of Prayer and Praise,* and other books. One of her latest projects is a satisfying devotional piece called *O Worship the King,* written in cooperation with John MacArthur and Robert and Bobbie Wolgemuth. The book explores the background and stories surrounding various well-known hymns, which are printed in the book, along with a CD of the Master's Choral group. Joni's story about the hymn "Man of Sorrows" will warm your heart, as it did mine. Three other books following this format are in production.

Another devotional that takes a look at hymns is *Spiritual Moments with the Great Hymns* by Evelyn Bence. It helps lift the heart to God in praise. Bence shares the background of each hymn, quotes some of the verses (which I like to sing), and ends with a prayer. Evelyn Bence has also written a thought-provoking book called *Mary's Journal.* I read this at Christmas time to refresh my understanding about the cost of the Incarnation.

My own prayers are often earthbound. I find great stimulus in reading the thoughtful prayers others have written. *Prayers for a Mother's Heart* by Ruth Graham makes a wonderful gift for a new mother—or an older mother. *The Valley of Vision: A Collection of Puritan Prayers and Devotions,* edited by Arthur Bennett, and *Prayers Written at Vailima* by Robert Louis Stevenson (a new insight into one of our childhood poets) are enriching. Look for *The Collects of Thomas Cranmer,* edited by C. Frederick Barber and Paul F. M. Zahl. One of my favorites is *A Diary of Private Prayer* by John Baillie.

Don't Miss This Author

C. S. Lewis's books are helpful to read and reread. He wrote nonfiction books on many subjects. Few writers have done more to stimulate clear thinking about great issues. *Mere Christianity* has helped thousands of readers understand what it means to believe in God. His *Screwtape Letters* not only delights; it instructs. The book is a series of letters from a senior devil to a junior devil about schemes to trip up those who believe. *A Grief Observed* shows Lewis's heart as he copes with the death of his wife, Joy Davidman. He wrestles with *The Problem of Pain* in a book with that title. Lewis was a prolific writer whose thoughts are as relevant today as when he wrote them. I can hardly imagine a mature person who hasn't read something helpful from his pen.

This chapter comes to an end—but the helpful books are more numerous than can be put into a single chapter. The resources are plentiful; the discipline to read and grow may not be. *Take and read*, and grow up on the inside—for your sake and for the sake of all who know and love you. And that includes God.

A book reads better which is our own, and has been
so long known to us that we know the topography of its blots
and dog's ears, and can trace the dirt in it to having
read it at tea with buttered muffins.

CHARLES LAMB

Books for the Stages of My Life Journey

Jesus with Dirty Feet by Don Everts

Ignore the very bad cover on this book. Written in "sense lines" (almost poetry), it offers a thoughtful and refreshing perspective on our faith—good for long-time believers, new believers, and great for those "on the way."

When God Interrupts by Craig Barnes

This book has been very instructive as I've looked back at the unexpected tragedy of my first husband's death at the hand of a drunk driver, and now in coping with new medical developments in my life. I've read, marked, and reread this book four times in the past few years.

Kitchen Table Wisdom
by Rachel Naomi Remen, M.D.

A collection of short (and good for reading aloud) stories/anecdotes from her years of practicing medicine, this book offers a lot of insight into living and dying, and was very helpful as we struggled with decisions about my medical treatment; a good reminder that, in the end, acceptance might be the best medicine. The author has a very eclectic approach spiritually, but offers a lot of wisdom.

RECOMMENDED BY
MARY JANE WORDEN CLARK,
AVID READER

Books That Inspire My Spiritual Life

Four Quartets by T. S. Eliot

A masterpiece series of four poems addressing connections between past and present, spiritual renewal and the nature of experience. Lines and passages from these poems have come unbidden to my mind for more than twenty years now!

The Cost of Discipleship
by Dietrich Bonhoeffer

I am always convicted by this call to sacrifice in the Christian life and its confident conclusion focusing on the believer's privilege to share Christ's incarnational life.

The Mind of the Maker
by Dorothy Sayers

A classic meditation on what it means to be made in the image of God and a brilliant exploration of the nature of the human and divine creative processes.

The Way of a Pilgrim (English translation)
by Anonymous

A classic tale of a nineteenth-century Russian peasant's quest for the secret of how to pray continually. What joy and goodness and plenty in this account of his simple and humble life of dependence on God's grace and the Spirit's leadings.

RECOMMENDED BY DONNA KEHOE,
COMMUNICATIONS CONSULTANT

Chapter 9

The Company of Others: Sharing Books

The pleasure of all reading is doubled when one is with another who shares the same books.

KATHERINE MANSFIELD

The moment I finished reading *The Holy Masquerade* by Olov Hartman I knew I had to share it with someone. The book wouldn't let me go; I found myself living inside its pages. I felt a terrible loneliness that I couldn't explain to those closest to me. I hounded my husband to read the book, and when he saw how much I wanted that, he sat down and read it. Then I had someone to talk to about how I felt about the characters in the story, about the theme of the book.

That was my most poignant time for the need to share. Sadly, the book is no longer in print, so it is difficult to share now.

There have been many other times when I've pushed a book on to a friend so that we could talk about it. I've found that book lovers are always recommending books to each other. They meet for lunch and suddenly one is scribbling down titles and, if they are like me, they discover them later in hardly readable form. When you say, "Have you read . . ." and the other person smiles with the kind of eagerness that says "Yes, and wasn't it . . . ," then you know a special kind of gladness over books.

It takes some sensitivity to do this wisely. Fitting people with books may be as difficult as fitting them with shoes. Sometimes we've read something that we think is exactly right for a friend or a family member; we push a book with the best of intentions, only to find that person isn't really into it. It can become awkward, lonely for me and embarrassing for you.

In a little book called *Prayers for Girlfriends and Sisters and Me*, author Evelyn Bence captures this dynamic:

> I bought her a copy of a book that touched me deeply, wanting to share the *ah-yes* that resonated through my being, the rush of the words that brightened my whole world. Too often I asked if she'd read it, opened it even. *It's right there on my night stand . . . I've been so busy.*
>
> Finally, she read a few pages—but only to get me off her back. It's time for me to lay off. She's not going to finish it. She's not going to get to the good stuff. The words that struck me with such force lie there in wait, in the dark, pressed between pages that may never be opened. Or maybe they'll be opened on the other side of a table selling secondhand (though never used) books.
>
> God, I can't make her read the book that changed my outlook on life. Even if she were to read it, I can't make her "get it" just as I did—the exact nuances. This disappoints me, frustrates me. I want her to open it, mark it, digest it, savor it. Catch the vision.
>
> Can you nudge her, please? Or—maybe it's time I realized: The words were a grace to me, not meant for her. Drop it.

Sharing doesn't always come out the way we had hoped. Instead of doubting our instincts and begrudging the intentions, we can wait until the moment comes when someone else obviously is ready for the words that changed our personal outlook. It will happen, but we can't make it happen.

Furnishing a Home with Books

Don't be too much of a neat-nik; some houses look like no one lives in them. Have books sitting around your living area where others might be enticed to pick them up and begin reading. Some women complain that their families are obsessed with television, but provide nothing else in the room to grab the interest of the people in it. Books are furnishings that provide warmth and invite investigation. I agree with Horace Mann who said that a house without books is like a room without windows.

Leave your books around the house in full view so others can be attracted to read what you have been enjoying. This may mean losing the book for a while. In a *Peanuts* comic strip, Lucy barks out, "All right, who took the comic book that was on this table?" Linus says, "Here, I'm sorry. I didn't know it was yours." Lucy, looking her ornery self, glares at him. "I suppose you read all the reading out of it!" Fortunately, all the reading can't be read out of books, and if the book gets someone else started reading, it may be worth losing it for a while.

Books about My Continent: Africa

Mukiwa by Peter Godwin

A memoir of a white boy growing up in Rhodesia (now Zimbabwe) in the sixties and seventies. A magical story, seen through the eyes of a child, turns into a vicious account of civil war seen through the eyes of Godwin the boy-soldier. Later Peter Godwin, an international journalist, returns to Zimbabwe to cover the massacre of thousands of the Matabele (Robert Mugabe's opposition) in the early eighties. *Mukiwa* alternates between being funny and tragic, reminiscent of Frank McCourt's memoirs in *Angela's Ashes*. *Mukiwa* is a welcome addition to the ever-growing body of African literature, a prophetic book in the light of Robert Mugabe's hatred for whites and flagrant disregard for the rule of law.

The Poisonwood Bible by Barbara Kingsolver

A finely woven tale of a missionary family's experiences in the Congo, seen through the eyes of each of the four daughters and the mother. The father, religiously zealous, but cruel and unfeeling, seems to have a strange mission, even baptizing people in a crocodile-infested river. Intriguing, complex, subtle—masterful writing. I would love to discuss this book with other Christians, because it is full of truths about missionary endeavors in Africa. However, Kingsolver's caricature of the male Christian missionary in Reverend Price begs some consideration and discussion. See also *Pigs in Heaven* and *Animal Dreams* by Kingsolver.

RECOMMENDED BY ROSEMARY MOORE, ATTORNEY AND MOTHER—SOUTH AFRICA

How did I get a boy I know to read *The Song of Hiawatha* by Longfellow? I didn't give it to him and say, "You ought to read this." Instead I left it on an end table, and he picked it up and was soon engrossed in it. At least make people curious to see what you are reading by leaving some books around. It will give you an opportunity to share about books. Children learn by being in the presence of books. (So do adults.)

On Being a Book Lender

A friend complained, "When I get hold of a book I particularly admire, I am so enthusiastic that I loan it to someone who never brings it back." Everything comes to him who waits but a borrowed book!

If the book you are lending means anything to you, do a favor for yourself and the person to whom you are lending the book. First of all, make certain your name is in the book. Then record the date and the name of both book and borrower in a small notebook. This is hard to remember if you are impulsive about lending, but it's a good habit to develop. For one thing, it gives you an opportunity to inquire about how the person liked the book and share ideas—besides assuring that the book is read and not just sitting on someone else's shelf. And a returned book allows you to share it with someone else. Occasionally a book is a throwaway in the sense that you don't want it back, but if you are reading good books, you will be able to use the book in your life and in the life of someone else if it is on your shelf instead of lost in the lending cycle.

Reading Aloud

We've always talked about books in our family, read favorite sections to each other, and tantalized one another about the marvels of the story. It's a good way for a family to feel together and laugh together and just plain *be* together. Sharing makes for a lovely companionship.

Anyone who has small children knows the delight of "read me a story." Our family is a read-aloud family. Something about the intimacy of being in the same room, sharing the same book, feeling similar feelings—which often means either smiling, weeping, or wide-eyed excitement over the plot—makes for a family closeness that is hard to define if you have never done it. Too many families stop reading aloud as soon as a child can read well enough to read privately. Don't neglect reading aloud!

We all want to stay connected to our children as they grow older, and reading aloud is one of the very best ways to do this. As Kathleen Lawrence noted wryly, "The memory of having been read to is a solace one carries through adulthood. It can cover over a multitude of parental sins." When you read aloud, you are creating an exclusive world for your family to enjoy together—a world that comes from a good book. You know the same people, go on the same adventures, feel the same things, know the same quotable phrases. Nothing I can think of is more binding than these times together. I feel so strongly about it that I would say that families who read together stay together. These families don't seem to have children who disrespect their parents' ideas or are deliberately rebellious against family standards. The family has grown their own private culture by reading and sharing ideas.

We've read aloud, not just with our own family, but also with other young people who have hung out at our house. We read to each other in our now-empty nest. We had a delightful time one summer reading the Narnia Chronicles aloud, taking turns and even recording them to send to our grandchildren. My husband is a great Winnie-the-Pooh reader, and his reading tapes are collector's items with some now grown-up kids who heard him read when they were young. Unfortunately, sometimes you can't find someone who wants to read aloud with you. We gave a copy of Seamus Heaney's *Beowulf* to our college-aged grandson, who wrote back saying, "I wish I had someone with whom to read this aloud. It reads so well." The idea of reading aloud may seem a bit much to you, but try it; you may like it.

Listening to books on tape is a good way to learn the wonders of reading aloud, especially when traveling. Most libraries stock these tapes, and the choice is amazing. We rarely take a trip that is more than an hour long without a book to listen to; it seems to shorten the distance! Time whizzes by and the journey seems less boring. If children are in the car they hardly ever say, "Are we there yet?" We've been known to decelerate and drive more and more slowly as we approach a destination because the story on tape is too good to leave.

The fun of this is catching. Two teenaged fellows (one of them our grandson) took a five-hour summer's journey to visit us, taking turns driving and reading to each other all the way to our cabin. The car had no air conditioning, but they drove with the windows up to enable the reader to be heard. They arrived sweaty but happy. It was a great book, they said, but it wasn't finished, so every night we heard them in their bedroom reading aloud before going to sleep. Is that a good friendship or what?

Giving Books

I treasure my book gifts, especially when they bear the inscription of the giver. A good book makes a great gift, a gift that keeps on giving. I don't *always* give a book for birthdays and Christmas, but people get pretty used to my flat packages. When my three-year-old neighbor boy opened his flat-looking package, so hopeful it was a toy, he cried out, "A book? I can't even read!" His mother and I still laugh over this. Many years later, that same neighbor boy, now graduating from high school, sent a note thanking me for yet another book, expressing his gratitude for my helping to make him a reader, saying that he planned to major in literature in college!

Cleaning out a file the other day, I found a letter from my sixteen-year-old nephew saying that he felt special gladness when he saw that someone from our family had drawn his name in the Christmas exchange because he knew he would receive some real "honey for my heart." He went on to say that he had already finished reading *Out of the Silent Planet* and was well on his way to completing *Perelandra*. He added, "I hope I'm not reading these too fast so that I miss something important." He ended his letter with a thank you, saying that as he looked over his bookshelves he realized how rich we had made him from the very beginning—he noted that we gave him *A Hole Is to Dig* when he was three years old!

I've had many thank-you notes over the years, but none that I value more than the ones from young people who have become readers. One ten-year-old sent me a *Redwall* book for my birthday this year!

Sharing Books Leads to a Book Group

The psychology of women lends itself to a keen interest in book groups. We like to engage life vicariously by reading—then to explore the emotional underpinnings of the lives of those we read about. We analyze and understand our own lives better through conversations, and we see the consequences of choice through someone else's life. All of which is a perfect setup for a book group.

Reading groups have existed for years, but recently their popularity has exploded, with book groups of every style, composition, and interest. Libraries now have book review groups, as do churches, senior-citizen centers, coffee shops, and even cyberspace. Chat rooms thrive around book talk, and book readers from around the world join in. You can pick up book reviews on the Internet from online bookstores like Amazon.com or Barnesandnoble.com. Sharing books is almost a contemporary pastime, but nothing quite matches a small group of live bodies sharing a book face-to-face.

Two from the Nineties Worth Chewing On

The Forgotten (1992) by Elie Wiesel

Malkiel Rosenbaum goes to the Romanian village of his father's birth, where the Jewish community had been destroyed in the last days of World War II, in order to discover the secret that his father, now losing his battle against Alzheimer's, desperately needs to uncover. Should certain horrific memories be buried because they might lead to revenge, or do they constitute the only firm basis for new life? How does memory link the generations to each other and to the God of Abraham, Isaac, and Jacob who is "source of all memory, that to forget is to abandon, to forget is to repudiate"? Elie Wiesel, more famous for his autobiographical *Night*, explores these questions that are crucial to our generation who has heard the Holocaust cry of "Never again" while we flip through TV channels, bored and restless and focused on ourselves.

The Sparrow (1996)
by Mary Doria Russell

Lured by the haunting music picked up by powerful radio telescopes, a small team of Jesuit missionary linguists and secular academics make first contact with an alien civilization on the planet of Rakhat. Even though they are pursing their goals for the glory of God, they precipitate a disaster for their new friends and themselves. Two questions swirl around the fate of the mission's leader, which have echoed throughout history: Where is God in human decision-making and suffering? How can colliding cultures respect and understand each other even as they change? Beautifully written. Some paperback editions include questions for group discussions. The sequel is *The Children of God*.

RECOMMENDED BY BARBARA HAMPTON,
TEACHER AND WRITER

How do people start groups? Some book lover has to begin it—someone who is eager to talk about what is in a book. Others join because they recognize that the commitment to read a book is a good discipline, something they might not do otherwise. They suspect they will get new insights from the other readers and expand their own horizons. The often unexpected benefit is the bonding that comes from sharing a book. As soon as two people agree to meet to talk about a book, you have begun a reading group.

Book groups have a long history. In 1891 Mary Houghton Harroun, a physician's wife in Santa Fe, Territory of New Mexico, gathered a dozen women to form a literary society, hoping to guard the literacy of its members and seeing themselves as "civilizers." They were pioneer women, many coming from places like Missouri or further east by covered wagons on the Sante Fe trail. The group they formed, called The Fifteen Club, still meets today and is quite elitist in that someone has to die before a new member can join. Their rules are firmly in place: fifteen members alphabetically take turns to present a book or an author, they serve only chocolates, and they "call the roll" at their meetings. Along with "Present!" each member responds with a researched quote or a current event that has caught her fancy. This may well be the longest-running book review group in the States. Certainly it is one of the most interesting, and Marian Meyer has written its history in *Santa Fe's Fifteen Club: A Century of Literary Women*.

Reading groups work best when members make their own rules about how often they meet (usually a month apart so that everyone has time to read the agreed-upon book), what they will read, and where they will meet. Rotating leadership and hosting seems to work best. Group size seems to be between six and twelve in the groups I polled. Committed members are essential, and smaller groups seem to work as well as larger groups, sometimes better. If the group is larger than eight, members begin to think their absence won't matter. Some basic compatibility among the members helps them to look forward to sharing together.

The social side of the group becomes increasingly important as the members bond and share ideas. That usually means food. Sometimes the social time and the food take more time than the book discussion. A book group in Nashville, Tennessee, plans a meal around the theme of the book, if the book lends itself to that. When they read *Under the Tuscan Sun* by Frances Mayes they had an Italian supper. When they read *Angela's Ashes* by Frank McCourt they ate an Irish menu.

What books should you read? Some groups begin because of interest in an author. One group, for example, decided to read C. S. Lewis's works. Another group meets to read mysteries. In many groups, the person hosting the next meeting chooses any book she wants the group to discuss and prepares to lead the discussion. (That has potential to bomb if group members don't know each other well.) More often the books are chosen ahead of time for a six- or eight-month schedule, and everyone gets the reading list. One group has decided to be really efficient. They work with a local bookstore and have books for sale at the meeting. Other groups let members pick up their books themselves either from the store or at the library. The Nashville group chooses to read four classics a year; otherwise the choice is open.

One group I belonged to for years is more a book-review group than a book-reading group. A group member signs up to give the review, chooses a book, and reviews it for everyone else. The disadvantage of this sort of group is that discussion is minimal because most group members are unfamiliar with the book; the advantage is that you get a good review, can ask questions about the book, and then decide if you want to read it. It's your group: make your own rules about how to do it, and change rules midstream if they don't work out.

Book selection depends on your group. Your own interests will dictate, but taking ideas from the books mentioned in previous chapters will help you decide. Also check out *The Book Groups Book* edited by Ellen Slezak. It contains a number of essays on book groups, plus it provides a listing of recommended titles in the back of the book. An even more helpful reference is *The Reader's Choice* by Victoria McMains, with brief book reviews and some questions for discussion.

Randy Hasper, minister of a church in California, decided to start a reading group to stretch the intellect and faith of members of his congregation. Today hairstylists and law officers, homemakers and house painters read Augustine, Bonhoeffer, Pascal, and Kierkegaard. In short, they read books that stretch them. And they love it. They started with three devotees of reading, and now eight to ten read together with an enthusiasm and loyalty that surprises him. Hasper says, "Most of us read what we never would have read on our own. Most of us understand what we never would have understood on our own."

Your group may not want to aim that high. My advice is not to aim too high or too low; you might lose people either way. Book choice is critical for the health of the group. Don't expect to be enthralled by every book you choose. You may want to give some a thumbs-down vote. Several groups rate every book on a scale of 1–5. Don't be afraid of big ideas and books that don't fit in a certain category; however, make sure the books say something worth reading. A book you choose may have significantly changed one member's life. Discussion is almost ready-made from such a book. Hearing of the controversy over the Harry Potter books, a number of adult groups chose to read at least one of that series so they could discuss it intelligently. (It's a good rule to never pronounce judgments on books you haven't read.) The best discussion happens when we relax, enjoy different perspectives, and learn from each other. We need to make room for disagreement, so that openness is the hallmark of the group.

Here are some good questions to help the discussion in a book group:

What is the author saying?
What themes run through the book?
What are the author's biases?
Does the book tell the truth?
What did you like best about the book?

Readers can access an Internet site that includes a host of free book discussion guides. The site is *http://www.randomhouse.com/vintage/read*. There are also links for information about the author and/or films being made of the book. Click on "Reading Group Guides" to find a list of what is available. Or begin by author or title. There is even a page of tips for leading good discussions and suggestions for the leader. Your reading group can add comments to the site via email.

Mother-daughter book clubs are growing in popularity, possibly spurred on by a book Shireen Dodson wrote called *The Mother-Daughter Book Club*. Shireen, a busy professional woman, came up with the idea after lamenting the lack of time she had to spend with her ten-year-old daughter. She was not getting through on the emotional level; they were not talking about life and ideas in a helpful way. When she mentioned the idea of a book club her daughter, Morgan, quickly came up with a list of friends she wanted to invite. Other mothers responded as warmly to the ideas as their daughters did. Ten busy mothers and daughters began meeting together to talk, laugh, and learn through the books they were reading together.

Obviously this kind of group serves a different purpose from the book groups discussed above, but it is a great idea to consider. Shireen

Dodson's book gives the details of their reading list and other helpful suggestions. This book group has succeeded in bonding mothers and daughters in ways they did not expect, boosting the self-esteem of many of the daughters and giving the mothers new insights into their daughters' values. Check with your library; they may have such a group already.

Boarding School Adventures

Any of these books would be a wonderful book to share with your young adult daughter.

A Time to Love by Margot Benary-Isbert
A young German girl and her Great Dane are sent away to a private boarding school in the country during the war. At Heilingwald she develops her love for music, meets her first love, and learns some valuable lessons about life and its heartaches.

Light a Single Candle by Beverly Butler
At age fourteen Cathy Wheeler loses her sight and is plunged into a world of changes and new experiences. She and her guide dog, Trudy, are enrolled in Burton Academy for the Blind. Learning Braille, acquiring new independence, and making valuable friends all help Cathy before she accepts the challenge of going back to public high school.

A Lovely Tomorrow
by Mabel Esther Allan
Frue Allan, a teenager growing up in London, is suddenly robbed of her home, parents, and future acting career when a rocket hits her city home on New Year's Eve 1944. She is packed away with her great-aunt far out in the country, and then enrolled in a boarding school where conditions are less than luxurious. Despite these difficulties, Frue eventually finds friendship, love, and even romance in her country home.

Bloomability by Sharon Creech
A young American girl whose job-hopping father moves frequently from state to state is taken in by her uncle and aunt for a year ("kidnapped," as she puts it) to attend their international boarding school in the Swiss Alps. There she learns about skiing, different cultures, and making lifelong friends.

New Worlds for Josie by Kathryn Worth
Tomboy Josie and her older sister, Elizabeth, leave their Midwestern home for a year to study abroad at a fashionable Swiss boarding school where everyone must speak French. Soon they realize that to be accepted by the European students they must learn to relate to their interests and accept that America isn't always first or best.

RECOMMENDED BY
SARAH JOY FELDHAKE,
HIGH SCHOOL STUDENT

Creative Book Sharing

I was invited to speak in a small town in northern California. The sponsors for this trip west were four young women who had opened a bookstore in an unused annex building alongside a church. Their shelves held a limited stock of their favorite books. This was not a highly financed project; it was Project Share in the best sense. Their aim was to encourage young mothers to read and to offer the kind of books that would enrich their lives. A black pot-belly stove provided

Discoveries from a Used Bookstore

My sister got me started on **Joseph C. Lincoln**, a writer she found in a used bookstore. Now I frequent used bookstores to look for Lincoln's wonderful stories written in the early 1900s about Cape Cod lighthouse keepers, old sea captains, and ordinary folk who live by the sea. When I find one, I know I will be reading late into the night, captivated by the memorable characters Lincoln creates in these seemingly simple stories.

Shavings is the nickname given to an odd fellow who whittles wood into windmills. Although he is teased and mistreated by others, the story shows his strength of character and his wounded heart.

Galusha the Magnificent. Everyone thinks Galusha is odd and not too bright, but they and the reader are in for a wonderful surprise.

The Woman-Haters. Two men try to hide from the pain in their lives in a remote lighthouse. A fun read—even better to read aloud in a group.

Cap'n Eri. Three retired sea captains may be lacking in social skills, but they more than make up for that in loyalty and courage. A little mystery, a little romance, and lots of laughs.

The Bradshaws of Harniss. When Zenas Bradshaw's doctor told him he must slow down, Zenas expected that his grandson would take over the family store. Instead Mark, caught up in flying, joins the armed forces to fight in World War II. This engaging story reveals courage, strength, and family loyalty as the family survives stressful months of separation, financial setbacks, and life-threatening events.

RECOMMENDED BY MARILYN TWINING,
ARCHIVES CONSULTANT

toasty warmth on chilly days; a braided rug covered the floor; a rocking chair was placed by the fireside; the sideboard held Staffordshire blue cups and saucers. The teakettle was humming on a small hot plate.

Young mothers walking their children in strollers stopped by for conversation, a cup of tea, and a chance to look at the books for sale. The "owners" took turns as hosts, ready to listen and to suggest books that would help make life bigger and better. It was more than a bookstore; it was a haven of loveliness, a friendship spot. Word spread quickly about the bookshop's charm; people began book-sharing in earnest, talking about ideas. The success of the outreach snowballed to the extent that they gathered a school gymnasium full of people to hear me speak—all of them touched by what was happening through the outreach of this bookshop. Sharing books reaps larger rewards than we can imagine!

The magazine *Arizona Highways* carried a story about a woman rancher named Winn Bundy, a booklover who hasn't let her isolation on a six-hundred-acre working ranch stop her from sharing books. She began the Singing Wind Bookshop in 1974 with $600 worth of books in her sprawling 1939 adobe ranch house. The home/bookstore sits at the end of a dirt lane about a half mile off the main road about twenty miles south of Tucson. Now her 2,400-square-foot bookstore meanders through several brick-floored rooms and boasts books on almost every subject. As her children moved out, Bundy turned bedrooms into book rooms with polished mesquite planks for bookshelves. Volumes line the rooms; books are tucked under windows and over doors. Once a year she hosts a festival for poetry reading, with special guests, jazz music, and good food. Suggesting books for folks who stop in to shop is her delight. When she is not talking books, she is out mending fences on the ranch or penning up pesky colts.

Reading this I thought of Stuart Brent, a well-known Chicago bookseller, who said, "It hurt me terribly if someone came in and asked for a book without letting me talk with him about it. The whole joy of selling a book was in talking about the ideas in it. It was a matter of sharing my life and my thought and my very bloodstream with others."

Another woman who loves books operates a used bookshop called First Editions on a back road about ten miles from St. Ignace in the upper peninsula of Michigan. The road is not heavily traveled, but word of this woman's savvy about books has kept tourists detouring to her establishment. She owns two houses and a garage. The smaller of the houses is crammed with used books, more orderly and organized than most stores, and so is the garage. Ask her about a title or an author and she may have one in a box in the garage if you can't find it on the shelf. When the bitterness of winter comes, she heads south and looks for more books.

Small inventory or large, independent bookstores usually have a mission to share books and get people reading. You participate in this mission every time you patronize one.

Finding Time for Reading

C. S. Lewis once said that the future is something that everyone reaches at the rate of sixty minutes an hour, whatever he does, whoever he is. We don't usually say it that way. We say, "I'm just so busy. I could never find the time for that." Which implies that someone else who is doing whatever *that* is has more minutes in an hour than we do. It's true that we can't do everything, but we do end up doing what we want to do, for the most part. That's hard to admit. We do waste time, but we don't like to admit that either.

Schedules are busy, but the people who read are the ones who have books right at hand to read. We need to think of wait-time as a gift. We wait for children to come out of school; we wait in the dentist's office; we wait a lot. Carry a book in your bag that you can pull out and read. A handy book encourages reading. Someone said that in our busy lives we should think in terms of taking four vacations a day—short breaks that refresh body and soul. What a place for a book.

A long time ago a friend told me, when I made the time complaint, that I would be surprised how many books I could read if I read fifteen minutes every night before going to sleep. I used the old "I'm too tired when I go to bed" excuse when he said this, but then I tried it and found that I planned for it. Reading became a way to wind down and relax, and I began to look forward to it. I'm not surprised at the large number of readers who write about reading in bed. There's even a book with the title *Reading in Bed*. "All good and true booklovers," wrote Eugene Field, "practice the pleasing and improving avocation of reading in bed. . . . No book can be appreciated until it has been slept with and dreamed over." Others would be quick to say that the time to read is any time; no apparatus, no appointment of time and place is necessary. Just a book.

Many women have husbands who are addicted to television—the kind of television that is a colossal waste of time. You might like to read, but he has the tube turned on. What to do? I can't tell you, but whatever the solution is I hope it means your husband starts reading more and gives you space to do so too. One solution is to split your time: sit with him for a while and then retreat. A half hour's good reading is food for the soul.

Some time ago Marshall McLuhan declared that books were obsolete. Then he wrote fifteen books to prove his point. Rumors continue to spread that books are no longer useful, with new technology and communication tools taking over the world. It's true that computers have given us a new world; it is easy to use up vast amounts of time searching the Web for information. (The computer can be every bit as much an enemy to relationships as the television.) But then visit your local Border's Bookstore or Barnes & Noble and find it crowded with people reading books, buying books, pulling books off the shelves, and you will see that the attraction of books is not diminished.

William Gass wrote about the conflict between the computer screen and books in *Harper's Magazine*. "Words on a screen have visual qualities, to be sure, and these darkly limn their shape, but they have no materiality, they are only shadows, and when the light shifts they are gone. Off the screen they do not exist as words. They do not wait to be reseen, reread; they only wait to be remade, relit. I cannot carry them beneath a tree or onto a side porch; I cannot argue in their margins; I cannot enjoy the memory of my dismay when, perhaps after years, I return to my treasured copy of *Treasure Island* to find the jam I had inadvertently smeared there still spotting a page precisely at the place where Billy Bones chases Black Dog out of the Admiral Benbow

Books I Read for Fun in Africa

The Lost Child and *On Our Own* by Anne Atkins

Atkins sets her stories in the future to explore the effects of grief and loss on children, and the long-term ramifications that current beliefs about abortion and marriage may have in our culture. Never overtly Christian (though she herself is one), her writing uses secular characters to explore questions about real meaning in life.

The Sacred Diary of Adrian Plass, Aged 37¾ by Adrian Plass

One of several hilarious, maverick tales by this British believe who pokes fun at Christian pretensions while sympathetically encouraging us on our journey. Sure to become family favorites.

A Prayer for Owen Meany by John Irving

Irving invents a child with unique gifts and handicaps who discovers that he has a mission in life, and helps the reader see events and people with new eyes. Once you let Owen Meany into your heart, you will never forget him.

Excellent Women by Barbara Pym
See description of book on page 73.

RECOMMENDED BY LINNEA BOESE, LINGUIST, BIBLE TRANSLATOR

with a volley of oaths and where his cutlass misses its mark to notch the inn's wide sign instead."

As a reader I love the adventure couched in that quote! I relate to the solidness of something in my hand, which I can read under a tree or slouched on a lawn chair. Ah, give me a book and let it even bear the marks of my jam sandwiches. And Lord, keep me from wasting too much time tracking down the details of this world on the Internet.

If time is a problem that you can't solve no matter what you try, look for short stories, for condensed books, for thoughtful magazines. Anything is better than nothing.

We all are stewards of our lives. We all have the same number of hours. Some may need to hone skills that allow the termination of conversations that are fun, but have gone past the useful time. Some may need to turn off the television. Some may need to learn to say no.

Whatever, you need to *guard your literacy*. It's a gift too wonderful to waste.

The wonderful thing about books is that they allow us to enter imaginatively into someone else's life. And when we do that, we learn to sympathize with other people. But the real surprise is that we also learn truths about ourselves, that somehow we hadn't been able to see before.

KATHERINE PETERSON

Afterword

The Roman poet Horace said the purpose of literature is "to teach and to delight." It reminds me of the fruit in Eden's garden—useful and delightful! That seems part of creation's pattern.

A literary work is part of God's created order. It is written because people have been gifted to write, to sub-create; and when we say, "What a fine book this is!" we are praising the Creator for making these gifts part of the human experience. We are delighting in the gifts of our fellow human beings. We appreciate the beautiful language and the emotion of a poem or narrative passage, and in doing so we proclaim "This is good!"

In a real sense we must learn *how* to read. It is more than reading words; it is seeing and understanding and discerning. There is no simple formula that teaches how to do this, just as there is no simple formula that tells you how to love your neighbor. It comes from experience, sometimes struggle, and then triumph. We learn to read by doing a lot of reading. There's no shortcut. Today I read books I once proclaimed "too hard to figure out" or "not too interesting," and I am surprised at how the book has changed!

In a day when people want to get there fast, to learn on the way to someplace else, and seldom sit down to ponder anything, readers form a special class of people. It is a society one joins by choice. You can let this world's stuff eat up all your time, or you can decide to build some inner riches. I resonate with Pete Hamill's comment on his growing library, which caused dismay to his family and to his accountant: "If I had not picked up this habit in the library long ago, I would have more money in the bank today, but I would not be richer."

The human story is about brokenness and redemption. These two aspects of life are revealed in different ways in literature, but they are the underlying themes in the universe and in good books.

There is a moral dimension to reading—a responsibility that is yours. Choosing books is like choosing friends. We always have to make decisions about the company we keep, and this is true of books as well.

Within these pages are some wonderful choices. I could wish you nothing more rewarding than hours of good reading!

Credits

"Stars in Apple Cores." Reprinted from *Polishing the Petoskey Stone*. Copyright © 1990 by Luci Shaw. Used by permission of WaterBrook Press, Colorado Springs, CO. All rights reserved.

"Man Cannot Name Himself" reprinted from *The Secret Trees*, copyright Luci Shaw, Harold Shaw Publishers 1976. Used by permission of the author.

"Forecast" reprinted from *Listen to the Green*, copyright Luci Shaw, Harold Shaw Publishers 1972. Used by permission of the author.

"Stopping by the Woods." THE POETRY OF ROBERT FROST edited by Edward Connery Lathem, © 1951 by Robert Frost. Copyright 1923, 1969 by Henry Holt and Company, LLC. Reprinted by permission of Henry Holt and Company, LLC.

"Dreams." From THE COLLECTED POEMS OF LANGSTON HUGHES by Langston Hughs, copyright © 1994 by The Estate of Langston Hughs. Used by permission of Alfred A. Knopf, a division of Random House, Inc.

"A Primate Termite." Copyright © 1942 by Ogden Nash. Reprinted by permission of Curtis Brown, Ltd.

"Matilda." Reprinted by permission of PFD on behalf of: *The Estate of Hilaire Belloc* ©: as printed in the original volume.

"Coats" copyright 1996 by the Estate of Jane Kenyon. Reprinted from *Otherwise: New & Selected Poems* with the permission of Graywolf Press, Saint Paul, Minnesota.

"To Know the Dark" from *Collected Poems by Wendell Berry*, published by Farrar, Straus and Giroux, LLC. Used by permission of the author.

Index of Authors

Achebe, Chinua, 59
Adams, Richard, 88
Aiken, Joan, 88
Albom, Mitch, 111–12
Alcott, Louisa May, 17, 30
Alexander, Lloyd, 43
Allan, Mabel Esther, 185
Allende, Isabel, 34, 59
Allender, Dan, 162
Allingham, Margaret, 77
Ambrose, Stephen, 118
Anderson, Neil T., 157
Archer, Jeffery, 75
Armour, Richard, 98
Atkins, Anne, 189
Augsburger, David, 158, 161
Augustine, 33, 103
Austen, Jane, 15, 61
Austin, Lynn, 94

Backus, William, 157, 159–60
Baillie, John, 171
Bainton, Roland H., 113
Baker, Russell, 108
Bakke, Jeannette A., 145
Baldwin, James, 71
Bangley, Bernard, 169–70
Barber, C. Frederick, 171
Barber, Noel, 80
Barnes, M. Craig, 166, 172
Belloc, Hilaire, 139
Benary-Isbert, Margot, 185, 82
Bence, Evelyn, 171, 176
Benchley, Robert, 98
Bennet, Arthur, 113, 171
Benson, E. F., 98
Bernstein, Sara Tuvel, 122
Berry, Wendell, 56, 69, 141
Betts, Doris, 68
Binchy, Maeve, 72
Birkerts, Sven, 31, 38
Bjorn, Thyra Ferre, 98
Blackmore, Richard, 29
Blake, William, 127, 134
Blamires, Harry, 37

Boa, Kenneth, 169
Bombeck, Erma, 101
Bonhoeffer, Dietrich, 111, 173
Bourke, Dale Hanson, 168
Bradbury, Ray, 89
Bradshaw, Gillian, 82–83
Brand, Paul, Dr., 118
Briscoe, Jill, 162
Brodsky, Joseph, 24
Brontë, Charlotte, 20, 63
Brontë, Emily, 63
Broyard, Anatole, 14
Buck, Pearl S., 101
Buckley, William F., 76, 105, 119
Buckley, William F., Jr., 105
Buechner, Frederick, 15, 40, 112
Buel, Joy, 110
Buel, Richard, Jr., 110
Bunyan, John, 60
Burnett, Frances Hodgson, 29
Burns, Olive Ann, 20, 48
Burritt, Amy, 115
Butler, Beverly, 185

Calvino, Italo, 51
Cameron, Alexander, 22
Campbell, Meg, 131
Card, Orson Scott, 89
Caro, Robert, 117
Carpenter, Humphrey, 112
Carr, Gwendolyn, 131
Carson, Ben, 107
Carter, Forrest, 84
Carter, Jimmy, 108
Castleman, Robbie, 123
Cather, Willa, 14, 55, 74
Catton, Bruce, 118
Cervantes, 60
Chacour, Elias, 118
Chambers, Oswald, 169
Chambers, Whittaker, 119
Chang, Jung, 101
Chapman, Marie, 160
Charles, Kate, 78–79
Chesterton, G. K., 76, 118

Christie, Agatha, 74, 76, 78
Clairmont, Patsy, 170
Clarke, Arthur C., 89
Clemens, Samuel. *See* Mark Twain
Cloud, Henry, 162
Coleridge, Samuel, 129
Coles, Robert, 118
Collins, Billy, 131
Colson, Charles (Chuck), 105, 158, 168
Colum, Padraic, 126
Connelly, Douglas, 151
Conway, Jill Ker, 111
Cooke, Alistair, 108
Cormack, Don, 123
Cornwell, Patricia, 77
Cowman, Mrs. Charles, 169
Cowper, William, 159
Crabb, Larry, 164
Creech, Sharon, 185
Crombie, Deborah, 79
Cronkite, Walter, 108
Crunk, T., 131
Curtis, Brent, 170

Dallimore, Arnold, 124
Dante, 96
Davidson, Diane Mott, 77
Davies, Robertson, 40
Davis, T. J., 93
Day, Clarence, 98
De Angeli, Marguerite, 28
De Bernières, Louis, 56
De Caussade, Jean-Pierre, 163
de Saint-Exupery, Antione, 88
DeJong, Meindert, 20
DeJong, Selina, 56
Dickens, Charles, 14, 25, 41, 62, 81
Dickinson, Emily, 140
Dickinson, Peter, 79
Dillard, Annie, 108, 120
Dinesen, Isak, 15
Dobson, James, 124
Dodson, Shireen, 184
Doerr, Harriet, 73
Donaldson, Stephen, 87
Dostoyevsky, Fydor, 40, 62
Douglass, Frederick, 106
Doyle, Arthur Conan, 74
Duncan, David James, 64
Dunn, Stephen, 131
Dunning, John, 79

Durrell, Gerald, 120
Duval, Scott, 151

Eareckson Tada, Joni, 108, 171
Earley, Tony, 70, 84
Edgerton, Clyde, 68
Edwards, Amelia, 115
Einstein, Albert, 35
Elegant, Roberts, 80
Eliot, George, 64
Eliot, T. S., 173
Elkins, Aaron, 79
Elliot, Elisabeth, 102
Elridge, John, 170
Endo, Shusako, 59
Erskine, Albert, 70
Evans, Mary Ann. *See* George Eliot
Everts, Don, 172

Faherty, Terence, 79
Farrel, Bill and Pam, 162
Faulkner, William, 70
Fee, Gordon, 151
Ferber, Edna, 55, 84
Field, Rachel, 28
Fischer, David Hackett, 116
Fischer, John, 94
Fish, Mary, 110
Fitch, George Hamlin, 146
Flavel, John, 113
Fleming, Jean, 124
Follett, Ken, 80
Forbes, Esther, 116
Foster, Richard, 157, 164
Foster, Sharon Ewell, 94
Francis, Dick, 38, 76
Frost, Robert, 129, 135
Fuller, Iola, 20

Gaebelein, Frank, 37
Gallagher, J. P., 115
Garcia-Marquez, Gabriel, 15
Gass, William, 189
Gertley, Jan and Michael, 125
Gilbreth, Frank and Ernestine, 98
Gill, Gillian, 74
Gilman, Dorothy, 75
Gire, Ken, 168–69
Godwin, Gail, 73
Godwin, Peter, 177
Goethe, 26

Golden, Arthur, 111
Golden, Harry, 99
Goudge, Elizabeth, 92
Grafton, Sue, 77
Graham, Billy, 105
Graham, Ruth, 171
Grahame, Kenneth, 30
Gray, Harold, 29
Green, Hannah, 55
Greenberg, Johanna, 55
Greene, Graham, 70
Gregg, Douglas H., 145
Grey, Zane, 85
Griffin, Emilie, 164
Grimes, Martha, 75, 79
Grisham, John, 76, 93
Grumbach, Doris, 29
Guelich, Robert A., 145
Gulley, Philip, 93
Guterson, David, 56
Guthrie, A. B., 85

Hagberg, Janet O., 145
Haley, Alex, 107
Hallie, Philip, 123
Hanff, Helene, 97
Hansen, Ron, 52
Hardy, Thomas, 63, 69
Harris, Mark, 167
Hartman, Olov, 175
Hasper, Randy, 183
Hasselstrom, Linda, 120–21
Hassler, Jon, 15
Hawthorne, Nathaniel, 64–65
Hays, Daniel, 151
Heaney, Seamus, 60
Heath, Aloise Buckley, 97
Hegi, Ursula, 80
Helprin, Mark, 56–57
Hemingway, Ernest, 66
Henkes, Kevin, 27
Henry, O., 74
Herbert, George, 140
Herriot, James, 22, 98
Hersey, John, 81, 102
Hijuelos, Oscar, 52
Hillerman, Tony, 75
Hilton, James, 69
Hiney, Tom, 123
Hirsch, Edward, 131
Hirshfield, Jane, 131

Hoban, Russell, 27
Holbrook, Teri, 79
Holm, Jennifer, 28
Holt, Pat, 123
Holt, Victoria, 81
Homer, 58
Hopkins, Gerard Manley, 135
Hornsby, Wendy, 79
Horowitz, Tony 120
Howard, Thomas T., 88, 130
Howarth, David, 122
Howatch, Susan, 73
Huang, Jim, 78
Hubbell, Sue, 121
Hudson, Bob and Shelley Townsend, 169
Huggett, Joyce, 145
Hughes, Langston, 138
Hughes, Robert, 80
Hugo, Victor, 58, 64
Hummel, Charles, 164
Hunt, Gladys, 123
Hunt, Irene, 20
Hunter, W. Bingham, 167
Hurston, Zora Neale, 43
Huxley, Aldous, 126
Huxley, Elsbeth, 80
Hybels, Bill, 167

Ingermanson, Randall, 95
Irving, John, 189
Irving, Washington, 70
Irwin, Grace, 92–93
Ishiguro, Kazuo, 55

Jacques, Brian, 88
James, P. D., 75, 77–78
Jellema, Rod, 129
Johnson, Barbara, 170
Johnson, James Weldon, 137

Kafka, Franz, 39
Karon, Jan, 29, 41, 48, 84
Kaye, M. M., 80
Kazin, Alfred, 46, 106
Keating, Thomas, 14
Keats, John, 26
Keeble, Midge Ellis, 121
Keillor, Garrison, 97
Kellerman, Faye, 77
Kellerman, Jonathan, 77
Kelley, Thomas R., 163

Kemelman, Harry, 76
Kenyon, Jane, 131, 134, 140–41
Kerr, Jean, 99
Ketterman, Grace, 123
King, Laurie, 78–79
King, Martin Luther, Jr., 118
King-Smith, Dick, 98
Kingsolver, Barbara, 25, 177
Kipling, Rudyard, 65
Kogawa, Joy, 56
Kreeft, Peter, 126
Kundera, Milan, 59

L'Amour, Louis, 83–84
L'Engle Madeleine, 20, 110, 141, 158
Lachman, Barbara, 82
Lamb, Charles and Mary, 60, 172
Lamott, Anne, 97, 106
Larrick, Nancy, 137
Latham, Jean Lee, 83
Laux Dorianne, 131
Lavransdatter, Kristin, 25
Lawhead, Stephen R., 80
Lear, Edward, 14, 139
Lee, Harper, 53
Lee, Li-Young, 131
LeGuin, Ursula, 89
Levertov, Denise, 134
Levitin, Sonia, 83
Lewis, Clive Staples, 14, 30, 35, 85–87, 89,
    105, 112, 126, 140, 166, 170–71, 188
Lincoln, Joseph C., 186
Lindbergh, Anne Morrow, 110
Loder, Ted, 134
Logan, Ben, 108
Longfellow, Henry Wadsworth, 137, 178
Lord, Bette Bao, 80
Love, Edmund, 98
Lowell, James Russell, 128
Lowry, Lois, 82

MacArthur, John, 171
MacDonald, George, 86–87, 92, 96
MacDonald, Ross, 78–79
Macke, David, 125
Mackintosh, Elizabeth. *See* Josephine Tey
MacLachlan, Patricia, 24
Macunovich, Janet, 125
Manchester, William, 116, 119
Mandela, Nelson, 106
Markandaya, Kamala, 25

Markham, Beryl, 108
Marsh, Ngaio, 76
Marshall, Catherine, 91, 116
Martin, Martha, 122
Martin, Tovah, 125
Masefield, John, 136
Massie, Robert K., 80
Mathews, Francine, 79
Mayes, Frances, 121, 182
Mayle, Peter, 97
McBride, James, 107
McCaffrey, Anne, 87
McCasland, David, 114
McCourt, Frank, 111, 182
McCullough, David, 117
McCullough, Donald, 162
McDowell, Josh, 167
McLuhan, Marshall, 189
McMains, Victoria, 183
McMurtry, Larry, 64
McPhee, John, 120
McReynolds, Kathy, 116
Mead, Jane, 70
Meberg, Marilyn, 170
Meddaugh, Susan, 27
Melville, Herman, 15, 65, 70
Meyer, Marian, 182
Michener, James, 80, 102
Millay, Edna St. Vincent, 136
Miller, Calvin, 141, 166, 170
Milne, A. A., 141
Mistry, Rohinton, 52
Mitchell, Margaret, 79
Montgomery, Lucy Maud, 22, 30
Morgan, Sarah, 110
Morison, Samuel Eliot, 119
Morrison, Toni, 66
Moule, Handley, 113
Mowat, Farley, 120
Muggeridge, Malcolm, 29
Muir, John, 119

Nash, Ogden, 139
Neff, LaVonne, 158
Nelson, Marilyn, 131
Newby, Eric, 115
Nieuwsma, Milton J., 82
Norris, Kathleen, 105, 122
Nouwen, Henri, 163, 168, 170

O'Brien, Michael, 95
O'Conner, Flannery, 70

Oates, Stephen B., 117
Ohanneson, Joan, 82
Olds, Sharon, 131
Oliver, Mary, 131
Ortberg, John, 162
Orwell, George, 89
Osborne, Rick, 124
Owens, Virginia Stem, 121

Packer, James I., 157, 166, 169
Paretsky, Sara, 77
Pargeter, Edith. *See* Ellis Peters
Pasten, Linda, 131
Paterson, Evangeline, 138–39
Paterson, Katerine, 25, 58
Paton, Alan, 53
Patterson, Ben, 158, 163, 167
Payne, Leanne, 167, 170
Pearce, Joseph, 114
Pearcey, Nancy, 168
Peck, Richard, 22
Pella, Judith, 96
Pender, Phoebe Yale, 110
Perry, Anne, 77, 79
Peters, Elizabeth, 79
Peters, Ellis, 54, 75
Peterson, Eugene, 29, 34, 158, 162
Phillips, Michael, 92, 96
Pickard, Nancy, 77–78
Pilcher, Rosamunde, 73
Piper, John, 163
Pipher, Mary, 125
Plaidy, Jean, 81
Plain, Bleva, 72
Plass, Adrian, 189
Plato, 33
Poe, Edgar Allan, 74
Polacco, Patricia, 27
Pollock, David, 102
Pollock, John, 114
Post, Melville Davisson, 74
Potok, Chaim, 25, 40, 53–54
Potter, Beatrix, 29
Proctor, Rob, 125
Pruitt, Elinore, 110
Pym, Barbara, 189
Pym, Barbara, 73
Quindlen, Anna, 21, 73

Rawicz, Slavomir, 84, 122
Reid, Van, 41

Remarque, Erich Maria, 81
Remen, Rachel Naomi, 172
Richter, Conrad, 84–85
Rinehart, Paula, 158
Rinker, Rosalind, 166
Rivers, Francine, 95
Roberts, Kenneth, 80
Robinson, Peter, 79
Rockness, Miriam, 114
Roe, Francis M. A., 110
Rolvaag, Ole E., 66
Russell, Mary Doria, 181
Ryken, Leland, 25–26, 37
Ryle, J. C., 113

Sampson, Lisa, 94
Sandburg, Carl, 116–17, 136
Sayers, Dorothy, 75, 126, 132, 147, 173
Schaap, James Calvin, 94
Schaefer, Jack, 84
Schaeffer, Edith, 168
Schultz, Charles, 156
Schwartz, Lynne Sharon, 23, 39
Seamonds, David, 157
Seeley, Mabel, 79
Sendak, Maurice, 27
Senter, Ruth, 169
Seth, Vikram, 64
Severin, Tim, 122
Sewell, Anna, 29
Shaara, Jeff, 81
Shakespeare, William, 46, 96, 128
Shaw, Luci, 132–33, 158
Sherline, Reid, 70
Shute, Nevil, 81
Sienkiewicz, Henryk, 14
Sittser, Gerald, 160
Sittser, Jill, 162
Skoglund, Elizabeth, 115
Slezak, Ellen, 183
Smedes, Lewis, 161
Smith, Betty, 17, 67
Smith, Dodie, 74
Smith, Hannah Whithall, 164
Smith, James Bryan, 164
Smith, Lee, 68
Smith, M. Blaine, 163
Solzhenitsyn, Alexander, 59, 81
Spangler, Ann, 169
Spyri, Johanna, 30
Starkie, Walter, 60

Stegner, Wallace, 20, 54–55
Steinbeck, John, 67, 70
Stevenson, Robert Louis, 14, 46, 99,
    153, 171
Stokes, Penelope J., 95
Stone, Irving, 80
Stott, John R. W., 167
Stout, Rex, 77
Stratton-Porter, Gene, 29
Strobel, Lee, 167
Suess, Dr., 33
Susanka, Sarah, 121
Swindoll, Luci, 170
Syswerda, Jean, 169

Tan, Amy, 72
Tan, Siang-Yang, 145
Taylor, Susie King, 110
Taylor, Sydney, 28
Teasdale, Sara, 135
ten Boom, Corrie, 107
Tennyson, Alfred Lord, 128
Tertullian, 33
Tey, Josephine, 75, 77
Thayer, Ernest, 137
Thayer, Helen, 122
Thielicke, Helmut, 145
Thirkell, Angela, 73
Thoene, Bodie and Brock, 95–96
Thurber, James, 96
Tolkien, 44
Tolkien, J. R. R., 86–87, 112
Tolstoy, Leo, 62
Tournier, Paul, 161–62
Townsend, John, 162
Trevor, William, 69
Trobaugh, Augusta, 94
Trollope, Anthony, 19, 63
Tudor, Tasha, 125

Turner, Jamie Langston, 93
Twain, Mark, 21, 41–42, 57, 70, 72
Tyler, Anne, 70, 72

Undset, Sigrid, 43, 64
Uris, Leon, 80

Van Reken, Ruth, 102
Verne, Jules, 89

Walsh, Sheila, 170
Walters, Minette, 79
Wangerin, Walter, 87, 155, 169
Warren, Robert Penn, 70
Weems, Ann, 134
Wells, Thelma, 170
Welty, Eudora, 70
West, Jessamyn, 65
West, Rebecca, 119
White, E. B., 96
White, John, 87, 124, 164, 168
White, T. H., 70
Whitlov, Robert, 93
Wiesel, Elie, 112, 181
Wilder, Thornton, 65
Willard, Dallas, 163, 166, 170
Williams, Charles, 78, 87, 162
Wilson, Dorothy Clark, 112
Winfrey, Oprah, 38
Wister, Owen, 85
Wodehouse, P. G., 41, 96–97
Wolgemuth, Robert and Bobbie, 171
Worth, Kathryn, 28, 185
Wouk, Herman, 80, 105
Wright, Vinita Hampton, 93

Yancey, Philip, 114, 118, 160, 168
Yates, Susan Alexander, 124

Zahl, Paul F. M., 171

Index of Book Titles

Across Five Aprils, 20
Acts of Faith, 70
Adventures in Prayer, 91
Adventures of Huckleberry Finn, The, 42
Affair, 73
Agatha Christie: The Woman and Her Mysteries, 74
Agony and the Ecstasy, The, 80
Ain't No River, 94
Alaska, 80
All Hallow's Eve, 88
All-of-a-Kind Family, 28
All Quiet on the Western Front, 81
All Rivers Run to the Sea, 112
All Things Bright and Beautiful, 98
All Things Wise and Wonderful, 98
Alphabet of Grace, The, 166
Amazing Grace, 93, 106
American Caesar: Douglass MacArthur, 116
American Childhood, An, 108
Amma: The Life and Words of Amy Carmichael, 115
Ancient Strife, An, 96
And the Sea Is Never Full, 112
And Then I Had Kids, 124
Andrew Connington, 93
Angela's Ashes: A Memoir, 111, 177, 182
Angle of Repose, 54
Angles of Light, 133
Animal Dreams, 177
Anna Karenina, 62
Anne of Green Gables, 22, 30
Annual World's Best Science Fiction, 88–89
Apostle, The: A Life of Paul, 114
Arizona Highways, 187
Ark, The, 82
Army Letters from an Officer's Wife, 110
Art of Forgiving, The: When You Need to Forgive and Don't Know How, 161

Art of the Kitchen Garden, The, 125
Arundel, 80
Assault on Eden: A Memoir of Communal Life in the Early 70's, 121
At Home in Mitford, 48
At the Back of the North Wind, 86
Autobiography of Malcolm X, The, 107

Babe, the Gallant Pig, 98
Back When We Were Grownups, 72
Baghdad without a Map: And Other Misadventures in Arabia, 120
Barchester Towers, 63
Baronet's Song, The, 92
Beacon at Alexandria, A, 82
Bearkeeper's Daughter, The, 83
Beasts of the Southern Wild, 68
Bedtime for Frances, 27
Beekeeper's Apprentice, The, 78–79
Bell for Adano, A, 81
Beloved, 66
Benchley Roundup, The, 98
Beowulf, 60, 179
Best American Mystery Stories Century, The, 78
Between Heaven and Earth, 168
Between Heaven and Hell, 126
Beyond Ourselves, 91
Bible for Blockheads, The, 151
Bible, the, 35–36, 47, 128, 130, 143–53
Big Rock Candy Mountain, 55
Big Sky, The, 85
Billy Graham, 114
Bird in the Tree, The, 92
Birds, Beasts, and Relatives, 120
Black and Blue, 73
Black Beauty, 29
Black Lamb and Grey Falcon, 119
Black Woman's Civil War Memoir, A, 110
Blessing Way, The, 76
Blessings, 72
Blood Brothers, 118

Bloomability, 185
Blue Bottle Club, The, 95
Blue Castle, The, 22
Bluest Eye, The, 66
Boat That Wouldn't Float, The, 120
Bold Love, 165
Bondage Breaker, The, 157
Bonesetter's Daughter, The, 72
Booked to Die, 79
Book Groups Book, The, 183
Booklist, 69
Book of God, The, 169
Book of Hours, The, 93
Book of the Dun Cow, The, 87
Born Again, 105
Bosom of the Lamb, 94
Bradshaws of Harniss, The, 186
Brat Farrar, 75
Breathing Lessons, 72
Brendan Voyage, The, 122
Bridge of San Luis Rey, The, 65
Bring Me a Unicorn: 1922–38, 109
Brothers Karamazov, The, 29, 62, 64
Byzantium, 80

Calico Bush, 28
Call, The, 102
Cap'n Eri, 186
Caring for Perennials, 125
Carnival Evening, New and Selected Poems 1968–1998, 131
Carry on, Mr. Bowditch, 83
Case for Christ, The, 167
Case for Faith, The, 167
Cater Street Hangman, The, 79
Catherine Marshall, 116
Celebration of Discipline: The Path to Spiritual Growth, 164
Chance or the Dance, 130
Chance to Die, A: The Life and Legacy of Amy Carmichael, 116
Chariot's Fire, 114
Charles Simeon: Pastor of a Generation, 113
Cheaper by the Dozen, 98
Chesapeake, 80
Child from the Sea, The, 92
Child's Garden of Verses, A, 14
Children of God, The, 181
Chill, The, 78
Chosen, The, 53
Christian's Secret to a Happy Life, The, 164

Christmas Carol, A, 62
Christy, 91
Chronicle of a Death Foretold, 15
Chronicles of Narnia, The, 14
Chronicles of Thomas Covenant the Unbeliever series, The, 87
Chrysanthemum, 27
Church Ladies, The, 94
Cimarron, 56, 84
Circle of Friends, 72
Circle of Quiet, A, 110
Civil War Diary of a Southern Woman, The, 110
Classic Poems to Read Aloud, 141
Cloister Walk, 106
Code of the Woosters, The, 97
Cold Sassy Tree, 20, 48
Collected Poems, 141
Collected Stories of Wallace Stegner, The, 70
Collected Works of Catherine Marshall, The, 91
Color of Water, The, 107
Coming into the Country, 120
Common Life, A, 48
Companions for the Soul, 169
Companions for the Spiritual Journey, 167
Compendium of Physic and Surgery, 51
Complete Book of Baby and Child Care, The, 123
Complete Works of Shakespeare, The, 20
Confessions, 104–5
Corelli's Mandolin, 56
Cost of Commitment, The, 168
Cost of Discipleship, The, 111
Country Year, A: Living the Questions, 121
County Chronicle, 73
Covenant, The, 80, 102
Crime and Punishment, 62
Critical Journey, The, 145
Crocodile on the Sandbank, 79
Crossfire Trail, 84
Crossing to Safety, 20, 55
Cross of Christ, The, 165
Crosswick Journals, The, 110
Cry of the Soul: How Our Emotions Reveal Our Deepest Questions about God, 165
Cry, the Beloved Country, 53
Cure, The, 83

Daily Readings from Spiritual Classics, 169
Dakota, 106, 122

Dare to Discipline, 124
Dark Canyon, 84
Dark Place The, 79
Daughter of Fortune, 34
Daughter of Time, The, 75
David Copperfield, 62
Deadly Drink of Wine, A, 78–79
Dean's Watch, The, 92
Death Comes for the Archbishop, 14, 55
Death in a Mood Indigo, 79
Death in Holy Orders, 75
Death of an Expert Witness, 75
Death of Ivan Ilych, The, 62
Deepening Your Conversation with God, 167
Descent into Hell, 87
*Desiring God: Meditations of a Christian
    Hedonist,* 165
Detecting Women Pocket Guides, 78
Devil's Dream, The, 68
Devotional Classics, 164
Dinner at the Homesick Restaurant, 72
Disappointment with God, 160
*Disciplines of the Holy Spirit: How to Connect
    to the Spirit's Power and Presence,* 145
Divine Comedy, 96
Divine Conspiracy, The, 170
Divine Yes, The, 165
Dog Who Wouldn't Be, The, 120
Don Quixote, 60
Don't Give In; Give Choices, 123
Door in the Wall, The, 28
Dragonriders of Pern series, The, 87
Dwight L. Moody, 114
Dying for Chocolate, 77
Dynasty, 80

Education of Little Tree, The, 84
Eighth Champion of Christendom, The, 54
84 Charing Cross Road, 97
Eleventh Commandment, The, 76
Emily Climbs, 22
Emily of New Moon, 22
Emily's Quest, 22
Emma, 61
Ender's Game, 89
Enter Sir Robert, 73
Eric Liddell: Pure Gold, 114
Eros Redeemed, 164
Evangelical Truth, 167
Evening Class, 72
Evensong, 73

Eve of St. Agnes, The, 26
Eve's Daughters, 94
Excellent Women, 73, 189
Exodus, 80
*Eyes of the Heart, The,—A Memoir of the Lost
    and Found,* 112

Fair and Tender Ladies, 68
Family Book of Verse, The, 141
Family Linen, 68
Far and Deadly Cry, A, 79
Farewell to Arms, A, 66
Far from the Madding Crowd, 63
Far Pavilions, The, 80
Fatal Shore, The, 80
Father, The, 131
Father Elijah, 95
Father Melancholy's Daughter, 73
Faust, 26
Fidelity, 69
Fields, The, 84
Finding God, 164
Fine Balance, A, 52
Firm, The, 76
First Among Equals, 76
First Easter, 91
Fisherman's Lady, The, 92
Five Bells and Bladebone, The, 75
Five English Reformers, 113
Flame Trees of Thika, The, 80
Flannery O'Connor: The Complete Stories, 70
Floatplane Notebooks, The, 68
Flower and the Nettle, The: 1936–39, 110
Forgotten, The, 181
For the Love of Books, 29
For Two Cents Plain, 99
Fourth Estate, The, 76
Franchise Affair, The, 75
Freedom from the Tyranny of the Urgent, 164
Friendly Persuasion, 65

Gaal the Conqueror, 87
Galton Case, The, 79
Galusha, 186
Gentle Insurrection, The, 68
Giant, 56, 84
Giants in the Earth, 66
Gifted Hands: The Story of Ben Carson, 107
Gift from the Sea, 109
Gift of Asher Lev, The, 54
Girl of the Limberlost, A, 29

Glamorous Powers, 73
Glass Lake, The, 72
Glittering Images, 73
God's Trombones: Seven Negro Sermons in
    Verse, 137
Godric, 15
Gods and Generals, 81
Godward Life, A: Savoring the Supremacy of
    God in All of Life, 163
God Who Hears, The, 167
Going Over East: Reflections of a Woman
    Rancher, 121
Golden Fleece, and the Heroes Who Lived
    Before Achilles, The, 125–26
Gone for Soldiers, 81
Gone With the Wind, 79
Good Earth, The, 101
Good Husband, The, 73
Gospel in Dostoyevsky, The, 62
Grace at Bender Springs, 93
Grace Disguised, A,: How the Soul Grows
    Through Loss, 160
Grasping God's Word, 151
Grass Widow, The, 79
Great American Short Stories, 69
Great Divide, The, 93
Great Divorce, 86
Greater Trumps, The, 88
Great Expectations, 14
Great Explorers: The European Discovery of
    America, The, 119
Great Joy, 169
Great Power, 169
Green Dolphin Street, 92
Green Journey, A, 15
Growing Up, 108
Guerillas of Grace, 134
Guilt and Grace, 161
Gutenberg Elegies, The: The Fate of Reading in
    an Electronic Age, 38

Habit of Being, The: Letters of Flannery
    O'Connor, 109
Hard Times, 25
Harper's Magazine, 189
Hawaii, 80
Heading West, 68
Healing for Damaged Emotions, 157
Hearing God, 166
Heart of the Family, The, 92
Heaven Tree Trilogy, The, 54

Heidi, 30
Herbs in Pots, 125
Herbs in the Garden, 125
Here and Now, 168
Here I Stand: A Life of Martin Luther, 113
Here We Are in Paradise, 70
Hidden Rift with God, The, 157, 159
Hiding Place, The, 107
Hill Bachelors, The, 69
Hiroshima, 81
Hobbit, The, 86
Hole Is to Dig, A, 180
Holy Invitations: Exploring Spiritual
    Direction, 145
Holy Masquerade, The, 175
Homecoming, 72
Home in the Bear's Domain, 122
Home to Harmony, 93
Honey for a Child's Heart, 123
Honey for a Teenager's Heart, 123
Horse-shoeing Husbandry, 51
Hotel Paradise, 75, 79
Hound of the Baskervilles, The, 74
Hour before Daylight, An, 108
Hours of God, Hours of Lead: 1929–32, 110
House of Light, 131
House of the Spirits, The, 34
How My Faith Survived the Church, 118
How Now Shall We Live?,168
How Reading Changed My Life, 21, 73
How to Read the Bible for All It's Worth, 151
Hudson and Maria, 114
Hundred White Daffodils, A, 141
Hungering Dark, The, 166
Hustling God: Why We Work So Hard for
    What God Wants to Give, 166

I Can Hear the Sun, 27
I Capture the Castle, 74
Ice House, The, 79
If Morning Ever Comes, 72
Iliad, The, 58
I Love Myself Best When I'm Laughing, 43
In a Dry Season, 79
In Little Place, 93
I Never Promised You a Rose Garden, 55
Inklings: C. S. Lewis, J. R. R. Tolkien, Charles
    Williams, and Their Friends, The, 112
Interrupted Life, An: The Diaries of Etty
    Hillesum 1941–43, 111
In This Sign, 55

Into the Depths of God, 166
Iron Scepter, The, 87
Irrational Season, The, 110
It All Started with Columbus, 98

Jacob Have I Loved, 25
Jane Eyre, 20, 63
Jayber Crow, 56
Jeeves, 97
Jesus Rediscovered, 29
Jim the Boy, 84
John Adams, 117
Johnstown Flood, The, 117
John Wesley, 114
Joni, 108
Journal of Hildegard of Bingen, The, 82
Journey to America, 83
Joy Breaks, 170
Joy Luck Club, The, 72
Joy of Listening to God, The, 145
Julie, 91
Just As I Am, 105

Kane and Abel, 76
Katherine, the Virgin Widow, 82
Killer Angels, The, 81
Killer Diller, 68
Killer Pancake, 77
Killing Fields, Living Fields, 123
Kim, 65
Kinderlager: An Oral History of Young
    Holocaust Survivors, 82
Kitchen God's Wife, The, 72
Knowing God, 157, 166
Knowing God's Will: Finding Guidance for
    Personal Decisions, 163
Knowledge of the Holy, The, 166
Kristin Lavransdatter, 25, 43, 64

Lady in the Tower, The, 82
Laird's Inheritance, The, 92
Lake Wobegone Days, 97
Land Circle: Writings Collected from the
    Land, 121
Land Remembers, The, 108
Last Full Measure, The, 81
Last Lion, The, 116
Last of the Breed, 83–84
Least of All Saints, 93
Legend of the Celtic Stone, 96
Les Miserables, 58, 64

Lest Innocent Blood Be Shed, 123
Letters and Papers from Prison, 111
Letters Never Sent, 102
Letters of a Woman Homesteader, 110
Letters of John Calvin, Selected from the
    Bonnet Edition, 113
Letters of J. R. R. Tolkien, The, 109
Let the Trumpet Sound: The Life of Martin
    Luther King, 117
Let Us Talk of Many Things, 119
Life Together, 111
Life with Father, 98
Light a Single Candle, 185
Light in the Window, A, 48
Light Princess, The, 87
Lion, the Witch, and the Wardrobe, The,
    30, 85
List, The, 93
Listening House, The, 79
Listening Prayer, 167
Listen to the Green, 133
Little Orphan Annie, 29
Little Pilgrim's Progress, 60
Little Prince, The, 88
Little Princess, A, 29
Little White Horse, 92
Little Women, 30
Locked Rooms and Open Doors: 1933–35,
    110
Lonesome Dove, 64
Longing for Home, 166
Longing for Love, 169
Long Walk, The: The True Story of a Trek to
    Freedom, 84, 122
Long Walk to Freedom, 106
Long Way from Chicago, A, 22
Long Way Home, The, 82
Loon Feather, The, 20
Lord of the Rings, The, 44
Lorna Doone, 29
Lost Child, The, 189
Lost Horizons, 69
Lost Keats, The, 79
Lovely Tomorrow, A, 185
Lucia's Progress, 98

Madame DuBarry, 82
Magnificent Defeat, The, 166
Making Life Work, 167
Man Born to Be King, The, 126
Man Called Peter, A, 91

Man Who Was Thursday, The, 114
Man with a Load of Mischief, The, 75
Mansfield Park, 61
Many Dimensions, 88
Mariette in Ecstasy, 52
Marquis' Secret, The, 92
Martha Speaks, 27
Master of Hestviken, 43
Masterpiece Theater, 108
Matter of Honour, A, 76
Me and My Baby View the Eclipse, 68
Means of Grace, A, 54
Memoirs of a Geisha, 111
Memories of the Great and the Good, 108
Memory of Junior, 68
Mere Christianity, 105
Mexico, 80
Middlemarch, 64
Midsummer Night's Dream, 96
Mind of the Maker, The, 132
Minister's Restoration, The, 92
Miss Mapp, 98
Mistress Pat, 22
Moby Dick, 15, 65
Moments with the Savior: A Devotional Life of
    Christ, 169
Monk's Hood, 75
Morbid Taste for Bones, A, 75
More Than a Carpenter, 167
Mornings on Horseback, 117
Moses, Man of the Mountain, 43
Mother and Two Daughters, A, 73
Mother-Daughter Book Club, The, 184
Mother's Heart, A, 124
Mr. Ives' Christmas, 52
Mr. Lincoln's Army, 118
Mukiwa, 177
My American Adventure: 50 States, 50 Weeks,
    115
My Antonia, 55
My Family and Other Animals, 120
My Name Is Asher Lev, 25, 54
Mystery of Providence, The, 113
My Ten Years in a Quandary, 98
My Utmost for His Highest, 114, 169

Narnia Chronicles, The, 14
Narrative of the Life of Frederick Douglass,
    106
Nearer, My God: An Autobiography of Faith,
    105

Nectar in a Sieve, 25
Nerve, Straight, Decider, 76
Never Too Late, 73
New and Selected Poems, 131
New Freedom of Forgiveness, The, 161
New International Version, The, 151
New King James Version, The, 151
New Living Bible, The, 151
New Revised Standard Version, The, 151
News of the Spirit, 68
New Song, A, 48
New Stories from the South, 70
New Worlds for Josie, 185
New Yorker Magazine, The, 96
Nicholas and Alexandra, 80
Night the Bed Fell In, The, 96
Night, 112, 181
Nine Tailors, The, 75
NIV Study Bible, The, 151
No Graven Image, 102
North to the Orient, 109
Northwest Passage, 80
Nothing Like It in the World, 118
Not So Big House, The, 121
Novels of Charles Williams, The, 88
Now and Then, 112
Number the Stars, 82

Obasan, 56
Odyssey, The, 58, 60
Of Love and Shadows, 59
Old Fox Deceived, The, 75
Old Man and the Sea, The, 66
Oliver Twist, 62
Oliver Wiswell, 80
One Corpse Too Many, 75
One Day in the Life of Ivan Denisovich,
    59, 81
100 Favorite Mysteries of the
    Century, 78
One True Thing, 73
Only Necessary Thing, The, 170
On Our Own, 189
On the Missionary Trail: A Journey
    Through Polynesia, Asia and
    Africa with the London Missionary
    Society, 123
Open Mind, Open Heart, 14
O Pioneers, 55
Oral History, 68
Orthodoxy, 114

O Rugged Land of Gold, 122
Oswald Chambers: Abandoned to God, 114
Otherwise, 134, 140
Our Only May Amelia, 28
Our Town, 65
Out of Africa, 15, 109
Out of the Silent Planet, 89–90, 180
Out to Canaan, 48
Overjoyed, 170
Oxford Book of English Short Stories, The, 70

Papa's Wife, 98
Parenting in the Pew, 123
Parenting Isn't for Cowards, 124
Parents in Pain, 124
Parish Papers, The: Three Complete Novels of George MacDonald, 92
Parker's Back, 70
Passing by Samaria, 94
Passionate Enemies, 82
Passion for the Impossible, A: The Life of Lilias Trotter, 114
Pat of Silver Bush, 22
Paul Revere and the Word He Lived In, 116
Paul's Case, 74
Paula, 34
Peanuts, 156
Pearl, The, 67
Perelandra, 89–90, 180
Persuasion, 61
Peter Rabbit, 29
Peter the Great, 80
Phineas Finn, 63
Pigs Have Wings, 97
Pigs in Heaven, 177
Pilgrim at Tinker Creek, 120
Pilgrim's Inn, 92
Pilgrim's Progress, 60
Pillars of the Earth, 80
Piping Down the Valleys Wild, 137
Place of the Lion, The, 87–88
Please Don't Eat the Daisies, 99
Poems 1968–1972, 134
Poetry of Robert Frost, The, 135
Poisonwood Bible, The, 25, 177
Polar Dream, 122
Polishing the Petoskey Stone, 133
Postcard from the Shore, 133
Poultry in the Pulpit, 22
Prairie Years and the War Years, The, 116
Praise Jerusalem, 94

Prayer for Owen Meany, A, 189
Prayer: Conversing with God, 166
Prayer: Finding the Heart's True Home, 157
Prayers for Girlfriends and Sisters and Me, 176
Praying the Scriptures for Intimate Worship, 169
Praying the Scriptures for Spiritual Growth, 169
Presence, The, 93
Pride and Prejudice, 15, 61
Prime Cut, 77
Princess & Curdie, The, 87
Princess & the Goblin, The, 87
Professor's House, The, 55
Promise, The, 53
Psalms of Lament, 134
Pursuit of God, The, 165

Quartet in Autumn, 73
Queen Lucia, 98
Quest for the King, 87
Quiet Neighborhood, A, 92
Quilt, The, 93
Quo Vadis, 14

Rabble in Arms, 80
Ragman and Other Cries of Earth, 87
Raney, 68
Reaching for the Invisible God: What Can We Expect to Find?, 168
Reader's Choice, The, 183
Reading in Bed, 31, 38
Reagan: An American Story, 117
Real Presence: The Glory of Christ with Us and within Us, 170
Realms of Gold, 129
Redeeming Love, 95
Redwall, 88, 180
Remains of the Day, The, 55
Remembering, 69
Remembrances and Winds of War, 80
Reporter's Life, A, 108
Resting in the Bosom of the Lamb, 94
Resurrection, 29
Retrieved Reformation, A, 74
Return, The, 83
Return of the Native, The, 63
Return of the Prodigal Son, The: A Story of Homecoming, 163, 165
Reversed Thunder, 34

Reviving Ophelia: Saving the Selves of
     Adolescent Girls, 125
Riders of the Purple Sage, 85
Right Ho, 97
Rilla of Ingleside, 22
Ring of Endless Light, The, 20
River to Pickle Beach, The, 68
Road from Coorain, The, 111
Romney's Place, 94
Rowan Farm, 82
Ruined by Books, 24

Sacrament of the Present Moment, The, 163
Sacred Diary of Adrian Plass, The, 189
Sacred Journey, The, 112
Sacred Romance, The, 170
Sacred Surprises, 168
Sacred Thirst: Meeting God in the Desert of
     Our Longings, 166
Saint Ben, 94
Saint Maybe, 72
San Francisco Chronicle, 146
Sanctuary Sparrow, 75
Santa Fe's Fifteen Club: A Century
     of Literary Women, 182
Saving Grace, 68
Scarlet Letter, The, 64
Scarlet Music, 82
Scarlet Pimpernel of the Vatican, The, 115
Scent of Water, The, 92
Scottish Collection, The: The Maiden's
     Bequest, 92
Seaboard Parish, The, 92
Seamstress, The, 122
Sea of Grass, The, 85
Secrecy, 72
Secret of the Old Clock, The, 78
Secrets of Heathersleigh Hall, The, 96
Secret Trees, The, 133
Selected Poems of Langston Hughes, 138
Señor Vivo and the Coca Lord, 56
Sense and Sensibility, 61
September, 73
Servant of Slaves, 93
Serving God: The Grand Essentials of Work
     and Worship, 163–64
Shadows of Ecstasy, 88
Shall We Tell the President, 76
Shane, 84
Share in Death, A, 79
Sharp Teeth of Death, The, 68

Shavings, 186
Shell Seekers, The, 73
Shepherd's Castle, The, 92
Short Story Masterpieces, 70
Silence, 59
Singer, The, 141, 166
Sir Gibbie, 92
Situation in Flushing, The, 98
Snow Falling on Cedars, 56
So Big, 55
Socrates Meets Jesus, 126
Soldier of the Great War, A, 56
Something More, 91
Some Wildflower in My Heart, 93
Song of Hiawatha, The, 178
Song of the Lark, 55
Souls Raised from the Dead, 68
Soul Survivor, 118
Source, The, 80
Southern Family, A, 73
Southern Selves: From Mark Twain
     and Eudora Welty to Maya Angelou
     and Kaye Gibbons: A Collection of
     Autobiographical Writing, 109
Southern Woman's Story, A: Life in
     Confederate Richmond, 110
Sparrow, The, 181
Speaker for the Dead, 89
Spirit of the Disciplines, The:
     Understanding How God Changes
     Lives, 163, 170
Spiritual Classics, 164
Splendid Outcast, The, 108
Spring Moon, 80
Stars and Song, 131
Stillness at Appomattox, A, 118
Stolen Lake, The, 88
Stones for Ibarra, 73
Stones from the River, 80
Stonewychke Legacy, The, 96
Streams in the Desert, 169
Suitable Boy, A, 64
Sula, 66
Summer of the Great Grandmother, The, 110
Surprised by Joy, 105
Susanna, 124
Sword Bearer, The, 87

Tale of Two Cities, A, 14, 62, 81
Tales from Shakespeare, 60
Tales of Mystery and Imagination, 74

Tanamera, 80
Tapestry, The, 72, 168
Taran Wanderer, 43
Tasha Tudor's Garden, 125
Taste for Death, A, 75
Teaching Your Child How to Pray, 124
Telling Lies, 79
Telling Yourself the Truth, 160
Temple, The, 140
Ten Fingers for God, 112
Tess of the D'Ubervilles, 63
Testament, The, 76
Testament of Devotion, A, 163
That Hideous Strength, 89
Their Eyes Were Watching God, 43
Theophilus North, 65
These High, Green Hills, 48
They Loved to Laugh, 28
Things Fall Apart, 59
Third Culture Kid Experience: Growing Up among Worlds, The, 102
Thirteen Clocks, The, 96
30,000 on the Hoof, 85
This Hallowed Ground, 118
This Is My God: The Jewish Way of Life, 106
Thousand Miles Up the Nile, A, 115
Thurber Carnival, The, 96
Til We Have Faces, 86
Time to be Earnest, A, 75
Time to Love, A, 185
To Kill a Mockingbird, 53
To Live Again, 91
Too Busy Not to Pray, 167
Too Many Cooks, 77
Tottering in my Garden: A Gardener's Memoir, 121
Tower of Geburah, The, 87
Town Like Alice, A, 81
Transgression, The, 95
Traveling Mercies: Some Thoughts on Faith, 97, 106
Travels in Alaska, 119
Treasure Island, 189
Tree Grows in Brooklyn, A, 17, 67
Trees, The, 84
Trial, The, 93
Trinity, 80
Trouble Sleeps, 68
Truman, 117
Tuesdays with Morrie, 111
Two in the Bush, 120

Ultimate Prizes, 73
Unafraid, 95
Unashamed, 95
Unbearable Lightness of Being, The, 59
Unchained Soul: A Devotional Walk on the Journey into Christlikeness from the Great Christian Classics, 170
Uncle Abner, 74
Undaunted Courage, 118
Under the Sun, 182
Under the Tuscan Sun, 121
Unholy Orders: Mystery Stories with a Religious Twist, 77
Unshaken, 95
Unspoken, 95
Unveiled, 95

Valley of Vision: A Collection of Puritan Prayers, The, 113
Velma Still Cooks at Leeway, 93
Vet in the Vestry, 22
Vicar's Daughter, The, 92
Virginian, The, 85
Voyage of the Dawn Treader, The, 86

Waiting Father, The, 145
Waiting: Finding Hope When God Seems Silent, 163
Walker in the City, A, 46, 106
Walking Across Egypt, 68
Wall, The, 81
War and Peace, 20, 62
Warden, The, 63
War in Heaven, 78, 88
War Within and Without: 1939–44, 110
Watership Down, 88
Way of Duty, The, 110
Weather of the Heart, 141
We Brake for Joy, 170
Wedding Story, A, 48
We Die Alone, 122
West with the Night, 108
What's So Amazing About Grace?, 165
What We Carry, 131
Wheel on the School, The, 20
When God Interrupts: Finding New Life Through Unwanted Change, 166
When the Snow Comes, They Will Take You Away, 115
When We Were Very Young, 141
When You Feel Like Screaming, 123

Where the Wild Things Are, 27
Whole Truth, The, 78
Wilberforce, 114
Wild Swans: Three Daughters of China, 101
Will Mrs. Major Go to Hell?, 97
Will to Live On, The, 106
Wind in the Willows, The, 30
Windbreak: A Woman Rancher on the Northern Plains, 120
Wisdom and Innocence: A Life of G. K. Chesterton, 114
With Malice Toward None: A Life of Abraham Lincoln, 117
Witness, 119
Wolves of Willoughby Chase, The, 88
Woman-Haters, The, 186
Women in the Wind, 121

Women of the Bible, 169
World Lit Only by Fire, A: The Medieval Mind and the Renaissance, 119
World of Mr. Mulliner, The, 97
Writing the River, 133
Wuthering Heights, 63

Xenocide, 89

Year Down Yonder, A, 22
Year in Provence, A, 97
Yearning: Living Between How It Is and How It Ought to Be, 166
Years of Lyndon Johnson: The Path to Power, The, 117
Yellow Room, The, 79

Zondervan Handbook to the Bible, 151